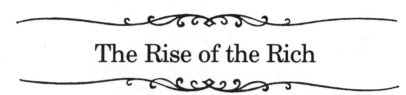

The Rise of the Rich

JAMIE CAMPLIN

St. Martin's Press
New York

Library of Congress Cataloging in Publication Data
Camplin, Jamie, 1947-
    Rise of the rich.

    Includes bibliographical references and index.
    1. Businessmen—Great Britain—History. 2. Great
Britain—Social conditions—20th Century. 3. Great
Britain—History—20th century. I. Title.
HC256.C34   301.44'1   79-4841
ISBN 0-312-68435-5

Contents

Illustrations

Preface

One day in October 1900 Alfred Harmsworth held a luncheon party at his Berkeley Square home.[1] Founder of the *Daily Mail*, Harmsworth had helped to revolutionize British journalism in the previous decade: he had demonstrated that news could be brought to a mass audience – and that money could be made in the process. The lunchtime conversation concentrated on the wealthiest men in the world. Joseph Choate, American ambassador from the Mid-West and scourge of British traditionalism, pointed out that such Americans as Andrew Carnegie and John D. Rockefeller were probably worth fifteen to twenty million pounds apiece. Harmsworth thought that the Tsar was richer; and as for Cecil Rhodes, he would one day be 'the greatest Croesus of all' since the development of Africa was bound to pour millions into his pocket, however extravagant he was. As it happened, Rhodes did not have long to live, but Harmsworth had made a more sensible prediction than his henchman Kennedy Jones, who argued that the company promoter Whitaker Wright would prove to have the greater fortune. Within a few years Wright's career had dissolved into bankruptcy, followed by suicide at the law courts after his trial for fraud,

Harmsworth, Carnegie, Rhodes, Wright – all are part of our story, and all had great fortunes. But the lives of many, perhaps most, of the very rich at the beginning of the twentieth century are missing from the social history of Britain. The role of the working classes has at last received its due in a wide variety of modern studies; and the aristocracy have always received disproportionate attention. History is written by the men in the middle and it is no wonder – for this and other reasons – that they figure largely in it. But those who made millions in the last decades of the nineteenth century, whose activities helped to create modern social and economic life, have largely been forgotten.

Contemporaries called them 'plutocrats', though the word should not imply a close-knit class, and generalizations made about them as a group, if offered uncompromisingly in this book, are often made in the consciousness that they are highly provocative; they are not meant to distract the reader from the central fascination – the history of several dozen quite remarkable individuals. Their greatest impact came in the reign of the king with whom many of them are closely associated – Edward VII – and I have therefore referred to the Edwardian period in my sub-title; but their lives would be incomplete without some examination of their nineteenth-century origins.

Looking back at the end of the first century of the money market in 1915, Ellis T. Powell remarked on 'the ceaseless and irresistible advance of the financial power, and the simultaneous weakening of those authorities which base their claims on political predominance, tradition, custom, precedent, conventions, expediency.'[2] The pursuit of power (occasionally and inadequately redirected to the pursuit of happiness) is the theme of the lives of all the plutocrats: power in economic affairs, in society, in politics, over individuals and communities. 'The plutocrat', said *The Encyclopaedic Dictionary* published in 1909, was 'one who has power or influence through his wealth.'

The battle for controlling dominion was not always pursued

publicly – the secrets of the plutocrats are not easily reconstructed. 'I had long learnt that history was not an account of what actually had happened,' Queen Victoria once confided to her diary, 'but what people generally thought had happened.'[3] Reminiscences are unreliable; the plutocrats themselves often left no certain guide to their feelings, no off-duty letters or honest diary comments. Most of them came from families without interest or concern in recording their place in history; and few of them have found serious biographers.

Nevertheless, I have been able to read with value nearly six hundred books and consult innumerable newspapers, magazines and other sources, in the preparation of this book. They have included a wide range of works by modern historians, to whose researches in a multitude of specialized fields I am greatly indebted: I have endeavoured to provide acknowledgment to them and to others in the notes on the text and apologize for any inadvertent omissions. Here I would like to record special further thanks to the Trustees of Broadlands, Hampshire, for permission to quote a number of letters from the royal family to Sir Ernest Cassel; and to the Archivist there, Mrs Mollie Travis, for her great courtesy and help. I am also most grateful to the following for their generous help in supplying illustrations: Mrs Anne Agapiou, Mr A. H. Boxer, Mr R. M. Hadfield, Sir Rupert Hart-Davis, Mr T. Insull, Miss Rosemary May, Mr Nicholas Phillips, Mrs Mollie Travis and Mr A. West.

Publishers by day are writers by night: their wives suffer accordingly. I offer most thanks to mine, not only for practical aid in typing a lengthy manuscript, but for acting as a spur in a variety of ways towards completion of the book.

Jamie Camplin
June 1976

Chapter 1

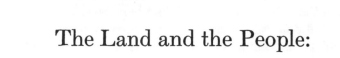

The Land and the People:
England Before the Plutocrats

Historians are in love with progress. In sixteenth- and seventeenth-century England they find a capitalist class of rising gentry ready to defeat a feudal king in the great Civil War of the 1640s. In the eighteenth century they present a dynamic trading nation working its way forward to a future of commercial prosperity; and the nineteenth is barely allowed to begin before a modern industrial economy is thrust upon the world. None of these descriptions is without an element of truth; but none of them reveals much about how the mass of the people spent most of their lives. For many centuries, down to 1850 and beyond, English civilization was a rural civilization; the land was the controlling influence on habits of thought, on everyday life and on the power structure of rulers and ruled.

In 1881 the American multi-millionaire steel magnate, Andrew Carnegie, took a trip from the Grand Hotel, Brighton, to the Caledonian, Inverness, in his native Scotland. Commenting on the people he encountered, he judged that, notwithstanding many notable exceptions, the British aristocracy was descended from 'bad men who did the dirty work of kings, and from women who were even worse than their lords'. He was happy to report – irreverently, and somewhat irrelevantly – that it was now hastening to an end very much in the manner in which it had been born.[1]

In the Middle Ages, certainly, the feudal nobility and their companions in dominance, the squirearchy, had been mainly noted for their might and military prowess.[2] But these abilities gave them land; and it is the association with land, passed down from generation to generation by primogeniture, that gave them an enduring control over the social, the economic and the political life of the nation. 'Palaces, halls, villas, walled parks all over England, rival the splendour of royal seats', observed Ralph Waldo Emerson, who twice came from America to visit the country, in 1833 and 1847. 'Primogeniture built these sumptuous piles.'[3] The younger sons and the daughters might not become paupers; it was rather that the landed inheritance had to pass intact to the heir, and his heir, for ever. At the beginning of the twentieth century the satirical magazine, *Truth*, quoted the aphorism, 'The eldest son must live on the estate; the younger sons on the State.'[4]

Land ownership brought power of a very special and all-pervading kind. At its simplest, it was expressed in economic terms. For most of the nineteenth century estate duty was minimal, and the bias in favour of landed as against personal property continued until the 1890s. For a long time, well beyond 1800, the land was also profitable; and this financial strength underpinned an unofficial hereditary control of church, army, government and everyday life. In the countryside, the great house in its park was the visible symbol of authority. When the Duke of Rutland had his twenty-first birthday in 1799, for weeks on end a place to live and sleep had to be found for everyone from upholsterers to bellhangers to stove flue-makers.[5] As late as 1847, when Lady Dorothy Nevill married her cousin Reginald (and was married by another cousin, the Rev. Thomas Walpole), it was all 'in the old English style – the tenantry drawn up at the gate, and all the neighbourhood jolly and gay with that robust happiness once the characteristic of English country life'.[6]

There is more to be said about the 'robust happiness', but the submissive tenantry were real enough. The country mansion, with church, village, labourers and servants, formed a closed and self-contained social system, with the landowners' family at its apex: Lady Frances Balfour, daughter of the Duke of Argyll, recalled that 'we used to be told that it was unnecessary for us to go to children's parties, as we were a party in ourselves.'[7] Even the country towns seemed to have no identity except as collections of shops – market places for the tenantry, as H. G. Wells called them. The landed proprietor probably appointed the clergyman, controlled most of the employment in his area, and ruled it through the Justices of the Peace. 'It is well said, "Land is the right basis of an Aristocracy"', observed Carlyle in *Past and Present* (1843): 'whoever possesses the Land, he, more emphatically than any other, is the Governor, Viceking of the people on the Land.'[8]

Until the coming of the railways, while roads remained poor, landed rule in the countryside was direct and personal. Charles Reade once drew three symbols to indicate the outlook of the county magnate: the smallest was that representing the importance of the Universe; somewhat larger was that for the British Isles; and the largest was 'The County'. There were even those who deliberately spelt 'County' with a capital 'C' to emphasize its place in the order of things when Lord Willoughby de Broke's mother came to Warwickshire in 1867.[9] Long after the House of Lords ceased to be of great importance in framing legislation, aristocratic power continued to be of account in the counties. Eustace Percy, one of the sons of the seventh Duke of Northumberland, even argued that aristocrats operated best outside national politics, in which they were uncertain in judging public opinion.[10]

Lord Derby, leader of the Conservative party, made clear his sense of priorities by refusing to come to London for months on end: much to Disraeli's annoyance. The fifteenth Earl actually turned down the Greek throne in 1865; to be a

European king could not compare with the attractions of being King of Lancashire. The Derby family typified landed rule in the provinces right up to 1914: 'Let the suffrage be universal, and Earl Derby stand for Lancashire, does anyone know any Hodgson who would have a chance?' was the question posed in 1885 after the franchise had been widened to include the agricultural workers the previous year.[11] After all, with a tenant whose family had followed his ancestor to Flodden Field more than 350 years before, Lord Derby was not a bad approximation to a feudal lord.[12] The fifteenth Earl, when he died in 1893, could boast 727 servants, gardeners and staff of other kinds; he left £62,000 to them in his will. His nephew, still enormously influential in the north, became Lord Mayor of Liverpool at the end of 1911, reinforcing the point that land dominated commerce.

The Earl of Derby was one of the last, perhaps *the* last, of his kind; but the extent of his powers serves mainly to show how much the landed aristocracy had to lose. It was clear, moreover, that ownership of land was a pre-condition of political power at Westminster, in central government, as well as in the localities. To begin with, the duties were not onerous, and it was understandable that one section of the community should have controlled the executive. As Ramsay Muir noted in 1910, government in the eighteenth century had been practically confined to the management of foreign affairs (for which it was natural that those who mixed in the Court circles of the chief European countries should exercise power), to the maintenance of a small army and navy (traditionally commanded by the upper classes), and to the relatively simple regulation of trade by a fiscal tariff (far removed from modern complexities).[13]

The exact point at which the House of Commons became a more important element in ruling the life of the country than the House of Lords is less significant than the dominance of both by a landed elite. As late as 1885 sixty families supplied – as they had for generations – one-third of the House of Commons, one-third of the effective sovereign body of an

Empire which included a quarter of the human race.[14] Three-quarters of the Commons in the century before the first Reform Bill in 1832 had been landowners or their near relations, and the landed, aristocratic influence remained disproportionate long after the £10 urban householder and 40-shilling freeholder had been given the vote by the great act that followed.[15] Bagehot described the situation in 1867 in his famous study of *The English Constitution*: Parliament dominated by the opinions of the landed interest, which controlled not only the counties, but many of the towns too. These were MPs with an intimate bond, based on common traditions, education and pursuits, tying them together. The merchants and manufacturers, by contrast, were 'a motley race. . . . Traders have no bond of union, no habit of intercourse; their wives, if they care for society, want to see not the wives of other such men, but "better people", as they say – the wives of men certainly with land, and, if Heaven help, with the titles.'[16]

The members of the House of Lords were no less of an elite, but not one based on an aristocratic caste of great antiquity. The House of Lords in 1910 could boast only fifty-four peers whose titles went back to the seventeenth century or further, only eleven to the fifteenth century or before. Indeed, no single male descendant of any of the barons chosen to enforce Magna Carta sat in the Lords by this time.[17] The descendants of the mercer Lord Mayor of London, Sir Godfrey Feilding, became Earls of Denbigh; those of another Lord Mayor, Sir Godfrey Boleine, were the Earls of Wiltshire. In well over forty years, it is true, Elizabeth I raised a mere eight commoners to the peerage, but the overall number of members of the Lords was small in this period – sixty-two in 1560, fifty-nine in 1603. The early Stuarts raised money by the sale of peerages: James I actually blackmailed Sir Richard Robartes into elevation from knighthood to baronetcy to barony.[18] Later in the seventeenth century Charles II created nearly thirty dukedoms, though a proportion of these were for the use of his bastard sons; he also employed agents for the sale of baronetcies. A little over a hundred years later, William Pitt the Younger actively began to exploit the political loyalty derived from the award of peerages.

Through the centuries, therefore, the blood of the House of Lords had been mixed with that of outsiders. S. Baring-Gould, himself quite a traditionalist, indicated how mixed the origins of the aristocracy must have been when he observed that anyone living in 1889 would have the blood of 1,028,096 people in them, if one looked at a mere 20 generations. Men's arteries, he said, were sluices, through which rushed the drainage of the whole social countryside.[19]

What gave the House cohesion was, once again, its connection with the land. Far into the nineteenth century, perhaps as late as the 1880s, ninety per cent of the aristocracy came from landed origins. Lord Derby's assessment of land-holdings, the first since 1086, became known as the 'New Domesday' survey, and showed that in 1873 four-fifths of the land was owned by a mere 7,000 individuals: of the peers among them, all but a small percentage held large estates. The authors of *The Great Governing Families of England* (1885) explained that 'aristocracy' was only another word for the great owners of land.[20] All kinds of property were socially important, but 'It seemed as if the word "land" had a peculiar virtue of its own which carried with it certain privileges. Elsewhere such privileges are conferred by birth; here, the land secures them.' This last observation came from the Frenchman Emile Boutmy, puzzled, perhaps, because France knew no similar system.[21]

The values of rural England reflected the characteristics of rural life. This was, in the first place, a small-scale society in which the rulers and the ruled knew each other on a personal (though not necessarily a friendly) basis. As G. S. Street acutely observed in 1910, the old society – before the twentieth century – was not entirely exclusive, but it did have another important characteristic: 'It was a large family, this small community, mostly related and mutually known. You were either in it or outside it.'[22] Society was small enough for Lady Palmerston to write in her own hand all the invitations to her parties in the middle of the nineteenth century.

Rural England was also a society intensely preoccupied by tradition. Consuelo Vanderbilt, the American heiress who married the Duke of Marlborough, could not understand why Guy Fawkes's attempt to blow up Parliament almost three centuries before should mean that her wedding date had to be changed from 5 to 6 November: only the first of a series of 'archaic prejudices' she encountered.[23] With tradition went deference: 'Even after he [the "old squire"] is insolvent, when everybody knows that ruin is but a question of time, he will get five times as much respect from the common peasantry as the newly-made rich man who sits beside him.' The writer, Walter Bagehot, deplored the fact that the peasants would listen to 'nonsense', rather than the new man's 'sense', but even he made an apparent value distinction in comparing idolatries of rank and wealth: in reverencing wealth we reverence not a man 'but an appendix to a man'; in reverencing nobility we reverence 'the probable possession of a great faculty' – an unconscious grace of life and fine manners, for example, which you may find in the middle classes, but which *ought* to be in a landed family.[24]

Stability was the obvious accompaniment of tradition and deference. Men do not plant trees for themselves, but for their sons and grandsons: the landscape of the countryside has no meaning without continuity; and change seems destructive to it. Aristocracy and change mix uneasily too, for aristocracy honours the dead and not the living, and looks to the ancestor for ultimate guidance and authority.[25]

Sir Bernard Burke's book on *Vicissitudes of Families* (1883) showed well enough that history was littered with examples of once-powerful names that had not survived, but it also revealed that the more distant a county was from London, and the more rural it was, the more lasting its old families were likely to be. Emerson had himself quoted the almost proverbial saying that a family living fifty miles from London would last a century, one at a hundred miles would last two centuries, and so on (though 'steam, the enemy of time, as well as of space, will dispute these ancient rules').

The descendants of the Saxon Gurth the Swineherd, or of Higg, the son of Snell, might not be able to trace their ancestry, but the sense of continuity on the land ran very deep. In 1850, Burke visited the hamlet of Finderne, about four miles from Derby, seeking traces of the family bearing the same name, which had lived there for nine generations from the reign of Edward I to that of Henry VIII. Not a stone was left of their ancient hall, but on the site 'Finderne's flowers', brought by Sir Geoffrey from the Holy Land, still grew, testifying to the immortality of the rural pageant. Lord Palmerston, about the same time, spoke to a Hampshire audience on a small estate in the New Forest which had once belonged to the lime-burner Purkis, who – according to tradition – picked up the body of William Rufus and carried the royal corpse in a humble cart to Winchester. Seven hundred years later the same farm, eight miles from Romsey, was in the hands of a yeoman of the same name, to whom it had passed by direct male descent.[26]

In one important respect later commentators, writing as representatives of an urban civilization, were wrong in their analysis of pre-industrial England. Read Boswell's *Life* or Walpole's *Letters* or the *Life of Selwyn*, advised the American George W. Smalley in 1911, and you would see a clear dividing-line between those in and out of Society: the eighteenth-century elite was 'a caste' into which you had to take the precaution to be born.[27] The England of the years before the Industrial Revolution in the later eighteenth century was certainly an unequal, superficially caste-like society, but that is not the same as saying it was a class society. An agricultural economy was dominated by a homogeneous group of 'gentlemen' – no more than one in twenty of the population – who had almost all wealth and power concentrated in its hands.[28] Individuals moved up and down the social hierarchy, but without any change to the overall values of society.

Everything was, we might say, dynamically stationary.

Ideas of 'class' are undeniably difficult to evaluate, connected to one's own intuition, and that of others, to accent, bearing, income, occupation, education.[29] Central to all such notions, however, is the awareness by a self-identifying group of the population of its status in relation to other groups in society. The 'rise of the middle class' has been placed far back in history, but there was never, until the nineteenth century, a close-knit class of town-dwellers unwilling to join the ruling gentlemen. A few large towns – London, Liverpool and Bristol among them – had populations with an urban outlook, but it was not until the great developments in textiles and iron, coal and steam-power, in the second half of the eighteenth century, that lasting changes began to be made to England's social structure.

It is to Marx that we look for the most explicit statements of class consciousness. He was the exemplar of the way the language of class developed at the hands of social commentators in the Industrial Revolution. 'Middle class' in particular, a phrase whose first use is generally ascribed to the Evangelical clergyman, Thomas Gisborne, at the end of the eighteenth century, was an excellent shorthand way of describing (and asserting) the self-conscious autonomy of the men who had made their way to fortune, or at least financial independence, from the new industries.[30] When Gregory King made his famous examination of society at the end of the seventeenth century, there was no need to distinguish the capitalist manufacturing entrepreneur who became such a familiar figure in the social analyses of the nineteenth century.[31] By then, for the first time in British history, a group of men could be distinguished not merely by its money but by the fact that it could not and would not be absorbed by the landed rulers, that it was proud of – and conscious of – its distinctive role.[32]

None of this should suggest that the Industrial Revolution destroyed the traditions – or the rulers – of rural England at a stroke. Progress in industry was accompanied by a revolution in agriculture, one part of which – the division of the open fields and common land of medieval England into separate and distinct fields and farms – tended to reinforce the economic control of the grandees over the people of the countryside. The traditional pattern of local government proved equally resilient.[33] A member of the Municipal Corporation Commission in 1838 declared: 'the refusal of the County magistrates to act with a man who has been a grocer and is a Methodist is the dictate of genuine patriotism; the spirit of autocracy in the County magistracy is the salt which alone saves the whole mass from inevitable corruption.'[34] For many decades landed interests openly tried to block reform, arguing that it was right that they should control expenditure in areas where they were the ratepayers – in the counties where they lived.

The selection of JPs was in the hands of the Lord Lieutenant, who made recommendations to the Lord Chancellor. Lord Braybrooke, in Essex in the 1860s, was not untypical in relying for advice on such representatives of the local squirearchy as T. H. Bramston. Here Mr Thomas, 'who lately kept a shop in Shoreditch', was judged unfit to serve, and it is likely that when Samuel Howard – who owned a large drug factory, and was a keen fox hunter – was found to be a gentleman in June 1863, it was because he was prepared to adopt the ways of rural England.[35]

Local-government reform came first to the towns, but there problems of sanitation and public health were too large to be ignored. The Municipal Corporation Act of 1835, by creating elective councils, took town government out of the hands of the Justices of the Peace, all men with freehold property worth at least £100. A bill to replace JPs in the counties by an elected authority was unsuccessful in the 1830s, though by 1871 the relief of destitution and the provision of sanitation and elementary education had been taken from their multifarious functions. The county police forces that developed from the late 1840s were, in most essentials, modern public bodies; and the new importance of paid local government officials was symbolized by the first issue, in September 1907, of *The Local Government Officer*, which recorded the foundation two years before of the National Association of Local Government Officers. But that was after well over a century of industrial and economic change.

Nor did the House of Lords succumb immediately to the new industrial wealth. Disraeli, in his novel *Sybil* published in the 1840s, painted a picture of plebeian aristocracy created by Pitt which bears little relation to reality. An acute social commentator at the end of the century pointed out that Pitt's new peers represented a very faint foreshadowing of the elevation of men actually engaged in commerce that was to follow later.[36] Besides, even the bankers among them had become landed gentlemen with large estates before receiving their titles.

Industrial riches were not an automatic substitute for feudal grandeur. The greatest Prime Minister of the first half of the nineteenth century, Sir Robert Peel, was opposed to any aristocracy, especially one of wealth, that was not based on birth or intellect.[37] By his time, it is true, the proportion of Lords per million of population was, perhaps, nearly thirty per cent greater than it had been under the first of the Tudors, Henry VII. Yet the first of the industrial peers, the cotton millowner, Edward Strutt, was not elevated until 1856, when he became Lord Belper. As the Manchester *Examiner* observed, 'It is something for those who claim to be regarded as the descendants of the mailed barons of England to admit into their order a man who not only has made but is making his fortune by spindles and looms.' Strutt's grandfather, Jedediah, was a partner of Richard Arkwright; his great-granddaughter married the Duke of Norfolk. Nevertheless, of only seven new peers in Queen Victoria's reign before 1885 who had a commercial or industrial background, several already had aristocratic connections, several made their mark in other fields.[38]

The influx of men without landed connections into the

House of Commons was more marked, but here too there were limits on what the existing establishment would tolerate. Jewish business interests remained unacceptable until after the middle of the nineteenth century. In the late 1840s Baron Lionel de Rothschild, father of the first Lord Rothschild, tried to overcome what one pamphleteer called, not quite accurately, 'the last remnant of political oppression which disgraces our community in England, and depresses their energies'.[39] The *Fortnightly Review* typified a range of opinion determined to prevent attempts to 'Judaize Parliament', and for more than a decade – despite winning a number of elections – the baron was abused and excluded from taking his seat. (As it happened, when he was finally successful, much more than a decade passed without him making a single speech.)

It may seem strange that the institutions of old England did not crumble more quickly in the face of fast-developing industrial and financial interests. Yet the successful industrialists of the early nineteenth century came from nothing, elevated by a hard, brilliant, selfish struggle; they needed first to survive, and that meant no leisure for social life, least of all for genteel imaginings. Aristocracy, the land and tradition had no meaning for them. For a long time they used their profits for furthering their own businesses rather than for self-indulgent luxury. They remained in day-to-day control of their factory-centred, family organizations: far removed from the Edwardian financier – most characteristically plutocratic of all the plutocrats.[40] As late as the 1860s Bagehot noted that there was not yet a large class of cultivated businessmen, able to leave their careers to pursue other ambitions. The men of business did not yet appreciate their own strength, though that would change in the future.[41]

The first industrialists do not people social histories of their period. A proportion gained public honours, found their way into local or national politics, but most cannot even readily be identified by the factories and towns which were their lasting monument.[42] It may be that social mobility declined for a time, as business became more complex: the rewards were potentially greater, the demands – on time and energy – were correspondingly more formidable.[43] In the 1840s and 1850s there might be rumours of Hudson, the railway king, and his wife, her dresses set in magnificence in proportion to the number of her guests; but these, Lady Dorothy Nevill remembered, were 'aristocratic days, when the future conquerors of Society were still "without the gate"'.[44] Money alone would not buy a way into London Society.[45]

The real revolution – the revolution that was to take the nation into the era of the plutocrats – was about to begin.

Chapter 2

Rural Dearth and Business Plenty:
the Economic Revolution After 1870

The story of the rise of the plutocrats is in two parts. It is first the story of an extraordinary transformation in the world economy in the years after 1870; and it is no less the story of the collapse of landed power in the same period – a collapse which the plutocratic beneficiaries of economic revolution were to exploit with unswerving ruthlessness.

The squire's creed had not changed much century by century: 'I believe in my father, and his father, and his father's father, the makers and keepers of my estate; and I believe in myself and my sons and my son's son. And I believe that we have made the country, and shall keep the country what it is. . . . And I believe in my social equals and the country house, and in things as they are, for ever and ever. Amen.' Mr Pendyce at Galsworthy's Worsted Skeynes (and Worsted Skeynes was every country house) did not seem ʈ ɔ ask much: to do his duty and carry on his estate and pass it on (enlarged if possible) to his son – those were the sentiments he sometimes expressed, and that were always in his thoughts. Yet by this time, 1907, clearly identifiable forces were destroying the squire's way of life; a last stand seemed in prospect: 'A great responsibility rests on us landlords. If *we* go, the whole thing goes.'[1]

As the First World War approached there was one thing about which everybody agreed; and what has been patiently reconstructed by modern historians in mortgage deeds and estate correspondence and rent-rolls was colourfully recorded in contemporary comment. When the formidable Lady Bracknell quizzed Jack Worthing on his eligibility as a suitor in Oscar Wilde's *The Importance of Being Earnest*, he was happy to confess that his income of £7,000–£8,000 came mainly from investments rather than land.[2] The real-life landowner – and shrewd man of business – W. Bence Jones noted in the *Nineteenth Century* in 1882 how reduced establishments and lessened expenditure were to be seen among country gentlemen on all sides.[3] Within twenty-five years landed property could be compared to a quicksand which engulfed large fortunes.[4]

The first and most obvious change to the land was economic; while profits from industry grew, profits from agriculture declined. Writing in the *Nineteenth Century* in 1882, Charles Milnes Gaskell described the position which was now threatened: 'For many years the landowner has been credited with the possession of the most valuable form of security; no other class of property has been supposed to vie with his, and among its chief recommendations has been the fact that it could not "run away", and the supposition that it was always increasing in value.'[5] Until at least mid-century, agriculture had benefited from the Industrial Revolution and a growing population with money to spend on its products. The Corn Laws helped to maintain the high prices of the Napoleonic period, and their repeal in 1846 made little practical difference so long as cheap imports were not available. The decisive developments that take us to the world of John W. Martin's *The Ruin of Rural England* (1901) came – as they did in industry – in the second and not the first half of the nineteenth century.[6]

Joseph Chamberlain's speech to an Ipswich audience in January 1885 was typical: 'I suppose that almost universally throughout England and Scotland agriculture has become a ruinous occupation.'[7] The years 1875–9 all saw poor harvests and the Royal Commission on the Depressed State of the Agricultural Interest followed immediately afterwards; disease added to the problems. Above all, again in the late 1870s, a great influx of cheap imports became possible: technical developments contributed; railways brought the goods to the ports; and fast sea transport completed the process which reduced the cost of sending one ton of grain from Chicago to Liverpool from £3 7s in 1873 to £1 4s in 1884. Milnes Gaskell, in his *Nineteenth Century* article, thought that 'The vast increase in the carrying power of ships, the facilities of intercourse with foreign countries, the further cheapening of cereals and of meat' were alone quite enough to frighten the squire. The agricultural interest managed to dominate the first Commission, and a drought in 1893 was followed by three more years of deliberations, but the actions taken did not include a return to protection.

Britain had been hit harder than other European countries because it had put all the emphasis on wheat and other grains, clinging to them in the self-righteous sentimentality of its agricultural spokesman, Henry Chaplin, himself an owner of 23,000 acres in Lincolnshire ('no one', said Lord Willoughby de Broke, 'was half such a country gentleman as Harry Chaplin looked').[8] Rents fell too, to such an extent that in some cases receipts failed to keep pace with costs. In the years 1855–9 agriculture, in the form of wages and profits, had provided twenty per cent of the net national income; the corresponding figure was just over six per cent in 1895–9, and if some stability returned in the years before 1914, there was no reversal of the trend – and no return to a system of semi-feudal landlord rule.[9]

The crisis came at a time when demands on the landowner's income were fast increasing. Milnes Gaskell argued that the size of the rent-roll in the 'New Domesday Book' – the analysis of land-holdings in the 1870s – gave no real insight into his position: mortgages and debts were common; servants' wages, the cost of horses and of game were all up; the outlay for his son's education at Eton had risen by nearly a third in twenty-five years, for his daughter's clothes by a half in the same period. His eighteenth-century forbears, living in better times, had left a house too big for him, too large to let, too good to pull down. The old Yorkshire saying had special point: Lord Rockingham had built a house at Wentworth fit for the Prince of Wales, Sir Rowland Winn one at Nostel fit for Lord Rockingham, and Mr Wrightson at Cusworth one fit for Sir Rowland Winn. Gentlemen were about to begin their century of non-conspicuous consumption, which comes up to the present day – an enforced pattern of life wholly alien to their former traditions, and one which they turned into a virtue; Milnes Gaskell advised them 'to lead a simpler life, to restrict . . . expenditure'. Even primogeniture was not an answer, for relations could not be forgotten: one member of the Northumberland Ridley family had to provide £10,000 each for his ten children.[10]

Some mitigated the effects of agricultural depression by turning away from corn to stock and dairy farming; and the distinction made by many writers between the 'corn' counties of the south and east and the 'grazing' counties of the north and west provided quite an accurate picture of relative prosperity. Corn interests were over-represented in the Royal Commissions, whereas the drop in prices allowed livestock farmers to benefit from cheap feed.[11] All this happened at a time when the lamb chop was taking the place of bread and cheese as a typical working man's dinner diet. Thus a landowner such as the Earl of Derby, who had property in different parts of the country, faced a situation in which his rents in Cambridgeshire showed a disastrous decline from 1870 to the mid-1890s, but those in Lancashire showed a healthy rise in the same period.

When James Caird discussed *The Landed Interest and the Supply of Food* in 1878 he alleged that landowners were failing to take advantage of 'a teeming, wealthy, meat-consuming people', as they could have done by treating their property in businesslike fashion.[12] But to some the difficulties were a positive spur. George Cadbury and Tom Bryan, in *The*

Land and the Landless (1909), described the gentry's response to plutocratic competition: many of them actually took more interest in exploiting the potential profit from their land in order to make the same show of affluence as the newly rich manufacturers.[13]

Of course the solutions were not simple, hardly to be found 'in the larger consumption of cabbages and strawberries by the English people', a comment of Milnes Gaskell's which found an amusing echo six years later when the great Gladstone, at a Hawarden flower show, appeared to offer the growing of strawberries as his main remedy for depression. W. Bence Jones was much more thoroughgoing in arguing that landowning was a business in the same sense as cotton spinning; naturally the old feudal ways had many appealing features, but it was no good looking back fifty years – to the 1830s – when the landlord only had to sit back in his armchair and watch the rents come in. Not that tenants necessarily wanted efficient owners – and Bence Jones's article provoked a rejoinder accusing him of showing 'How to Abolish the Tenant-Farmer Class'.[14]

The evidence at least suggests that English landowners as a body were probably no less efficient than industrialists in the same period; many of them used commonsense methods to increase their incomes.[15] The growth of the professions, of high standards in the law, surveying, banking, land agenting, were ultimately further signs in the decline of hereditary privilege, but for much of the nineteenth century they could be used by the landed aristocracy to their own advantage. When Sir James Graham was about to sell a large part of Netherby in the 1820s, his agent, John Yule, protested: 'plebeian though I am, I cannot bear to see it go out of the possession of an Honourable old family, who have always been beloved by their retainers, into the hands of a Hard-hearted grinding speculator.'[16] State aid for agricultural improvements – more than thirteen million pounds from 1846–81 – helped to mitigate the worst effects of strict family settlement, by which the 'landowner' was no better than a 'life tenant' in the

Sir Ernest Cassel, Sir Thomas Lipton and Alfred Harmsworth are among those that covet Edward VII's throne in this drawing by Max Beerbohm

Maurice de Hirsch; from
the 'Men of the Day'
feature in *Vanity Fair*
26 July 1890

Sir Julius Wernher

sense that he could not sell or mortgage his property. The Settled Land Act of 1882 at last allowed the landed proprietor to sell land subject to family settlement – provided the sum raised was kept in the family – though this too was a portent of an age which put monetary security before the integrity of the landed estate: it offered the way out of financial crisis, and the end of a way of life.

In the villages themselves, there was a visible change from 'peasant thrift' to 'commercial thrift', forcibly described by George Sturt, who had inherited a small family business supplying farmers' needs, and who catalogued *Change in the Village* in 1912. Gone were the people who 'with their own hands raised and harvested their crops, made their clothes, did much of the building of their homes, attended to their cattle, thatched their ricks, cut their firing, made their bread and wine or cider, pruned their fruit trees and vines, looked after their bees, all for themselves'. The peasant had become the spender of money at the baker, coal merchant and provision dealer; and if he spent money he had first to make it.[17]

Even the Central Chamber of Agriculture, founded in 1865 to promote agricultural interests, showed the landowners responding to the new pressures on them, rather than leading. Its Chairman admitted that the 'long immunity of the land from attack [for Whigs and Tories were alike of the landed class] not only resulted in apathy among those landowners who still held seats in Parliament, but also in their individual knowledge of the industry becoming, with rare exceptions, practically atrophied.' His Chamber never seemed to have the true cohesion of the old landed interest, and when in November 1909 it was proposed that a deputation should be sent to the Marquess of Crewe (Liberal Leader in the Lords) and the Marquess of Lansdowne (the Tory Opposition Leader) to complain about the effects on the land of Lloyd George's famous budget, 'There was a very animated debate . . . opponents of the motion (ten in number) being Members of Parliament sitting on the Government side of the House'; and when the deputation finally went, Crewe and Lansdowne declined to meet it. The power of the 'Railway Interest' made a fascinating contrast. In 1904 an inquiry was made into the different rates charged by railway companies for carrying home as against foreign and colonial farm produce. The new masters exercised their power in packing the committee to their advantage.[18]

It was readily understandable that the landowner felt his power slipping away from him. For many decades articulate, noisy attacks had been made on him almost as if he was a feudal baron, ruling over his neighbourhood by military force.[19] It did not matter that the actual importance, earlier in the century, of the Chartist Fergus O'Connor's National Land Company, or, more recently, of Henry George's land reformers, was small. Ireland, always the odd fellow in the British Isles, was wholly exceptional in having a Land League instrumental in changing the land system.[20] But a string of legislation seemed to confirm the landowner's belief that the world was plotting against him. The Tithes Act of 1891 made tithes payable by the owner and not the tenant of the land; and a series of Acts included, in 1908, a strengthening of the tenant's claim to compensation against his landlord for unreasonable behaviour.[21]

More significant were measures directed against the privileges of land ownership, especially dearly loved sporting and shooting rights; the Ground Game Act of 1880 removed the landowner's right to protect pheasants and other game which had often destroyed his tenants' crops, and the process did not stop there. In January 1881, in the North Riding of Yorkshire, a tenant farmer stated that 'he saw no reason why the landlords should not have winged game *at present*';[22] and an Act of 1906 gave tenants the right of compensation for damage caused by such game, which only the landlord had the right to kill. The landowners who had always dominated hunting even found this favourite of pastimes threatened; subscription hunting, more or less the rule by 1900, was a sign that increased costs, as well as legislation, could add to the sense of oppression.[23]

The overall consequence of all these changes was that the land declined rapidly as a source of employment. The number of male agricultural labourers in England and Wales declined by a third in the thirty years after 1871, while the population as a whole increased by a considerably greater proportion in the same period. The Liberal politician C. F. G. Masterman called it 'the largest secular change of a thousand years: from the life of the field to the life of the city'.[24] Industrial growth may have set the pace in the first half of the nineteenth century; Britain may have been the most urban population in the world at mid-century; but the real drama came later. The relative profits from agriculture and industry in 1855 and 1913 speak for themselves: agriculture dropping from 57 million pounds to 46 million, industry, despite long periods of depression and fluctuation, surging forward from 123 million to 517 million.[25] A 'second' Industrial Revolution was the counterpart to the crisis on the land: it transformed the world in the second half of the nineteenth century and provided riches on a scale never before seen in Britain.

Population statistics were revealing. England and Wales: 1801, 9 millions; 1851, 18 millions; 1911, 36 millions. Greater London alone grew from just over a million to much more than seven millions in the same period. The result was an urban landscape of a new kind, for in the past living in a large town had still meant living within walking distance of the countryside: at the beginning of the twentieth century a Liverpool man of fifty might still remember viewing the sea across the open fields which had by then become Bootle.[26] For men who had never seen a city, the first great towns of the Industrial Revolution must have shocked the consciousness; but now, for a new generation that might never have seen anything but endless miles of houses and factories and shops in a wholly urban existence, what meaning could there be in the rhythms of rural life?

Large-scale industry and technological progress helped to cater for the fast-changing urban society. Big business had been known before – in coal-mining long before 1750, in engineering or cotton spinning from the 1780s. But the older industries of the first Industrial Revolution, especially coal and iron, were later able to take advantage of the improved transport facilities and sophisticated methods of financing that developed as a response to the needs of a national economy and an Empire enjoying rapid expansion; the whole of Europe in 1880 did not produce as much coal as Great Britain a little more than thirty years later.[27] A whole range of massive consumer industries grew in harmony with the needs of a much-altered market-place: the cocoa of Cadbury and Rowntree, the tea of Lipton, the soap of Lever – these were the typical products of the age.[28] New processes, specialized machines, entirely new industries altered the pattern of traditional living. Internal combustion engine and electric light, mass-produced newspapers and synthetics – all were part of a technological revolution that made its first impact in the second half of the nineteenth century, above all in the decades that followed the 1870s, until the First World War.[29]

For the first time both Europe (amidst the imperial expansionism of the 1880s) and America (after the Civil War gave an enormous boost to industrial interests) embraced the elements of mass civilization: the scale of industry and city life, the influence of communications, technology and education on everyday life, the very size of the population – these are the identifying characteristics of contemporary existence. The picture needs only one qualification. In the early days the benefits of industrial civilization were very unevenly distributed through society. In 1874 even Gladstone expressed the fascination of the conquest of nature, but he was unhappy to note that the employers had derived more than the workers from the technological revolution.[30] In this last observation he pointed towards an important truth: the system which gave riches to a small elite had not changed; almost everything else in the world had.

'Inventions facilitate big operations', Andrew Carnegie wrote in 1900. Since he had begun his career several decades before, the locomotive had quadrupled in power; the steamship had become ten times bigger, the blast-furnace had seven times more capacity – and there was no sign of a slackening in the trend.[31] He understood the process well because he – with the other men of business, the plutocrats – were the principal beneficiaries in a brief but astonishing period preceding our own era of institutional and corporate power. The plutocrats looked back to the era of individual achievement, and they looked forward to the impersonal future – to remote rule at the head of the modern business corporation.

This was the background that enabled one of the most distinguished historians of the late nineteenth century to observe: 'There has probably never been a period in the history of the world when the conditions of industry, assisted by the great gold discoveries in several parts of the globe were so favourable to the formation of enormous fortunes as at present, and when the race of millionaires was so large.'[32] In one sense, the American experience seemed more spectacular than the British, for Rockefeller and Guggenheim, Gould and Harriman won wealth of staggering proportions in a country that had known barely a century of independent existence. Britain's ascendancy in the world economy reached its high point in about 1870, when her foreign trade figures almost matched those of France and Germany, Italy and America combined. But if Britain was no longer, by the last decades of the nineteenth century, a country unfamiliar with modern civilization, it was the staging-ground for a social and economic experiment in which the traditions of a thousand years were to be shaken by businessmen whose mastery of their environment gave them power of a wholly new kind.

There may have been as many as eighty men who died in Britain between 1901 and 1914 leaving more than a million pounds. Some of these were aristocrats, some have been forgotten and some have lives which may never be reconstructed – no one now has heard of Raphael the merchant banker, Quilter the stockbroker, or Loeffler the engineer. For others the historical record is clearer. When Barney Barnato –

East End slum kid and financial genius – died in 1897 he left nearly three million pounds. Sir Julius Wernher and Alfred Beit, partners in South African diamond and gold, had fortunes amounting to nearly twenty million pounds between them. Sir Ernest Cassel, German-born star of the international financial community, was still worth seven millions in the post-war austerity of 1921 in which he died.[33]

The plutocrats were quite distinct from the growing numbers of moderately wealthy, middle class who were acquiring respectability in the period, and whose pretensions were further diluted in the hands of what C. F. G. Masterman called the 'Suburbans': the inhabitants of 'Acacia Villa' and 'Camperdown Lodge', or of 'Homelea', 'Belle View' and 'Buona Vista' – contiguous dwellings in Beaconsfield Road, Upper Norwood.[34] Naturally the story of aspiring middle class and plutocrats overlapped at many points, but the Edwardian radical Arthur Ponsonby identified a species of 'hardheaded genuine plutocrat', untouched by moral scruple or old-fashioned gentlemanly refinement: an altogether tougher breed.[35] These men had the will, and the resources, to drive for the top, in an elitest struggle that dramatized the deep divisions in British society. Their millions seemed all the more amazing while 'the Multitude' lived the life of the proletarian city – a devastated landscape under a grey sky, erected almost overnight for an industrializing society; and while the 'Prisoners', at the bottom of the social pyramid, lived and died an unseen, almost animal-like existence.[36]

The stakes were high. The life expectancy of a poor man born in 1900 was about thirty years; the rich man could look forward to double that. As the old society faded and the age of the masses closed in, there was a short period in which new men – the plutocrats – rose to immense wealth at a speed which perhaps knew no precedent in the history of the world. After 1914 restrictions and taxes and socialism were to make life more difficult for plutocracy as well as aristocracy. But, for the moment, there were those ready to seize the oppor-tunities provided by revolutions in technology and communications, by vast, rich markets and the development of the world overseas. The years from 1870 to 1914 – the exact borderlines are blurred – were the years in which individual economic skill, making use of the anti-individualistic tools of modern civilization, was to produce a fascinating phenomenon: the rise of the plutocrats.

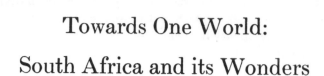

Chapter 3

Towards One World:
South Africa and its Wonders

Millionaires and How They Became So was published in 1884. It perfectly expressed the atmosphere in which the plutocrats came to prominence. 'We do not propose to teach "the gospel of greed" but rather to tell the method of success. Every true man has a laudable desire to be rich.' The message was complacent: 'There is not wealth enough in the world for every man to be rich. It follows as a necessity that some must be poor if others are to be millionaires'; and it was simple: 'we have been struck by the similarity of method which each millionaire has adopted to become rich. The only secret of their methods has been hard work in starting life, and dogged perseverance once started.' The analysis was, perhaps, true as far as it went, but more significant was the fact that – with the exception of such aristocrats as the Duke of Sutherland, or the Duke of Northumberland – most of the gigantic fortunes had been made since the invention of steam-power.[1]

Steam-power had its most profound effect on communications: mass production was meaningless in a world without fast and effective means of distribution. By 1896 the united capital of British railways had reached £1,000,000,000: if a man had started to count it, sovereign by sovereign, at noon on 1 January 1897, at fifty sovereigns a minute, day and night, it would have taken him until 9.20 am on 11 January 1934 to finish. Two railways had even acquired hereditary directors, as if they were baronial institutions: Sir Watkin Wynn of the Great Western and the Duke of Sutherland of the North-Western.[2] In the thirty years before 1870, 125,000 miles of railways were built in the world; in the thirty years after 1870 the figure reached 360,000 – in a sense, the railway age came much later than the period with which we associate it.[3]

The efforts of the railway pioneers were not accompanied in the main by the modern methods of organization and finance of those that followed; nor by huge financial rewards. But later in the century, the fortune of Baron Maurice de Hirsch, grandson of the Bavarian court banker and friend of Edward, Prince of Wales, amounted to twenty million pounds, perhaps more. The core of his fortune came from railway development, for in 1868 he launched East Hungarian Railways, with support from the international bankers Bischoffsheim and Goldschmidt (for whom Sir Ernest Cassel once worked), and the long-term intention of linking the lines of Austria-Hungary to those projected from Constantinople and Adrianople. Delighting in the incessant intrigues of the Ottoman Empire, obtaining first-class technical and financial backing, he achieved a brilliant, far-sighted, devil-may-care conquest with the Oriental Railway Company and his other enterprises.[4]

'Turkish Hirsch' – the nickname came from his railway-building activities – was a truly cosmopolitan figure. His origins lay in Munich, but he controlled his business empire from London, from Paris, from Brussels, from his Central European estates. The German ambassador in London, Baron von Eckhardstein, observed that towards the end of his life, Hirsch 'lapsed into an almost incomprehensible lingo in which he mixed up English, French and German': 'And those sind die Karpaths', he would tell visitors on the terrace of his castle, which overlooked the Carpathians.[5] Railways knew no national boundaries and their builders thought in terms of international riches.

One Edwardian businessman recounted a tale which reinforced the message learned from the spread of railways. In the year AD 212, the Emperor Caracalla, who ruled jointly with his brother, heard from the Praetorians that he might become sole Emperor of Rome if he returned from Britain without delay. He crossed Europe in sixteen incredible days, killed his brother (among others) and succeeded. In 1827 the British ambassador in Rome was told that he might become Prime Minister if he went immediately to London: he – it was George Canning – took sixteen days, and duly took office. So much for 1600 years of progress. The speed and the extent of change in the world was limited by the speed and range of communications.[6]

Experience of life outside Great Britain became much more common in the nineteenth century, especially as sea transport became faster after mid-century, and with it came the opportunity to invest or seek money in what became the greatest Empire the world has seen. In 1900, the British Empire was half as large again as it had been in 1870; and some countries which never became part of it were developed largely with British capital.

The attacks by J. A. Hobson (*Imperialism*, 1902) and H. N. Brailsford (*The War of Steel and Gold*, 1914) on the export of capital, and the Marxist interpretations of Empire that have found much favour and disfavour ever since, are not much guide to the atmosphere of money-making, which reached its extreme expression in South Africa. John Buchan's David Crawfurd and *Prester John* (1910) are more to the point: ' "You see, Davie," ' Crawfurd's uncle explained, ' "you don't know the rudiments of business life. There's no house in the country that would take you in as a common clerk, and you would never earn much more than a hundred pounds a year all your days. If you want to better your future you must go abroad, where white men are at a premium." ' And, indeed, in South Africa Davie successfully thwarted the plans of John Laputa, trying to revive the empire of Prester John, the legendary King of Abyssinia. In an adventurous triumph over treachery, rascally half-castes and native spears, he made his fortune: 'My money seemed pleasant to me, for if men won theirs by brains or industry, I won mine by sterner methods, for I had staked it against my life.' The epilogue abandoned romance – of one kind, at least – in the discovery (not by the hero) of a diamond pipe and its development as the Aitken Proprietary Mine, 'one of the most famous in the country'.[7] Buchan dedicated the book to Lionel Phillips, who would not have found it inappropriate; he had himself come from England as a young man to make a fortune in diamonds and gold, and – in the aftermath of Dr Jameson's famous raid on the Transvaal in 1895 – to face a death sentence and eventual reprieve.

The story of the opening up of South Africa is as fascinating as it is significant: as J. B. Robinson, most unpleasant of millionaires, wrote in 1900:

It is my opinion that few men in England have any adequate conception of the future importance of South Africa . . . we are laying the political foundations of a continent which will be the keystone of the arch of our Empire. The resources of the Transvaal are endless. It is seamed with rich minerals of every kind. Its population, under a modern administration, will go up by leaps and bounds.[8]

What a land of contrasts! 'An atmosphere of exquisite purity, skies of intense blueness, spells of perfect calm, seasons of divine exhilaration, alternate with blasts of scorching wind, with thunderstorms of unsurpassed severity, with occasional tempests of hail, snow, and rain, with periods of pitiless and destructive drought'; and the history matched, with periods of calm followed by war, rebellion and bloodshed. Odd that we should go to the insensitive Robinson, this time writing in 1887, for such an observant description.[9]

One of the other pioneers in the diamond fields recalled the situation in 1870: the whole of South Africa was virtually bankrupt, with a British pound obtainable only at a premium . . . no railways, no markets of importance . . . a Boer population which consisted as much of self-sufficient hunters as anything. . . .[10] Such was the country in which a man would tell you that diamonds were the droppings of ostriches, in which in 1852 the missionary John Campbell had marked on his map the spot where he camped on the banks of the Orange River by the word 'diamonds' – and no one cared about what he called these 'trifles'.

Sporadic diamond finds in the second half of the 1860s were quietly received, until in 1869 a farmer, Schalk van Niekerk, was shrewd enough to pay a Hottentot shepherd boy 500 sheep, 10 oxen and one horse for what was eventually to be called 'The Star of South Africa', a diamond which soon changed hands in South Africa for £11,200, was then sold through London jewellers to the Earl of Dudley for £25,000 and was on the market again in 1974 for £225,300.[11] Sir Richard Southey, Colonial Secretary when news of the find broke, is said to have portentously announced: 'Gentlemen, this is the rock on which the future success of South Africa will be built.' The immediate result was a rush of ten thousand diggers in less than two years to the banks of the Vaal River – into which the Orange River flowed – and more discoveries on the adjoining Boer farms; in July 1871 finds at Colesberg Kopje accounted for the foundation of the famous town of Kimberley (christened after another British Colonial Secretary).

Sir Osbert Sitwell, who saw the effect of the plutocracy on the Edwardian London of his boyhood, made his own judgment on the South African diamonds, which expressed a spirit of 'unparalleled materialism'; they lacked 'the icy blue fires of those that came from Brazil'.[12] His comment would have sounded odd indeed in the early years when (one pioneer recalled) 'the future magnates were . . . merely "maggots" financially', isolated hundreds of miles from Cape Town.[13] J. B. Taylor (later a partner in Wernher, Beit & Co.) travelled as an eleven-year-old boy on a monthly journey by mule from the coast, source of all supplies: at Kimberley tinned foods caused ptomaine poisoning, mealie-meal was £3–4 a *muid* sack, water was two miles from camp. Clouds of dust would blow down their tents, covering their bedding and cooking with an inch of filth; rain and hail storms might follow.[14] Julius Wernher wrote home of a place with no grass, few trees, yellow sand broken by muddy water, and a great wide plain with patches of green: there was nothing more to say.[15]

The claims were dug directly by the side of the inadequate tracks; vehicles and animals would fall down them; deaths often resulted.[16] Kimberley deaths in one year in the 1880s amounted to more than 3,000 from a population of 20,000, a figure which included over 50 murders. As late as 1891 the most adventurous of English aristocrats, Lord Randolph Churchill – 'done with politics', as he wrote to his wife from Mafeking, and trying 'to make a little money for the boys and for ourselves' – could only describe the land through which he passed as 'this God-forsaken country'.[17]

Many of the names of the early diggings told their own story: Forlorn Hope perhaps more appropriate than Larkin's Flat. The mining was carried out in chaos; at first diamonds were found on or near the surface, but once digging went deeper, it was not long before open workings deteriorated for lack of attention and capitalization. The politician J. X. Merriman grasped the essence of the matter in a letter to the sourly ubiquitous Robinson in January 1886: 'Briefly, I am quite satisfied that amalgamation on a basis which will bring millions of foreign capital into the Colony will be the salvation of the whole country.'[18] By this time companies had developed from the individual diggings and were in danger of killing each other, just as the early diggers had often ruined each other in mad confusion.

For once history's anecdotes may not be far from the truth. One day Cecil Rhodes is said to have asked Alfred Beit what plans he was considering. Beit, a short, plumpish figure, doubtless rolled his large, prominent, thoughtful brown eyes as he replied: 'I am going to control the whole diamond output before I am much older.' Firmly on the historical record is the statement he made at the first meeting of the new De Beers Consolidated group, after success had been won, in May 1888: 'When I saw the necessity and desirability of getting that control of the Kimberley Mine, I put my whole heart into it, and after a while it got to be a matter of sport, and then I went into it still more heavily.'[19] Beit had been born in Hamburg in 1853. His father was a merchant without the physical stamina to maintain the momentum of his business; the family took its lead from his mother – a strong, domineering, economy-conscious figure ('all that Beit wanted', said Rhodes, 'was to be rich enough to give his mother £1,000 a year').[20] His uncle, Dr Ferdinand Beit, was the founder of the German chemical industry ('We', said Alfred, 'were the poor Beits').[21]

He first encountered Kimberley as the representative of the merchants D. Lippert & Co. in 1875 and, though there are many recollections of him dreamily stroking his feeble moustache, his ability was soon in uncharacteristically immodest evidence: 'I found that very few people knew anything about diamonds; they bought and sold vaguely. . . . Of course, I saw at once that some of the Cape stones were as good as any in the world.'[22] In 1878 he set up on his own as a diamond merchant and in the eighties became associated with Wernher and his partner, Porges.

Julius Wernher came from Darmstadt, in the grand duchy of Hesse, where he was born in April 1850 as the eldest son of a railway engineer who knew Robert Stephenson and Brunel. Julius started work in a Frankfurt bank and, on being posted to Paris, was caught in the Franco-Prussian War, in which he served in the cavalry and the occupying army. His Paris employer armed him with a letter of introduction to Jules Porges in London and early 1871 found him on the other side of the world, in South Africa, as assistant to Porges's partner, Charles Mège, in his diamond-buying activities. Within little more than a year he was able to write home confidently: 'I am already indispensable to my Frenchman'; and their joint interests soon included the ownership of diamond mines in the Kimberley fields. The most important friendship he made was with Alfred Beit, and the two became partners in January 1890 when Porges retired.[23]

Beit and Wernher had met Rhodes in the early days: Rhodes – abstracted and silent as a young man, pictured by one of his contemporaries leaning moodily against a street wall in Main Street, Kimberley, his mouth firm, his chin strong, his profile massive, impassive, waiting to leap into actions which would carry him to great heights, and great despair.

Rhodes's problem was that he could never keep a sense of proportion: like many of the characters in this book he was immensely able and immensely naive. Dr Jameson hit the root of the paradox when he asked: 'Where are you to find so large a man of ideas combined with so big a man of action?'[24] Rhodes was a founder of the De Beers Mining Co. Ltd in April 1880 while still in his twenties – just ten years after he first came to South Africa for health reasons. He impressed the impassive Liberal politician Haldane 'as a splendidly energetic man of affairs, with a wide outlook and great capacity for getting things through'.[25] His failing health gave urgency to everything he did and though, with the exception of Beit, he disliked financiers, he saw the need for money to finance his aims. But such aims: when he first drew up a will, in September 1877, the estate was to help establish a secret society 'the true aim and object whereof shall be the extension of British rule throughout the world'.[26] In session after session in the Cape Parliament he made clear his desire for 'a united South Africa to the Zambesi': 'it is as if I were a little sailing-boat on Table Bay, and knew exactly what port I am aiming for'.[27]

He told a special meeting of De Beers shareholders in March 1880 that his ambition was not merely to make their company the richest and greatest but also 'the most powerful company the world has ever seen'.[28] The message was evidently appealing, and the Rev. F. Verschoyle forcefully answered the attacks made on him in the *Contemporary Review* by J. A. Hobson. 'Luxury, ease, and the reputation of wealth he valued . . . at nothing.' Money as an end in life was not worth the labour; it was money as an instrument that was supremely well worth getting, 'the true lever of Archimedes to move the modern world'.[29]

And the means of acquiring that lever? Well, 'Ask little Alfred' provided the best answer to that question. Beit often appeared misleadingly inattentive, but had brilliant powers of observation and intuition when any financial question arose. Frank Harris, who interviewed him for the London magazine *John Bull* shortly before his death in 1906, noted a nervous hesitation in his manner until he began to talk business, when 'he came to perfect self-possession'.[30] In 1885, after a long period of amalgamation, there were still more than fifty private holdings, more than forty companies with interests in the seventy acres of the chief mines: the Kimberley, De Beers, Dutoitspan and Bultfontein.[31] The battle that followed centred on the Rhodes–Beit interests and those of the cockney genius, Barney Barnato. Rhodes's methods were crude when he finally met Barnato: he talked of peace and plenty in a prosperous British Africa, and tried to buy Barnato out. Beit, on the other hand, could raise substantial institutional backing, and was in close touch with European financiers, above all with Nathaniel Rothschild, who once chided Rhodes with the curt judgment, 'our business is to get diamonds, and we are not a philanthropic association'.

Not that victory came easily, nor did it result in the extinction of Barnato, who sat on the board of the De Beers Consolidated Co. which was set up in 1888, powerful enough to control the diamond production of the world. The Cape Town *Lantern* recorded the occasion by portraying Rhodes and Barnato providing the heads for the Kimberley Janus, at the door of the temple of the mining industry. The trust deed put no limits on the scope or geographical range of its investments; in its time it was the largest corporation in the world.

Frank Harris misread the situation, and misunderstood Barnato's character, when he pointed to the mystery of Beit's success over Barnato, 'who had reached Kimberley years before him, and who had never cared for anything in his life but money, and had sought it night and day with the meanness of avarice which collects pennies and saves crusts'.[32] Barnett Isaacs – Barney Barnato – came from the Whitechapel slums of London, born in 1852 in this home of alcoholism and bullying, crooks and prostitutes, and – for some – resolute cheerfulness. His skill in predicting share price changes made him fortunes many times over; and he could still perform effectively in the Chair – in Rhodes's absence – at the first Annual General Meeting of De Beers Consolidated, despite preparation which consisted of drinking and gambling for many nights before.

But his special gift was as a salesman not as a wooden-faced financier. He had arrived in South Africa with only £30 and 40 boxes of cigars to sell, and his acting talents are seen to good effect in the pictures which survive of him at Kimberley in 1870 as the Admiral in 'Black-Eyed Susan' and the auctioneer in 'The Octoroon': never was so strange a prototype for a millionaire. He was later able to claim: 'there is nothing this country produces I have not traded in, from diamonds and gold, right through wool, feathers and mealies, to garden vegetables.'[33] A Beit or a Rothschild might be unimpressed, but in the general uncertainty which his activities often fostered – there were many slumps, as well as booms, in the early years – others were happy to respond to the magic of his appeal: 'If I had proposed to make a tunnel from the Bank of England to Johannesburg, they would have snatched at the shares, without waiting to hear a single detail of the scheme'. Megalomania mixed with massive achievement.[34]

'Mr Beit said little, but supported Mr Rhodes; but the notion of using the diamond mines to create an Empire did not recommend itself as good business to Mr Barnato': the understatement, describing their meeting in 1887, came from one of

Rhodes's early biographers.[35] Of course Barnato enjoyed influencing President Kruger of the Transvaal in the furore that followed Dr Jameson's Raid, but the economic power that enabled him to do so was what he understood – and his nephew, Solly Joel, was one of the prisoners. Beit's reaction against politics was even stronger, and it was through constantly deferring to Rhodes on political matters that he showed most misjudgment: on the eve of the Boer War, dining with Sir Drummond Chaplin in Hamburg (Chaplin with his wife, Beit with his mother), he declared: 'Rhodes tells me that Kruger will climb down to any extent rather than fight.'[36] War followed. Beit had acquired a keen interest in furthering the aims of Britain from Rhodes, but Frank Harris was close to the truth – rather rare for him – in asserting that his instinctive aversion to political enterprises was matched by his overriding concern with his profit-and-loss account.[37]

At the Commission of Inquiry which followed the Jameson Raid Beit admitted spending nearly £200,000 in support of the furtherance of the non-Boer population's rights in the Transvaal – if necessary by violence – though he denied prior knowledge of the Raid. The Report exonerated him from the charge – made by the radical Labouchere – that he had used the Raid to carry out bear operations for his firm's profit. But many people noted the effects of the upheaval; Lady Sarah Wilson, who had first met Beit on her way to South Africa in 1895, watched the departure of the boat carrying him to the London Inquiry: 'Mr Beit looked ill and worried; Mr Rhodes, on the other hand, seemed to be in robust health, and as calm as the proverbial cucumber.'[38]

Rhodes told the former Prime Minister, Rosebery – in a conversation recorded by Rosebery in his betting book – that the Raid had cost Beit and himself £400,000, but it was the persistent worry, not the money, that took its toll.[39] In 1901 Arthur Markham MP repeated accusations that Wernher, Beit and the members of their company were thieves, swindlers and warmongers, and an out-of-court settlement provided no real compensation. Two years later, Beit's re-election to the Board of the Chartered Company was questioned in the Commons.

Wernher watched all this with even greater alarm. At the time of the Raid Beit was working hard acquiring a British character, partly by supporting British interests, but Wernher warned him against all political involvement. Rhodes pushed him on; Wernher drew him back: a situation which was mirrored in financial matters too. 'Rhodes could never have achieved what he did at Kimberley nor in Rhodesia without Beit,' observed Lionel Phillips, who became a partner in Wernher, Beit & Co. after the Raid, 'and Beit in turn might have landed himself in terrible financial troubles but for the wise head, the cool judgment, and the clear vision of Wernher.'[40] Wernher's calm and solidity harmonized with the imposing weight of his body: he eschewed intuition and gambling for facts – and he made more money than any of the South African magnates. He never had to face crisis unprepared and he often rescued Beit from making mistakenly bold purchases in the market at the wrong time. 'Silent and self-contained', was the judgment of Barney Barnato's first partner, Louis Cohen (who was neither).[41]

Wernher's self-analysis ran on the same lines: 'I am not one of those people who create fortunes by genius or new combinations, and lose them again and win them again. I only walk well-known paths, but I walk steadily . . . not out of conviction, without, indeed paying too much attention to my own point of view.'[42] It was, perhaps, excessive caution which led him to make one of his rare mistakes. The Society magazine *Vanity Fair* was delighted to report in January 1908: 'Every now and then we have a pleasant case in which a millionaire parts with his money almost as easily as if he were some impecunious devil living from hand to mouth.' A Paris electrical engineer, Lemoine, obtained £60,000 from Wernher through his claim to have discovered how to make synthetic diamonds, and though his trial for fraud followed, 'The whole mad case only shows how the most cautious men are sometimes caught by the wildest propositions.'[43]

Sixty thousand pounds was, in fact, a small price to pay for the opportunities provided by South Africa: 'You know that we are so big in this country', said Wernher, in a comment that indicated confidence rather than expressed unreality, 'that what is good for the country is good for us.'[44] For after diamonds came gold, discovered on the Witwatersrand plateau in October 1885, before which it had only been found in alluvial deposits or in quartz veins.[45] The following year the Rand was declared a public gold-field. 'The incalculable element which we call luck was always one of the chief attractions of the Rand', J. B. Taylor's brother explained: 'and sometimes luck changed rapidly and sensationally, confirming the faith of those who believed in it.'[46] As Beit pointed out, however, there was much early scepticism among the men who had the resources to create a modern industry. Ferdinand de Rothschild, who spent three weeks in South Africa in 1894, recorded cautiously: 'it must not be forgotten that the deeper you work into the ground the greater is the difficulty and the expense.'[47] Rhodes himself feared that Beit, in becoming too involved with gold, would cease to support him, and failed to see the potential which was to create the city of Johannesburg and multi-million-pound riches.

Beit, on the other hand, mastered both the technical and financial problems of developing the gold-mines. He was instrumental in obtaining the best engineers from all over the world to cope with deep-level mining, and he found the capital to support them; he reckoned that each of his mines required a million pounds in order to maximize returns, but he refused to use their potential for the easy money of share speculation. He could not look to London, where the big banking houses did not appear to be interested in gold, but through Rudolph Kahn of Paris, in particular, he obtained European finance: Crédit Lyonnais from France, the Deutsche Bank from Germany, in the end the Rothschilds – all participated, entrusting to Wernher, Beit & Co. enormous sums for investment in the gold industry.[48]

Beit had first visited the fields in 1886 after agreeing to

guarantee more than £80,000 for J. B. Robinson's debts, and sending Robinson, with a further £25,000 capital, on a trial exploration. Robinson had almost bankrupted himself working against Rhodes and the diamond amalgamations; Beit saved him, but had no illusions: 'it was difficult to work with him, or rather impossible. If you know him you will know that.'[49] Beit's money was used by Robinson to secure for them both what later became some of the richest gold claims, but their uneasy period of co-operation soon ended.

Robinson's ability was never in doubt; Robinson's life was Robinson against all his fellow men. There was no sentiment attached to the nickname of 'The Buccaneer' that was soon given to him; it merely reflected his ruthlessness. 'A robust, well-built man, alert, pugnacious, full of energy, with florid features, strong jaw, and keen blue eyes, which pierced you like a diamond drill': his biographer, Leo Weinthal, was laudatory.[50] 'Sour-visaged and unsympathetic, he looked as yellow as a bad apple, and green with spleen like a leek . . . he had no personality, no magnetism, but resembled a mortal who had a tombstone on his soul': his contemporaries were not.[51] He saw himself as the one man who had appreciated the importance of the gold-fields, while others laughed at land purchased from impecunious farmers as 'Robinson's cabbage patches'. But there is an unpleasant smell that followed his entire career, leading to his ultimate humiliation when he tried to buy his way into the House of Lords.

One thing Robinson could truly claim; unlike the other diamond and gold magnates, he came from a pioneering family and, at the age of seventeen, had fought with a burgher commando of the Orange Free State in the Basuto War of 1865; he knew South Africa as his own country, and spoke the *taal*. In this respect his credentials were unexceptionable. But many of the other pioneers had been Jews – Julius Mosenthal and his brothers, for example – and much of the British hostility to the millionaires when they arrived in Britain was encapsulated in a baldly xenophobic accusation by the popular novelist, Marie Corelli: 'though the King is now "supreme Lord of the Transvaal" there is no chance whatever for British subjects to make fortunes there, the trades being swamped by Germans, and the mines controlled by Jews.'[52] There was this – and the sheer money-making madness of it all. Merriman's wife expressed the unreality of the reality in December 1888: 'I found Johannesburg in a most tremendous state of excitement. . . . Even "Barney Barnato" says he has never seen such excitement. They tell me the Exchange was the scene of mad excitement – men taking their coats off and shrieking like maniacs – fortunes were made and lost in hours.' One man made £20,000 in a day, another £9,000 in an hour . . . and, she added to her stodgy husband: 'I do hope you will make something out of it.'[53]

Chapter 4

The Financiers: New-style

The lessons from the Empire were these: that guts and enthusiasm and enterprise counted, but that the biggest rewards went to those using the sophisticated methods of modern finance. Saemy Japhet, who had started as a junior with the banking firm of Emil Schwarzschild in Frankfurt in 1873 and set up on his own in November 1880, was a young man in the important years. His first two decades in business were the most important banking years in the history of the world to that date: 'Currencies were consolidated and stabilised, the finances of many countries like Spain, Portugal, and Turkey had been reorganized, banks had built up powerful organizations and Bankers had to become experts in all fields, creating, building up and supporting new industries . . . the experiences gained in home enterprises were used and applied in other countries, resulting in huge profits.'[1]

It was not until the 1870s that industry abandoned traditional sources of capital – its own profits and the landed rich – for financing its operations.[2] Railroads and telegraph systems, steel and chemicals, demanded large amounts of long-term credit. In the late eighteenth century there had been no banks at all in Leeds or Sheffield and a manufacturer might have had to go a hundred miles from remote parts of Yorkshire or Lancashire to find banking facilities.[3] By 1903 a leading City authority could observe that 'so completely have the existing institutions responded to the calls for branches that England as a whole may be said to be well-nigh overbanked'.[4]

The change was not merely measured in numbers but in the organization of banks. Legislation in 1826 allowed joint-stock banks to develop, and the failure of the City of Glasgow Bank in 1878 helped to precipitate the important Companies Act of the following year: 'the shareholders had to pay up £2,750 for each £100 share', Japhet recalled; 'Since that time there have been no banks with unlimited liability.' Above all, the growth in international trade made necessary the provision of elaborate systems of international payment, with the Bank of England in a controlling role. The industrial capitalism of the early Industrial Revolution had given way to the finance capitalism of modern western society – not necessarily the complicated *Das Finanzkapital* of the Marxist economists, but, at its simplest level, a new way of developing the world through the provision of large-scale and long-term investment finance.

Japhet visited London for the first time in 1886. It made an immediate impression on him as a place where he might make his fortune: sufficiently attractive to enable him to ignore the fact that he had no significant financial resources, no personal knowledge of the market, faltering English, few important connections and a variety of enemies. London became his head office, with branches (by 1900) in Berlin, Frankfurt and Hamburg. As the capital of the most powerful nation on earth, London was 'the banker of the world' – an epithet applied to it in the unlikely circumstance of a paper read to the American Bankers' Association in 1901.[5] That able propagandist of British supremacy, Hartley Withers, was only recording facts when he wrote: London is 'pre-eminent as the money factory. Its money is not only more genuine, that is, more undoubtedly convertible than that of any other centre, but is also under certain circumstances both more easily and cheaply produced to suit the convenience of the user.'[6]

Since the early nineteenth century the City had been dominated by what has been called 'a sort of financial aristocracy': the investment bankers, 'the mighty loan-mongers, on whose fiat the fate of kings and empires sometimes depend', as Disraeli (who obtained advice from Lionel de Rothschild) called them.[7] The fortune of the London Rothschilds on the death of Lionel in 1879 may have been £100,000,000: 'these descendants of a petty hawker of the Frankfurt ghetto seem to be the very personification of earthly riches', wrote an early historian of the family, Ignatius Balla, in 1913; 'Neither Rockefeller, nor Carnegie, nor Astor, nor any other Transatlantic prince of finance, has capital equal to that of the Rothschilds.'[8] Perhaps because of their sustained banking success in many countries they never lost their special air of being a house apart from the others; as the journalist and writer T. H. S. Escott noted at the beginning of Edward VII's reign, they had managed to maintain a perfectly distinct position of their own, despite competition – whether aristocratic or plutocratic – of an unprecedented kind.[9]

Time had always been a great sanctifier and by then there were new victims for the Society journals: 'in these *fin de siècle* times of untoward smartness', declared the short-lived *Men and Manners* in 1893, 'it is something to be able to say of wealthy men that they strove to eminence and power by no weapons other than those of honour and industry'; and this certainly applied in the case of 'The Rothschilds: An Unique Record', as the magazine described their achievement.[10] Social enhancement combined with business caution. Nathaniel, first Lord Rothschild – son of Lionel and head of the firm in our period – preferred not to risk capital if he could avoid it: 'it's like putting your finger into a machine – the whirring wheels may drag your whole body in after the finger'. The consequences often seemed salutary: the Barings made a gigantic profit from the flotation of Guinness Breweries,

which the Rothschilds had turned down, but the Barings –
through unwise commitments elsewhere – faced crisis in the
1890s.[11]

Others were quick to grasp at opportunities which had not
existed when the Rothschilds first emerged from the ghetto;
and of these one name stood out. When Japhet was in need of
capital in 1909, 'I looked about, but in reality in one direction
only: Sir Ernest Cassel.'[12] He arranged to see Cassel and made
a short, concise statement, for it was as well to keep to the
point with Sir Ernest, who always listened attentively, but
did not care to have his time wasted. The response was rapid:
'I have always heard nothing but good about you and your
firm', Cassel said, 'and I am prepared to accept your offer [the
immediate need was a guarantee of £200,000]. Are your books
properly audited and who is your accountant?'

Japhet's reply was acceptable; 'Good,' the financier
continued, 'my chief secretary Kritzler will call on you; he
will go through the list of your clients and will report to me. If
his report is satisfactory, and I have no doubt it will be, we
will discuss details and conditions. And now tell me something
about your business.'

Japhet did so, and a second meeting followed at Brook
House, Cassel's London home, in which he was confined to
bed by gout. Already Japhet had announced to his partner,
Gottfried Loewenstein, that their firm would henceforward
enjoy the support of the most influential man in the City,
though Cassel – lying in bed with his swollen knee – was
quick to point out that he had not only relied on Kritzler's
report, but sought additional information from Berlin.
Congratulations from many City men followed – Lord Rothschild among them – and for the next ten years Cassel was the
most active of sleeping partners.

Not that automatic success was guaranteed: rewards were
high; losses could be great. In 1912 W. H. Muller of Rotter-
dam, one of the leading Dutch merchant banks, proposed to
Cassel the formation of a syndicate to acquire gold-mining
concessions in Siberia. Muller and Cassel, who between them

subscribed half the capital, managed to cope with the problems of getting machinery and men to such an inaccessible region, but the Bolsheviks were a different matter; and all was confiscated by the new Soviet regime.

Moreover, not even the aid of the newspapers owned by Lord Northcliffe, with their much-vaunted power to topple governments, was always enough to ensure a profit. In the same year as the Siberian venture Japhet & Co. underwrote £500,000 for the London store of Waring and Gillow, which had first approached Cassel for fresh capital in 1910; 'I shall take everything you cannot place', Cassel told Japhet, and was left with £250,000. Kennedy Jones, Northcliffe's chief editor, had given the issue a good press, and this had given them the mistaken confidence not to use a broker to place the debentures. No doubt, as Cassel said, 'Hard work, good information and then instinct are the keys to success',[13] but that explained everything and nothing.

Jacob Cassel of Cologne conducted a banking business of no great size; his death, and that of his elder son, Max, in 1875 came a year after his wife's, Ernest Cassel's mother. Ernest, who left school at fourteen, began with the Eltzbacher banking firm in his native town, but the real opportunities were international in scope, and he moved rapidly from the commission merchants Blessig, Braun & Co. in Liverpool (January 1869) to a clerkship with the Anglo-Egyptian Bank in Paris (April 1870), to Bischoffsheim and Goldschmidt in London (in the upheaval of the Franco-Prussian War).

'Dear Sir', he wrote to Bischoffsheim (Maurice de Hirsch's brother-in-law), 'I apply for the position in your office and refer you to my former chiefs, Messrs. Eltzbacher, Cologne. Yours sincerely, Ernest Cassel.' Certainly, as Japhet noted, 'The letter breathed a rare self-confidence.'[14] But there was ample scope for abilities to be demonstrated, and Cassel showed his immediately in disentangling the affairs of the New York, Pennsylvania and Ohio Railroads, in which his firm was heavily involved. A salary of £200 per annum had become a manager's salary of £5,000 when he was only 22, in

1874, after his skills had helped the firm through a serious crisis involving the finance of the Nicaraguan Canal.

The *Daily Telegraph* was not alone in describing the Cassel story as a 'romance of finance',[15] but the rational key to the romance was an ability to think on the massive scale demanded by a world developing more rapidly than ever before, together with the single-minded determination to pursue the details as well as the grand design. A number of finance houses saw the potential of the Swedish iron-ore mines but grew tired of the difficulties; Bischoffsheim and Goldschmidt had money tied up in the under-used Swedish Central Railway, linking the coast with the mines inland. It was Cassel himself who was responsible for introducing the Gilchrist-Thomas process – at the time ignored in England – for the conversion of phosphoric iron-ores. Mining and railways, docks and shipping interests proliferated, providing the core of his fortune, which was already perhaps £150,000 in 1881 when he was not yet thirty.[16]

Backing from Hirsch enabled him to set up on his own in 1884 and his reorganization of the Louisville and Nashville Railway, in conjunction with the Frankfurt-born Jacob Schiff of Kuhn, Loeb & Co., launched him with success. About 1,500 letters from Schiff to Cassel survive, and demonstrate not only the intimacy of their own relationship – 'the most faithful friend I have ever had'[17] – but that of the international financial community. It could hardly have been otherwise. Of course Cassel concerned himself with domestic matters of importance – he underwrote the construction of the Central London Underground Railway and played a vital part in financing the development of Vickers – but his operations overseas were spectacular. He arranged the finances of the Mexican Central Railways, issued the 1893 Mexican government 6 per cent loan, the 1895 Chinese 6 per cent loan and the 1896 Uruguay 5 per cent loan. Above all, his coat glittering with the order of the Knight Commander of St Michael and St George (from the British government) and the Grand Cordon of the Medjidie Order (from the

Egyptian government), he was the 'Maker of Modern Egypt'. In the twenty-five years from 1882 to 1907 England is said to have made nearly 120 promises to evacuate Egypt while at the same time pursuing policies which confirmed her hold over the country. Cassel does not find his way into the account – a non-Western view of Anglo-Egyptian relations in the period – that makes this point.[18] Japhet, by contrast, has a paragraph of superlative praise for him – opening up the country, aiding civilization, bringing peace between the races, enriching the whole land . . . and making an enormous amount of money.[19] The Khedives of Egypt owed large sums to the European powers, but the economic arguments for damming the Nile coincided with the strategic considerations of Cromer, the Consul-General in Egypt, and the government in Britain. Cassel's scheme was presented to the Prime Minister at the end of 1897: the contractors Aird & Co. agreed to construct the dam for two million pounds; Cassel's company, the Irrigation Investment Corporation, would pay them as the work proceeded in return for bonds repayable in half-yearly amounts of £78,613 – the repayments to be financed from the revenue that would come from the newly irrigated land. 'They were offered', in Winston Churchill's judgment, 'what was, upon the whole, the best investment in all history.'[20]

By 1914, the author of *Egypt in Transition* could record: 'this great engineering triumph may be said to have repaid its cost already.'[21] Cassel had been there – behind the scenes, unnoticed – when the Khedive, Lord and Lady Cromer and a splendid array of other dignitaries had assembled for its opening by Queen Victoria's youngest son, the Duke of Connaught, in 1903. His role in the economic development of the country was fundamental: half the initial share capital of the National Bank was taken up by him in 1898; he was a prime mover in the formation of the Agricultural Bank in 1903; he purchased from the Khedive, in partnership with French financiers, the 250,000 fertile acres of Daira Sanieh for £6,500,000 – all this against opposition, at home as well as abroad.

Sigmund Münz has left us a marvellous picture of him at Marienbad, favourite resort of his great friend, King Edward VII, shortly after the death of the King: 'His wealth, influence and connections place such power in his hands that one feels oneself in the presence of a creator and controller of vast unseen forces – Swedish ore-combines, Egyptian cotton, American railways, Turkish politics – all these various interests absorb his attention.' He might be aptly named *'Ernestus Britannicus, Ernestus Germanicus, Ernestus Africanus,* and *Ernestus Americanus'.*[22] Here was Cassel on the eve of retirement, still powerful as the short, but tumultuous era, of which he was one of the least publicly lauded but most significant spirits, itself drew to a close.

Not all the financiers of Cassel's period had his magisterial presence; there was more to the City than that. When W. Arthur Woodward took his readers on a morning's tour of the Stock Exchange in February 1896, he noted: 'Neither the Rothschilds, nor Mr Barnato – erstwhile acrobat and still juggler – nor any of the famous bankers and large speculators whose names are most familiar with the public, are actual members of the House.' Money-making was a many-sided activity, in which chance could play an important role. 'The Stock Exchange itself is an enormous oblong hall, which . . . reminded me of the gaming rooms at Monte Carlo,' Woodward observed. 'The vicissitudes of the Stock Exchange are, in fact, like those of the *roulette* or *trente et quarante* table.'[23]

The 10,000 square feet of the New House of the Exchange, opened in 1884, symbolized the spirit of the age. In the eighteenth century it had often been hard to find any stocks in which to invest – Alexander Pope's father evidently abandoned the search for investment in disgust and kept his money in a strong box.[24] As *The Times* noted in the 1840s, however, the development of the railways encouraged even the clergy to abandon scripture for script.[25] By 1914 approximately 4,500 securities were quoted on the London Exchange.

Financial education did not keep pace with financial opportunity. In the second half of the nineteenth century the real value of assets was often hidden; groups of companies made non-existent profits recorded in paper transactions; and disillusioned Society members turned against the very men to whom they had sold their names to give respectability to speculation.[26] The Stock Exchange, incorporated after the Royal Commission of 1877 gave it the monopoly power to licence brokers, was subject to very little government control. There had always been men, who – like Edward Ponderevo in *Tono-Bungay* – offered the proposition that the road to wealth lay through filling the most expensive bottles with the cheapest liquids, but the opportunities now provided by modern company promotion were endless.

The most effective criticism of the system was a record of its results. There were plenty of warnings. The Report of the Stock Exchange Commission examined the cases of such disasters as Charles Lafitte and Peruvian Railways, both liquidated within two years, and concluded that the Exchange had been used to float companies without real existence.[27] Naturally some people in the City knew what they were doing, notably the much criticized 'Hebrew millionaires and plodding Germans'. *The Times* obituary of the Jewish financier, Lord Swaythling, declared that 'To hear his exposition of a situation which might involve not only "triangular" but even "quadrangular" arbitrage operations was an intellectual treat.'[28] But the City Editor of the same paper – whose function was itself a sign of the times – warned against 'a weltering chaos of uncertainty and haphazard guesswork, based on figures that often mean nothing – or worse than nothing, because they seem to mean so much – and on gusts of opinion blown hither and thither by causes which have no logical connection with the merits of the stocks affected'.[29]

The mania was at its height in the 1890s, when the crash of the Liberator Building Society in 1892 was followed by the flight of Jabez Balfour, a former Liberal MP, to South America, when in 1894 the failure of a finance company compelled the resignation of A. J. Mundella from the Cabinet, and when Ernest Terah Hooley (according to the *Financial Times*) 'came upon the City . . . like a whirlwind, and literally carried all before him'.[30] The *Buffalo Sunday Morning News* may not have been America's most respected newspaper, but it expressed a popular view in observing: 'As a spectacular money-maker . . . Hooley is a much more interesting individual than Cecil Rhodes, Alfred Beit or Barney Barnato. . . . No wonder he is the most popular man in England, and as much sought after as if he were a prince of Royal Blood.' The *Spectator* put it slightly differently in complaining of 'beggars . . . suddenly raised from dunghills to sit among princes'.

Hooley was born in Nottinghamshire in February 1859, son of a lace-maker – a trade which he followed for a while but abandoned (as he claimed in his 'autobiography') because there was no money, no 'big money', in it. As understudy to John C. Cottam, he quickly learned the means of attracting money to dubious enterprises, and his own early ventures included the Atmospheric Evaporation Syndicate (Limited) and Rio Luna Mines (Limited). 'My great business', he explained, 'was to buy something without the money to pay for it, sell it for as much as I could, and get out with the profit.' In 1896 he set up his headquarters at the Midland Grand Hotel in London, where he exuberantly ran up bills of £250 a week, 'determined to make a million or go smash'.

Plans were made before dawn in the morning, and the rest of the day saw constant entertaining, arrival and despatch of telegrams, delivery of proofs and new prospectuses, board meetings, signing of transfers, the frou-frou of perfumed skirts – and aristocratic chatter from 'The Hooley Peers'. For here, as one contemporary account noted, was 'the ugly phenomenon of men of high social position accepting director-ships in doubtful or over-capitalised companies, and receiving secret payments as the price for their names'. Hooley set the fashion for 'guinea pig' directors on the boards of public companies – and thereby claimed to have saved many a noble family from ruin. He 'got hold of an earl' (in fact Lord

The Yellow Drawing-Room at Sir Julius Wernher's Bath House, decorated in late eighteenth-century French style and photographed in 1911

Alfred Beit

Cecil John Rhodes

De La Warr) and offered him £10,000 to find a duke or half that for 'ordinary' peers.

Of the Hooley companies launched in 1896 – and they went well into double figures – the Singer Cycle Company had Lords Ashburton and Greville as trustees for the debenture holders, the Dunlop Pneumatic Tyre Company had Lords Albemarle and De La Warr, plus the Duke of Somerset, on the board, the Swift Cycle Company had Lord Randolph Churchill as Chairman. Not all, of course, were crooked, and Dunlop soon acquired 'the requisite commercial leaven' in 'that very new man' Mr William Harvey du Cros and his son Arthur. But, in the words of Miss Julie Mackey's song, performed at the Palace Theatre,

> What a shame he didn't stop
> After his three million 'cop'
> 'Schweppes' soda' proved a useful 'prop'
> Now, like the corks, he's gone off pop!

The 'cop' was the launching of Dunlop; the 'prop' came in 1897, with Lord March as Chairman and De La Warr involved yet again ('the latter being, as will be observed, particularly handy whenever directorates were concerned').

Some very shrewd businessmen were attracted by the Hooley schemes. Sir Blundell Maple, one of the earliest of Edward, Prince of Wales's millionaire tradesmen friends, put £10,000 into the company which was to be formed to exploit Pedersen's Cycle Frame. In February 1898 Maple threatened to tell the story of the company's affairs to the newspapers if his money was not returned; he got it back, but the other shareholders – provided with promises only – watched helplessly as Hooley filed his petition for bankruptcy on 8 June 1898: there were 414 creditors. The promoter blamed his fall on the payment of large commissions in connection with the formation of companies (we would probably call them bribes) and on blackmail by the press (if he meant that he paid large sums both to encourage and suppress comment, that was true). What was certainly at fault was a system that allowed the ignorant to lead the blind. Hooley admitted that he knew nothing of 'high finance': he turned down, for example, one of the few genuinely successful patent medicines of the period, the American Carter's Little Liver Pills. As he said, without being completely disingenuous, 'It would give me the greatest pleasure in the world to make everybody's fortune.'

Not that bankruptcy finished his career (least of all, as we shall see, his social career): in 1900 he bought the Siberian Goldfields Development Co. Ltd, registered in May with capital of £1,000,000, and said to have been given exclusive rights to exploit the fields from the Tsar. A bribe of £10,000 to his contact in the Russian Embassy in London led, initially, to withdrawal of the official disclaimer that had appeared in *The Times*, but the dissatisfied shareholders petitioned for the winding up of the company in July 1901. The Sapphire Corundum Company Ltd, which went into liquidation in August 1903 with a deficit of £805,845, was not an isolated case; and though the brilliant advocate, Rufus Isaacs, secured his acquittal on fraud charges in 1904, he went to prison in 1912 for false pretences over a property deal. Even after the war, photographed as the model of a cynically sinister figure, he was to be found dealing in cotton-mill shares, enjoying his third bankruptcy (with liabilities of £686,000), and – in 1922 – returning to prison.

Cassel, and men like him, succeeded because they understood the creative role of large-scale finance in the modern world. Hooley, and men like him, succeeded because they exploited the general ignorance of that same role. But both were part of the same story.

Chapter 5

The Discovery of the Consumer:

Plutocracy at Home

One day in the mid-1890s, Ernest Hooley called at Port Sunlight, not far from Liverpool, undecided as to whether he should try and purchase the great soap-manufacturing firm of Lever Brothers. William Hesketh Lever, well on the way to creating the company that on his death in 1925 had factories in twenty countries, issued capital of over £56,000,000 and 85,000 employees, was unimpressed – though he did pick up an unintended tip from the promoter on the worth of Bovril shares.[1] Forty-four in 1895, Lever had made a magnificent escape from the 'island of middle-class comfort set in a sea of poverty and drabness' into which, in his own words, he had been born.[2]

Bolton in his youth was the incarnation of the self-help city – an organized chaos of labour, smoke and dirt, which the strongest dominated in gawky grandeur. Lever himself, son of a grocer well able to pay his seventh child and elder son the substantial sum of £800 a year at twenty-one, treasured the ideals of Samuel Smiles's book, *Self-Help*, a presentation copy of which was given to him on his sixteenth birthday. He is seen in early pictures with the face of Lancashire commerce: quiff of greasy hair, long side-burns, plumpish but firm

features except for the heavy chin, tight, if not mean, mouth
and thick neck. The image did not change much as the years
passed. He was never poor, but the Society magazine *Town
Topics* was right to call him 'Self-made in the sense that he
can stand in the middle of his works and his model village and
think of the days when a couple or so of his clerks on inverted
soap boxes, a horsehair chair or two, and a desk were his staff
and his office furniture.'[3]

It seems clear that Lever was the driving force behind the
expansion of his father's business beyond the confines of
Bolton, calling eventually for a Wigan warehouse which he
managed. Indeed, James Lever had some doubts about the
wisdom of developing in size until the firm had no rival in
wholesale grocery between Liverpool and Manchester. His
son's first job was cutting and packing soap and 'Whether it
was this early association, at the age of fifteen, with soap that
caused the subject of soap to get into my mind I do not know;
but it did get into my mind, and the year I was married I
turned my attention to soap.'[4] The market was there as never
before, for the Industrial Revolution had brought heavy
concentrations of a fast-growing – and dirty – population. At
the beginning of the nineteenth century, there was no soap in
the slums; there was no money to buy it – and often no
water, save what could itself be bought in the street.[5] The
nonconformist God, beloved of the self-help industrial town,
was a clean God, however, and luckily his people, as the
century progressed, became richer in worldly goods. Lever
simply applied the back cover homily of his own salesmen's
magazine, *Square Deals*: 'Business is not a game of chance. If
you know the rules and will apply them with energy and
intelligence, your work will be pleasant and success sure.'[6]
Soap was not going to be superseded quickly.

Lever, perhaps not quite truthfully, said that he was 'as
ignorant of soap-making as a baby in arms';[7] invention was
unnecessary, for money was to be made simply by doing
something better than it had ever been done before.[8] He did
not begin by manufacturing his own product, but in 1885 his

father's rather unwilling loan helped him to buy a six-year lease on a Warrington soap works: his first year's output was 20 tons a week, his second 450 tons. Port Sunlight, which became the centre of his empire, was built on land cheaply acquired on an undeveloped section of the Mersey in Cheshire, and manufacturing began there in January 1889.

The principles which he later directed at his salesmen in *Square Deals* were the principles which led to his own success. 'Square dealing' itself was 'the only basis on which permanent success may be built'; more important in practice was constant energetic work – Theodore Roosevelt's admonition, 'Success comes only to those who lead the life of endeavour', was quoted approvingly. The 'natural-born salesman' was not right for the modern world: the 'scientific salesman', the captain with a compass aboard, was better prepared for emergencies. The magazine kept strictly to business, for Lever Brothers was not 'a school for philanthropy' and its aim was to sell all the soap it could, avoiding all distractions.[9] Lever did not believe in chance; he believed that opportunities came to everyone in different forms and a process of 'mental stocktaking' would lead to correct assessment of the possibilities; characteristically, he told his audience in the Gladstone Hall, Port Sunlight, on New Year's Day 1916 that no successful man 'can claim more than that he took advantage of the opportunities as they came along'.[10]

To look at any selection of Victorian city photographs is to be made aware that the Victorian age was the first great age of advertising. Fifty pounds were spent on advertising in Lever's first year in soap: and 100,000 times as much in the next two decades.[11] All the emphasis in the early years was on promoting Sunlight Soap – by advertising, prizes and other devices – to the fast-growing working-class market: just literate enough to respond to basic emphasis on the virtues of cleanliness, or what appeared to be something for nothing. Today, we are over-familiar with such methods; then they were new; and never have they been pursued so energetically. In 1899 the Secretary of the Soap Makers'

Association complained of a case in which a schoolteacher at a Board School had been distributing advertisements and prizes promoting Sunlight Soap and other products.[12] The example was both trivial and – repeated a million times in different forms – the key to success.

Growth was controlled in the early years, with careful and not over-ambitious use of profits to finance expansion: 'It is only a question of growth . . . steady growth each day.'[13] In the 1890s new products were introduced: 'Lifebuoy' in 1894, with the power to disinfect and the good sense to use up the residual oil left from producing 'Sunlight'; 'Lux' soap flakes in 1899. Other companies were swallowed up at home and, because England was not the world, Lever looked overseas too. He first visited North America in 1888, before Port Sunlight had even opened, and travelled 15,000 miles studying American methods and arranging agencies. He liked the American style and on his voyage round the world from September 1892 to March 1893 went to Chicago, where the World Fair was in construction: 'the Americans have every cause to feel proud of this monument of their energy'.[14] Agencies were converted into manufacturing companies to avoid tariff barriers; promotion devices were directly exported (a startled Swiss population on the shores of Lake Geneva found themselves in the middle of a gigantic washing competition, the *Fête des Blanchisseuses*, on Easter Monday 1899). The purchase of 300,000 acres in the Solomon Islands in 1905 was one of a number of acquisitions directed at obtaining raw materials: negotiations with the Belgian government led, in 1911, to enormous tracts of land in the Congo passing into Lever control.

The Lever style was absolutist. According to his commercial enemies he was 'more ruthless, more autocratic, more dogmatic than Napoleon';[15] according to himself, 'no man has any excuse for making the same mistake twice over'.[16] He encouraged weak flattery by his hostile reaction to criticism; most respected him, but this was not a man to arouse more positive feelings. His son's neutral conclusion was that so

much of his father's existence was devoted to his business and
its development that his life, and the history of the company,
could only be told sensibly together.[17] The glass cage which
formed his office at Port Sunlight – situated above the halls
where his clerks worked (and were watched) – symbolized the
way he ran the company. His brother, who had feared rapid
growth, had a nervous breakdown in 1895 and died in 1910.
Lever Brothers became a limited company in 1890 and went
public in 1894 with a capital of one and a half million pounds.
By 1902 William possessed all the ordinary capital, retaining
it until his death, while the preference shares, as an expression of his supreme confidence, were made available to
the public. Board meetings were a formality; overall policy
was Lever's decision alone.

The joint-stock company, successfully used in the development of the railways and much boosted by legislation of the
1850s and the 1860s which legalized limited liability, changed
the character and scale of British industry. As the City Editor
of *The Times* observed in 1910, 'The joint stock system has
immeasurably quickened the pace of all kinds of commercial
and industrial development.'[18] It was none the less true that,
as Andrew Carnegie – supreme millionaire among the millionaires – noted in 1891, the business concerns which had given
Britain power were, with hardly an exception, 'the creations
of the individual millionaire'. All the plutocrats faced the same
problem; they needed the joint-stock company to take their
creations from the large to the giant, but by using it they
ultimately found themselves, as Carnegie put it, 'no longer in
the race'. 'Promotion' into a joint-stock concern, he thought,
was like promotion from Commons to Lords; it limited the
push, the masterfulness, the excitement and, above all, the
authority of the industrialist.[19] Here, as elsewhere, the plutocrats were on the edge of the contemporary world – using
the techniques of the new world to triumph over the old order,
techniques which were also to destroy their own individual
pre-eminence in our own age of corporate control.

These tensions were clearly visible in Lever's progress. His company had perhaps forty per cent of the entire domestic market by 1914; of the overseas factories only that in Japan had been a real failure. He loved the success: 'One can go to places like the Congo, and organise, organise, organise, well, very big things indeed.'[20] But the problems for one man, however remarkable, were crushing: when war broke out not only Japan, but the companies in Austria, Sweden, South Africa and China were not making profits. Some time before, he had written to one of his few confidants, Joseph Meek, head of the Australian operation, complaining of a series of problems that had threatened to wreck the company: the high price of raw materials, fierce – and sometimes unfair – competition, and what he described as 'the *Daily Mail* attack'.[21]

The high price of raw materials in the early 1900s led the chief soap manufacturers to establish a group for mutual benefit in July 1906. Lever had watched with disquiet his competitors adopting his own methods; he had tried, unsuccessfully, to stop the giving away of prizes for collected wrappers. The last few years before 1906 witnessed an advertising campaign by all the manufacturers on such a scale that diminishing returns were the inevitable consequence. And when the *Daily Mail* and other newspapers owned by Lord Northcliffe violently attacked the restrictive practices that followed, the consequence was the engaging spectacle of two plutocrats locked in a struggle from which neither could ultimately benefit.

It is worth noting that Lever's plans would have limited the advertising in Northcliffe's newspapers, but it is probable that the newspaper proprietor liked the sense of power that went with a crusade. Lever was portrayed as a grasping, rapacious figure, owner of 'Port Moonshine', the Soap Trust shop in which 'We don't care about you. We want more of your money'.[22] Threatening libel, and annoyed by Northcliffe's men, Lever refused to settle out of court; Northcliffe employed Rufus Isaacs to represent him, but to no avail. Lever received the largest sum ever awarded for a libel action in Britain, and other actions that followed involved North-cliffe in the loss of £250,000. The money was contemptuously given to Liverpool University, but another result – from all the bad publicity – was a decline in sales; two years later Lever estimated his losses at considerably more than £500,000. There were no more plans for amalgamation.

One remarkable friend of both Lever and Northcliffe had unsuccessfully tried to bring them together: Sir Thomas Lipton.[23] '*Veni, vidi, vici*' fully summed up the Lipton career, according to Charles Bateman, writing in 1901; and, indeed, there are few rags-to-riches tales to match it.[24] If Lever had washed the teeming masses of the cities, Lipton was to feed them.

Kennedy Jones, Northcliffe's lieutenant, was born in the same mean Glasgow street as Lipton, 'only we lived at the better end of it'.[25] Lipton's father, originally an Irish tenant farmer, moved to Glasgow, worked in a warehouse, as a time-keeper in a paper-mill and eventually managed to open a small shop. As a boy Lipton was, he said, at least 'rich in the possession of parents whose home influence was always of the best', though it was perhaps more important that his boyhood experience showed him 'the "race" is usually won by the swift *and* the strong'.[26] His first jobs were with a firm of stationers – aged nine and at the equivalent of twenty-five new pence a week – and then with some shirt manufacturers, but he had fled to America, land of promise, before his fifteenth birthday in 1865.

The romance is not wholly inappropriate; at Chicago in 1896 he told his audience how he always visited the room in New York in which he had first slept, whenever he crossed the Atlantic: 'You may smile. You have always travelled first class,' he said: 'I once was not able to.'[27] America was an important influence; 'it sharpened me and I always felt that I got a good commercial training there'.[28] That 'commercial training' included three years on the rice plantations of South Carolina, working six days a week until his health collapsed, and a period in a grocery store in New York – 'that tremendous city, which, all my life, has been like a lode-star to me'. The streets of New York were not, in the aftermath of the Civil War, paved with gold, but they offered a particular kind of experience; and 'I went home to make my fortune, thus reversing the usual order of things.'[29]

At twenty-one he opened a grocery shop in Stobcross Street, Glasgow; the necessary capital was only £100, but within six weeks he was in a position to take on an assistant. The growth that followed was not a mysterious process. All the plutocrats worked fanatically hard, with a puritanical disregard for social life, while they acquired their fortunes – their later ostentation was in some sense a reaction against the early years. For years, summer and winter, Lipton often worked from 8.30 in the morning until 11 at night, 'toiling, rejoicing', and rushing for the last train from Glasgow Central Station. 'If I got enough to eat and a nice bed to rest in for six out of the twenty-four hours I was well content' – a pattern of life which continued long after he acquired support from managers and buyers and accountants.[30] He never gambled, never drank, never smoked; and all visible signs of a brief romance in 1885 were rapidly suppressed.

Ceaseless, untiring personal work was the explanation Lipton himself gave to *Pearson's Magazine* of his success, though, as the magazine noted, there was nothing in his bearing to indicate the overwrought businessman.[31] He was always an optimist and thought that there was something 'buoyant and healthy' in the attitude; photographed at twenty-seven, 'already on the way to fame and fortune', he appears relaxed – but not too relaxed – and self-confident; with tough, but not cruel, eyes; surprisingly slender fingers, a large walrus moustache hiding the mouth; neat – but not too neat – hair and suit. He wanted no partners, and disliked loans: 'if you stick to business, business will stick to you.'[32] The breathless, rambling, repetitive and often inaccurate biography by his friend Captain John J. Hickey, of the New York police force, put it with splendid bluntness: 'he knew how to make money, and what was more, he knew how to keep it, and make it double, thereby fooling the high hatted swells of London.'[33]

Hard work was not enough. Lipton was quick, he said, to grasp 'how great can be the Power of Advertisement'.[34] In 1877 an advertisement was made to resemble a Scottish one pound note and had to be withdrawn because of the confusion that followed; but his keen pricing made its slogan quite accurate: 'Great Irish ham, butter, and egg market. Ham, butter and eggs given elsewhere for the value of one pound, given here for fifteen shillings.' In 1887, on the occasion of Queen Victoria's Golden Jubilee, he wrote to her asking 'whether your most gracious Majesty would be pleased to accept the largest cheese ever made'. The Queen's Private Secretary, Sir Henry Ponsonby, politely pointed out that Her Majesty could not accept presents from private individuals, but Lipton, sensing the publicity value, gave the correspondence to the press. Much criticism followed, but Lipton's moved a stage further towards becoming a nationally known name.[35]

Large cheeses, which he used as the centre-piece of street processions, were not just used for noisy promotion, for Lipton began importing them from America. His aim was always to cut out the middleman and he made regular trips to Ireland, attending the markets and buying for cash; the same principle was at work in his purchase of a Chicago slaughter-house, able to kill and dress 300–400 pigs a day. When he was criticized in the American press for creating a 'corner' in American pork to pay the expenses of his yacht in the America Cup, he pointed out that 'I am always dealing in the commodity on a large scale'.[36] And this was the key to providing grocery and dairy products for the working classes who were at last in the position to afford them. In noting that 'The poor man's 20s is as good as the rich man's £1', he was not propagating a social philosophy; he was showing how to make money.[37]

A Glasgow procession was also used to announce the advent

of Lipton's tea in 1889. 'Everybody in Glasgow was thus brought to know that I had this article to sell. My tea went like wildfire, and its large success has continued ever since.'[38] When tea wholesalers had approached him, he had discovered the profit possibilities in the product – especially if sold in bulk at a lower price, carefully graded into clearly labelled packets. He went himself to Ceylon and acquired estates there, which he was to modernize and use to undercut his competitors. Tea had been drunk for several centuries, but import duties remained high into the 1850s and it was only the development of the Indian variety that created a raw material suitable for the new mass market.

By the time Lipton turned to this new product he had thirty shops with, in 1889, a turnover of one and a half million pounds: in 1880 he had twelve branches in the Glasgow region; he opened in Leeds in 1881, in Liverpool in 1883, and London in 1888, in Westbourne Grove, scaring 'local buttermen out of their old and profitable prices', according to the *Paddington Chronicle*.[39] When *Pearson's Magazine* interviewed him in 1896, he had sixty shops in London alone, his Chicago slaughter-house produced a million pigs a year, his London headquarters contained 12,000 chests of tea, and he owned the largest tea estates in Ceylon. Not mentioned, or still in prospect, were the Bermondsey preserve factory, the Old Street coffee-roasting plant, the Shadwell wine and spirit vaults, Kent fruit gardens, and stores in Hamburg and Constantinople, Stockholm and Copenhagen.

It was after Lipton's mother and father died in 1889, 'leaving me a sad and very lonely man', that he moved to London and pursued his activities with even greater, quite obsessional zeal.[40] Growth and diversification gradually forced him to reconsider his proud boast that not so much as a farthing of outside capital had been used in the development of his business from the first tiny Glasgow shop.[41] Lipton's became a public company in 1898, amid scenes in which – according to Northcliffe's *Daily Mail* – the whole City went mad: applications for no less than £40,000,000 of stock were received. Already Lipton's was beginning to suffer from lack of decentralization, the sort of paranoic central direction that could lead to boardroom discussion of 'Repairs. Harrogate: Cycle Tyre 7s 6d'.[42] The profit figures from 1898 to 1914 fell far short of investors' hopes, yet, for the moment, Captain Hickey caught the mood with perfect inelegance:

But those blokies thought that there was a gold mine in the knowledge of this great tea merchant, for Tom Lipton was growing greater and greater every day, so they implored him to organize a Lipton Limited and they handed over their wealth, and Sir Thomas organized the greatest corporation the world ever knew and it was known the world over as the Lipton Limited.[43]

The sad old butler in Galsworthy's *The Island Pharisees* (1904) was nostalgic about the past. It went almost without saying that 'there was gentry then. . . . There wasn't so much o' these here middle classes then.' But he also thought it worth noting that there were 'none o' them Amalgamated Stores, every man keepin' his own little shop.'[44] No one who is unaware of what retailing was like before Lipton's time will begin to understand how he was so successful. As late as 1856 Francis Wey, Paris visitor to London – go-ahead capital of the first industrial nation – recorded: 'shopkeepers do not extol their wares, they seem quite indifferent as to whether you make or do not make a purchase. . . . I had the greatest difficulty in getting the assistant to show me more than two fingers of each glove, as though displaying the entire article was beneath his dignity.' The cashier took his money as if he was receiving a charity subscription; and the parcel was handed to him by a shopman 'with a benevolent expression as though he were making a small gift'.[45]

   All this changed with the advent of chains of retail shops, a process which began in the 1850s with, for example, the newsagents W. H. Smith and J. Menzies, and was extended to the main consumer trades in the 1870s. By 1914 there were as many as sixteen firms with more than 200 branches, seven – including Lipton's – with over 500; and that did represent a revolution.[46]

Some of the causes have already emerged. Even in the early stages of industrialization Britain was a country of local, at most regional, activity, especially in economic life. The coming of mass-production techniques compelled mass, nation-wide distribution, as did the availability of cheap, standardized foods in the last decades of the nineteenth century. A recognizable pattern of middle-class demand emerged as Britain became the centre of world trade, of an Empire, of international finance and industry. A fully industrialized, urban nation was also a nation of working-class demand for goods to be widely and cheaply available – above all, for basic foods, always the biggest item in the working-class budget.

The shops themselves began to standardize all essentials, from fittings to produce. Blending and mixing and grinding were gradually abandoned. The *Shopkeeper's Guide*, published in 1853, had actually recommended that many goods should only be made up on demand;[47] a different spirit informed R. K. Philp's *Handybook of Shopkeeping* in 1892, by which time the substitution of clear, fixed prices had largely brought to an end 'higgling' with the shop-keeper.[48] Many of the multiple shops integrated their production and distribution and, like Lipton, tried to cut out the middleman. And everyone made use of such technologies as food-canning, helped by a new process of tin-plating which took the sale of canned vegetables from 400,000 cases in 1870 to 55,000,000 in 1914.[49] The one less definable factor of importance was the individual, for the battle against the old ways was not won without a fight. The first Lord Devonport recalled in a matter-of-fact tone, with a hint of pride:

From 1880 onwards we opened branch after branch in town and country under the now-familiar name of the

International Stores. . . . As may be imagined, we encountered a good deal of prejudice and hostility – prejudice on the part of the old-fashioned public, to whom the idea of multiple retailing was new and strange, and therefore suspect, and hostility on the part of the trade, who held the distinction between wholesale and retail as sacrosanct.[50]

The department store reflected the same developments, though there is some debate about the date at which these stores first emerged; Bambridge's of Newcastle is said to have used price tickets as early as 1830, but the great age came long after the 1860s had established Wanamaker, Altman and Marshall Field in America.[51] The buildings themselves were the first noticeable feature: their plate-glass windows, their gas-lights, their lifts, their sheer size – all proclaimed that they were part of the new world. (*Punch* depicted a lost 'shopman', asking one of his own customers the way back to his own toy department.)[52] They were found in central locations, now readily accessible through the new transport systems. The range of goods offered was enormous; their display unprecedented. The 1882 Maple's Catalogue contained everything from 'Officers' Barrack Furniture' to '1 Housemaid's Box @ 2s 9d'.[53]

J. B. Maple was virtually in control of the firm his father had founded in 1840 by this time. The showrooms covered 'more than five acres' and 'no one can form an adequate conception of the magnitude and variety of the stock without a personal visit'. Among the 24,000 families who had done business there in 1881, apart from those who paid when they purchased, were 'nearly all our own Royal Family, besides the other Courts of Europe, Principal English Railway Companies, Metropolitan and Provincial Clubs, and other large Public Institutions, as well as many Government Works'. Maple's, like the other big stores, itself became a social centre. The palaces of commerce had 'democratised luxury', in Emile Zola's phrase.[54]

Once the country was being fed, clothed and groomed on a national basis, it was natural that it should be educated and informed in the same way. In the 1860s and 1870s no newspaper had a mass circulation in the modern sense; the most that can be said is that *The Times* was known internationally. As late as 1850 the British government penalized journals through the duty on paper; as early as 1905 the *News of the World* reached a circulation of one million. In the years between there were revolutionary changes in production which went hand-in-hand with revolutionary changes in the market for news.[55]

The Forster Education Act of 1870 and those that followed into the new century ensured the creation of a national system of primary and secondary education as the First World War approached. The newly educated population that resulted was greedy for reading matter. The 'more rapid production and scientific distribution of newspapers', as Alfred Harmsworth – later Lord Northcliffe – put it, made it possible to satisfy the demand;[56] the telephone and telegraph changed the character of the information presented. Telegraph cables crossed the Channel in the 1850s, the Atlantic in the 1860s.[57] Guglielmo Marconi acquired the first patent in wireless telegraphy in 1896; and the *Queen*, founded by Mrs Beeton's husband Samuel as a 'Ladies' Newspaper and Court Chronicle' in 1861, exuberantly exclaimed: 'the telegraph is going to do without wires; we are going to talk to each other half way round the world. . . . Hooray! Here indeed opens up a glorious vista.'[58]

No one was kind about the men, the newspaper barons, who made use of these conditions. H. G. Wells's Cossington, not far removed from a caricature of the real-life Alfred Harmsworth, was 'a *poseur*, a smart tradesman, and a very bold and wide-thinking political schemer', changing from day to day: 'He had a vanity of sweeping actions, motor-car pounces, Napoleonic rushes, that led to violent ineffectual changes in the policy of his papers.'[59] Stephen McKenna's Sir John Woburn rose from nothing 'to drug the sense of a nation, to render an impassive people neurotic, to debauch the mind of a generation.'[60] Marie Corelli's vicious and unscrupulous David Jost might work through newspapers with quite different political allegiances, but they had the same ultimate purpose: the control of public opinion.[61]

The stereotype certainly did not apply to Passmore Edwards, the son of a Cornish carpenter and publican, who campaigned in the 1850s, in *Intellectual Tollbars*, against the taxes on knowledge – on paper, advertisements and journals themselves. His early career showed just how difficult it was for an able proprietor to succeed before conditions changed: 'I thought that, if I could write for periodicals owned by others, I might start and own one myself'; but 'It was no easy matter, more than half a century ago, when the taxes on knowledge were in full swing, and before modern Education Acts came into operation, to commence and establish a magazine, with experience and without capital, or with capital and without experience; and, of course, doubly more difficult to achieve success without both money and experience.'[62] His first venture, *The Public Good* (1850), did not pay; nor did those that followed, until he acquired *The English Mechanic*, *The Building News* and, above all, in 1868 *The Echo*. Through this last paper he became the pioneer of the halfpenny daily for the London working classes at a time when most people had not fully seen the potential middle-class audience for news.

Three years before this, in 1865, a Dublin barrister who was later to die of drink became the father of the first of his seven sons – christened Alfred, and in time to shake British society far more than the earnest Edwards.[63] 'Journaliste à 15 ans. Directeur de journal à 20 ans. Proprietaire de 60 journaux à 40 ans. Le "Napoléon de la Presse". L'homme d'affaires. L'administrateur. Le patriote': this was the enthusiastic shorthand description by Andrée Viollis in 1919.[64] Alfred Harmsworth grew up amidst middle-class poverty and dignified decay: 'As long ago as I can remember, I was determined to be rid of the perpetual and annoying question of money.'[65] As a boy he seems to have pursued a variety of bizarre money-making ideas, from a 'silk-hat reviver' to 'Tonk's Pills – Cure all Ills'; and it may have been his feelings for his mother, to whom he sent some message nearly every day of his life, that influenced him most. As Viollis said, 'Quand on étudie la vie d'un homme célèbre: "Cherchez la mère", devrait-on dire. Dans le cas de Lord Northcliffe, on cherche et on trouve.'[66]

In the early 1880s, in his school magazine, he noted that *The Times* was generally thought of as the premier journal of the world, but his most important early experience probably came from the work he did for the Newnes publications, whose tone was best conveyed by the fact that in 1883 they gave a house in a prize competition on the sole condition that it should be named 'Tit-Bits Villa'. Harmsworth thought about going to Cambridge, began to read for the Bar, and abandoned both for free-lance journalism; and then came a period out of London (for health reasons), gaining experience with Iliffe and Sons of Coventry.

There were easier ways to make one's fortune – Harmsworth himself wrote *One Thousand Ways to Earn a Living* for Newnes – but he still managed to save a thousand pounds by the time he was twenty-one. His key observation of journalism in the 1880s was devastatingly simple: 'most of the English newspapers were edited for what might be termed the "highbrow" classes and were not interesting to the masses.'[67] Later, in self-justification against his critics, he saw his achievement not in terms of 'the march of wealthy syndicates' but as the giving way of 'the printer with the newspaper' to 'the newspaper with brains'.[68] Those brains sought out a new, mass audience; and within a year of forming his own business, he launched (in 1888) *Answers*, which achieved a weekly circulation of one million in five years and was the first of what were later to become the journals of the Amalgamated Press.

According to the banner headline on *Answers* No 1, dated 2 June 1888 but actually printed after No 3 had launched the magazine with answers to invented questions, the magazine was 'Interesting Extraordinary Amusing', with information

'On Every Subject Under the Sun'. If you wanted to know that in 1795 it was calculated that all the flour used by British hairdressers in a year would have made 5,314,280 quartern loaves, this was the place to look.

It is not difficult to satirize *Answers* and its founder, as the disgruntled W. L. George discovered in writing of *Zip* and its proprietor, poorly disguised as Harmsworth. What cannot be denied is that Harmsworth, in his own words, 'knew from the first just what people wanted to read',[69] and that the methods used to reach those people were adventurous: *Answers* started in the tiniest of one-room offices, but built up a circulation of more than 48,000 in its first year. Copies were given away to spread the word (Harmsworth claimed to have invented this device); publicity came from an *Answers* pipe, *Answers* prize dogs and toothache cures. One of the few mistakes was to refer to the Prince of Wales as 'Tum Tum' because of his weight: it was the aristocracy, not the newly educated, that wanted to make fun of the heir to the throne.

New magazines soon followed, several a year. Harmsworth's self-styled 'Schemo Magnifico' was to kill his opponents by pushing them out of the market-place by the weight of his own enterprises: *Comic Cuts* ('Amusing without Being Vulgar') and *Halfpenny Marvel* and *Pluck Library*, for example. Later, *Answers* was used to boost his first venture into daily journalism: 'Since we purchased the *Evening News* last September [1894], we have added nearly 400,000 copies a week to its circulation. We paid £25,000 for the paper, lock, stock and barrel, and we would not sell it for £100,000, or indeed, for any figure.'[70] The *Evening News*, founded in 1881, had failed as a newspaper and lost Conservative interests a great deal of money: its success gave Harmsworth a new status. He made very sure that everyone heard about its transformation, for the prizes went to those who shouted the loudest.

The same approach was developed in a more important way in 1896: 'Four leading articles, a page of Parliament, and columns of speeches will NOT be found in the *Daily Mail* on 4 May, a halfpenny.'[71] The first issue of the *Daily Mail* does

not look like a revolutionary document from the vantage
point of the tabloid 1970s; it did not have screaming headlines
across many columns; it carried respectable small ads. and
announcements of births, marriages and deaths (copied from
other papers) on page one. Within a year, however, its impact
was thought important enough for inclusion in a survey of
Social Transformations of the Victorian Age: 'The *Daily Mail*
has shown a busy generation which reads its papers as it takes
its lunch standing at a buffet' how easy it is to present 'the
essence of the day's news'.[72] Nothing better symbolizes its
appeal to the newly literate, urban population than the two
parts of its headline on the eve of the First World War: 'Bank
Rate Doubled: King not to go to Cowes'.[73] Readers, many of
them office workers, enjoyed the thought that they were
being made (briefly) aware of important matters of economic
policy – the slogan 'all the news in the smallest space'; they
still preferred to read about royalty, to become spectators at an
aristocratic peep-show.

No wonder the old elite missed the point; they had always
been used to deference, but this was not the deference of the
defeated. When the Prime Minister, Lord Salisbury, dismissed
the *Mail* as 'a journal produced by office-boys for office-boys',
he showed how little he understood the country he ruled was
becoming a country of office-boys – many of them on their
way to becoming office managers. There were 367,215 copies
of the first issue sold, nearly a million at the height of the
Boer War in 1900, and, though some decline was visible in the
years that followed, constant successful attempts were made
to ensure the paper itself was news – the £10,000 prize, for
instance, for the first flight by aeroplane from London to
Manchester.

The process was not magical, though it seemed so. Mistakes
were made, notably in 1900 when the story of 'the Peking
Massacre' in the Boxer Rebellion turned out to be a plot
hatched by the rulers of China for their own purposes. The
Daily Mirror, started in October 1903 as a paper aimed at
women, lost at least £100,000 before its relaunch with illustra-

tions; and then had to wait several decades before social change allowed its proper development. The *Observer*, Harmsworth owned from 1905–12, was never much more than a nuisance, even if its circulation rose – at a cost – sharply. None of this could change the fact that the search for profit had made startling changes to journalism: as the new century began, Harmsworth had an income of £150,000 a year, with capital worth nearly a million pounds; in 1905 a public company, Associated Newspapers, was formed to run the group, and we can begin to identify a modern newspaper industry.

Harmsworth himself was sometimes careless with money; and he was constantly resisting the vital pressures of advertising space. Riches gave him the independence to pursue his own ends; finance was not his chosen vehicle in the pursuit of power. He made a virtue of this: 'Newspaper owners should certainly have no association, direct or indirect, with financiers', he wrote in 1903. He had been roundly abused as one of 'a certain number of fools' (as Labouchere's magazine *Truth* put it) who had paid a high price for Rhodes's Chartered Company stock and seen it fall, and whose judgment on national issues could have been affected.[74] In a sense this was true: he wanted absolute freedom to control opinion, and that meant freeing himself from influences and pressures.

His experience with *The Times* is the exemplar of this obsession. Ever since the retirement of J. T. Delane in 1877 *The Times* had been in decline. When Sir Ernest Cassel was staying at Windsor Castle in November 1907, he told Lord Esher that he – and several others – had been approached by the owners of *The Times* for £200,000; Esher noted in his diary: 'Cassel will not find any money unless the *management* is in new and competent hands.'[75] Cassel and Northcliffe – by this time Harmsworth had acquired a title – both sought power, but the financier and journalist had slightly different routes to the summit. Northcliffe acquired *The Times* in 1908, and most subsequent writers seem to have been mesmerized by the assertion printed in the paper: 'There will be no change whatever in the political or editorial direction . . . which will be conducted by the same staff on the independent lines pursued uninterruptedly for so many years.'[76] At most, he is shown battling against a traditional national institution, asking for help – as in the famous Beerbohm watercolour of *Evenings in Printing House Square* – as he feels 'the demons of sensationalism rising'. He did, gradually, use the methods of the *Daily Mail*, but he was never able to make the deeper changes that were necessary to give him the sense of control he needed.

Northcliffe was destroyed by success: the more power he had, the more possibilities presented themselves, the more everything seemed to slip from his grasp – the pursuit of power became, in the end, the pursuit of madness.

And yet, on the way, life could be good: Northcliffe's will was proved at £3,500,000 in February 1923. What happened when he – and the other members of the plutocracy – took time off from making money, we shall now see.

Chapter 6

In at Last: the Social Revolution

To possess a million pounds in 1900 could be very frustrating. How was the world to comprehend the magnitude of your achievement – and the power it gave you? An essay 'On Money' in the first decade of the twentieth century argued that those who worked for riches knew no other purpose than the making of more riches: money-making was an end in itself. A more sophisticated view, however, insisted that money was only a means to an end.[1] The plutocrats' problem, having perhaps made more money in less time than any other group of people in the history of Britain, and that in a society with deeply traditional values, was one of self-identity, defining their status to themselves – and others. According to the American ambassador in London, they turned away from money-making in order to pursue the cultivation of the mind and the arts of living to perfection.[2] The historical record shows something different: the plutocrats made an assault on society in two separate, but connected ways: by parading the wealth they had won through the public display of luxury, and by using that wealth to ape the life-style of the existing establishment.

Lionel Phillips rationalized the plutocratic love of luxury

by describing it as 'the hallmark of civilisation'; everyone benefited from luxury, he argued, for 'the greater the abundance, the variety, and the utility of commodities that contribute to the comfort and elevation of mankind, the wider the field of employment'.[3] But there were other, more cogent reasons for spending money as well as making it. Thorstein Veblen's *The Theory of the Leisure Class*, first published in 1899, is a key document of the period – written precisely at the time plutocratic power was coming to its height in both America and England. Veblen, who was the son of Norwegian emigrants to Wisconsin, showed how exemption from employment had been the economic means of identifying the upper classes ever since predatory warlords had first shown their prowess by seizing land and property.

In time property had become the conventional basis of esteem. Through the centuries the mere possession of wealth, which was at the outset valued simply as an evidence of efficiency, became identified in the public mind with merit. Wealth or power, moreover, had to be seen, 'for esteem is awarded only on evidence' – the evidence, for example, of 'a constantly increasing differentiation and multiplication of domestic and body servants', whose utility lay not in the amount of work they did, but rather 'in their conspicuous exemption from productive labor', which underlined their master's wealth and power.[4]

Not all the first-generation millionaires delighted in publicly paraded luxury; most of their children did. Dr Frederick Mott, pathologist to the London County Asylums, argued in 1914 that 'self-made men not infrequently form the first step in the process of degeneration. . . . The selfishness and meanness or the cunning, avarice, and moral guile by which they have succeeded in amassing a fortune for their children to spend selfishly is the first evidence of degeneracy.' The parents, for purely selfish reasons, succeeded by work and abstemiousness; the children, with the same selfish instinct but no need to work, acquired vicious habits and criminal propensities, which often led them to prison or the mad house. *The Times*

found all this 'rather sweeping' but did not doubt that it
contained a germ of truth; W. A. Smiles, Samuel Smiles's
grandson, wrote indignantly to protest at the dismissal of
'self-help' doctrines.[5]

Part of the difference in the generations could be explained
by the fact that the plutocrats had a rough ride from Society
in the early days – something their more sophisticated
children did not have to face. Mrs Ismay, wife of a shipping
magnate, kept a diary account of her experiences in London
in May–June 1881, in a tone of excited wariness, happy to be
there, but obviously overawed by her experience:

1 June 'At a Ball at Mr Millais'. About 800 there. Saw a
number of London Fashionables!'
8 June 'Tried to get into the Albert Hall, but could not
owing to the crowd.'[6]

The emphasis on luxury – by both the plutocrats and their
children – also had a more simple root: the opportunities
available. At the beginning of the twentieth century a bachelor
in London with only £1,000 a year could still manage a flat in
Mayfair and a servant (which might account for £150); he
could dine at his club for 4s, at a good restaurant for perhaps
10s; his evening clothes would not cost him more than
11 guineas from the best tailor in Savile Row. Even his
week of admittance to the Royal Enclosure at Ascot could be
obtained for only £2.[7]

A magazine examination of 'The Social Future of England'
by the Fabian William Clarke, just before Edward VII came
to the throne in 1901, referred to an apt description of the
country as 'the paradise of the rich, the purgatory of the
poor, and the hell of the wise'. Whether the saying was true
or not, it was certain that for the rich there was no more
pleasant a place to live than England. 'Here the rich man can
say with that *confrère* of his in the Gospels, "Take thine ease,
eat, drink, and be merry." ' The climate was not ideal, but
there were many other important advantages: the quality of

the servants and the sport; the variety of luxuries in the shops; the absence of revolution or even an instinct for equality; and an easy growth of vested interests well looked after by Parliament. The rich American could escape from nerve-racking pressures, the rich Australian from daily monotony.[8] The process that was to make England the pleasure-ground of the world's richest people had begun.

Consumption was much in evidence in Edwardian England. Price Collier, who wrote about the country for an American newspaper audience, noted with distaste the 'prodigal expenditures' on drink ($750,000,000) and on sport ($220,000,000) in the Britain of 1906–7, though he laid much of the blame on the working classes.[9] C. F. G. Masterman faulted 'the enrichment of a new wealthy class . . . and the effort of some old-established rich families not to be pushed under in display by these alien intruders', which turned 'modern life into a huge apparatus of waste': a competition for luxurious indolence as mad as the armaments race.[10] The 'wanton waste' described in E. J. Urwick's *Luxury and Waste of Life* (1908) was rivalled only by the rich of Imperial Rome, dining off dishes of nightingales' tongues at £60 each. The 1885 Whiteley's catalogue had included a picture of LUXURIOSUM, a splendid garden chair with awning – one of a characteristic range of consumer goods. Even Lady Colin Campbell's *Etiquette of Good Society*, revised in 1911, was in no doubt that 'with the rapid strides of civilisation and refinement comes the love of luxury and the desire for means to gratify it'.[11]

Money was not only spent, but spent ostentatiously. The economist Arthur L. Bowley, who studied the change in the distribution of national income between 1880 and 1913, could find no statistical evidence that the rich as a class were getting rapidly richer in real income immediately before the First World War. But he pointed out that a few motor-cars could, in a week, provide a demonstration of 'wasteful and arrogant expenditure' over several counties; and he was prepared to suggest that wealth, 'without increasing as a whole more rapidly than population', was passing 'into the possession of persons who enjoyed ostentatious expenditure'.[12] Marie Corelli had her own way of saying much the same: 'why should we call the Roman Heliogabalus a sensualist and voluptuary? His orgies were less ostentatious than many social functions of today.'[13]

Ever since Edwardian times the rich, most of them, have tried to hide their riches from public view; then they could feel the security of knowing that their ostentation would meet approval from all but a relatively few – and, in their own way, equally ostentatious – social critics. Whatever else might be said about the Edwardian environment, no one could describe it as unobtrusive: its music was the music of Elgar, its architecture was characterized by overpowering display, its applied arts sought to show the costliness of the object, not the beauty of the design.

Photography and film widened the range of visibility in a literal sense. Robert W. Paul filmed the 1896 Derby; the Pathé film library contains film of Queen Victoria's Diamond Jubilee: Victoria's funeral, Edward VII's accession, his funeral, were all recorded on film.[14] Though the fashion for portrait photography had begun in the 1860s, technical changes later encouraged the use of photographs to record social occasions of all kinds. The Duchess of Devonshire's famous fancy-dress ball of 1897 was recorded in pictures and the photographs were later collected together and specially bound; the albums were available only to the few, but anyone could – and nearly everyone did – buy photographs of such Society celebrities as Lady Randolph Churchill. One magazine of the period, in an article on X-ray photography, pointed out that civilization was the relentless foe of privacy, but it was clear that those whose privacy was invaded encouraged the process.[15]

The Times, in 1912 and in serious mood, asserted that the work begun by Society journalists in bringing 'the secrets of the English governing class . . . into the back-kitchen and the bar-room' had been completed by the camera: now 'the shop girl and the schoolboy not only know that the Countess of X brought her daughter to some fashionable reception and that Lady Y looked pretty in grey and silver at the racecourse, but they may actually behold these personages taken in unguarded moments in their habits as they live.' Those who used to listen at the keyhole were engaged in an exciting, if undignified occupation: now the whole of Society had become like an open shop window in which ostentatious luxury was revealed to the most casual glancer.[16]

Winning a place in Society through conspicuous consumption went hand-in-hand with the pretence of living the life of the country gentleman – so long the arbiter of social acceptance. As a consequence, there were those to observe bitterly how 'you would find in the remote countryside, in historic houses containing chapels with the tombs of Crusaders, men "with names like Rhenish wines" entertaining queer companies of appropriate friends.'[17] The process had begun in the early Industrial Revolution, when the building of Willersley Castle by the textiles manufacturer Arkwright provided only one example from many; and later the difficulties of the landed gentry after the 1870s had the effect of bringing much-needed money to provide a superficial restoration of country-house society.

Society in the Country House (1907) complacently quoted Montalembert, who – on a visit to England in the 1850s – decided that the best omen for the social and political future of the country was the *marchand enrichi*.[18] Bernard Shaw's Malone, American immigrant son of an Irishman who had died in the Great Famine, gave the story a different tone: 'Me and me like are coming back to buy England; and we'll buy the best of it. I want no middle class properties. . . . I have the refusal of two of the oldest family mansions in England. One historic owner can't afford to keep all the rooms dusted: the other can't afford the death duties. What do you say now?'[19] The aggressive tone of the concluding question was an accurate guide to the realities of power.

Why should there have been this desire to conquer what had already been displaced? On the simplest level, of course, rural life could be very pleasant. Mahdo Singh, Maharajah of Jaipur, visited Lord Curzon's Kedleston, near Derby, when he was in England for Edward VII's coronation. 'I watched the rabbits playing on the green turf, and I thought I could sit watching these little creatures in the sun, and could rest there for ever, playing a flute, and I wondered how English sahibs could ever go to India.'[20] Sentimentality became attached to life in the green fields of England, the more so as rural society went into decay. The printed papers of the Patriots' Club in the first years of the twentieth century quoted approvingly the poem by George Bartram:

Old England, gracious wielder of the spell
Of pastoral beauty, janitress benign
Of green Arcadian temples, matron-belle
Robed rich of rustic glory, it is well,
Yes, past all boasting, to be son of thinc.[21]

In private, as well as public, the same image was recorded: George Sturt, friend of Arnold Bennett, noted in his diary in December 1899: 'Some of these days I shall go in search of a village. . . . A village inhabited by Peasantry: rounded in by its own self-supporting toil, and governed by its own old-world customs.'[22] Everywhere the image persisted of smiling rustics in snowy smock-frocks, the children with cheeks as red as the apples in their orchards, the buxom wives at the gates of their little white cottages: rural health and wealth and plenty.[23] The cheer was very faint indeed, for the alternative picture, once forcibly expressed by H. G. Wells, who thought the country boys 'displayed a sort of sluggish, real lewdness – lewdness is the word – a baseness of attitude. . . . In the English country-side there are no books at all, no songs, no drama, no valiant sin even.'[24]

A more practical attraction of country life was the deference of a deferential society. When Consuelo Vanderbilt arrived at

Woodstock station on her way to Blenheim she was greeted by a red-carpet-on-the-platform, mayor-in-scarlet-robes reception. There might be prejudice to face (it was explained to her that Woodstock had a Mayor and Corporation before America was discovered),[25] but a new sort of popularity was in prospect for those with modest pretensions: 'Your City banker or merchant', declared *The Times* on 26 January 1892, 'spends his money freely, and he does not expect too much subservience from the shop-keepers amongst whom his family live, with the result that he is widely respected.'[26]

Above all, complete social acceptance depended on acceptance by the existing rural hierarchy; and that was best achieved by adopting their way of life. So long as the incumbent of the manor house was the magistrate, centre of social life, wielder of economic power in his control of local employment, his position would find its aspirants. The result was a curious sort of pretence. H. G. Wells, whose Bladesover House in *Tono-Bungay* was based on Up Hill in Sussex, brilliantly conveyed the Edwardian rural atmosphere:

The great houses stand in the parks still, the cottages cluster respectfully on their borders, touching their eaves with their creepers, the English country-side . . . persists obstinately in looking what it was. It is like an early day in a fine October. The hand of change rests on it all, unfelt, unseen; resting for awhile, as it were half reluctantly, before it grips and ends the thing for ever. One frost and the whole face of things will be bare, links snap, patience ends, our fine foliage of pretences lie glowing in the mire.[27]

The fact that all the social comment on the plutocratic purchase of rural England distracted attention from the point that already many of the *nouveaux riches* saw no necessity to acquire the large estates that they could well afford. A number of the richest – the City banker Swaythling, the brewer Burton, Winterstoke of Imperial Tobacco – bought only a few thousand acres;[28] and even more treated the country as a weekend escape rather than a way of life. The very word 'week-end' was first used in *The Times* in 1892,[29] and by 1914 it seemed commonplace for *Punch* to talk of 'the passing of the old families and the advent of the week-end "merchant princes" '.[30]

A number of writers described the men – rich Jews, newspaper proprietors, manufacturers – who copied the life of the gentry from Friday night to Sunday morning in the manner of what H. G. Wells called 'pseudomorphs'. 'They entertain themselves and their friends', said Masterman, 'in the heart of an England for whose vanishing traditions and enthusiasms they care not at all.'[31] Country-house hospitalities seemed like prolonged London dinner parties; there might not be money to be made in the country, but there was the opportunity to spend what had been made elsewhere. Relaxation was an additional advantage – 'a heavenly boon of comparative rest', according to *The Tatler*'s Lady Lilith, 'which permits one to get to bed somewhere about midnight . . . forty-eight blessed hours of surcease from the malady of "going-on-somewhere" which is the St Vitus' dance of modern society.'[32]

Lady Monkswell, who week-ended several times at Sir Julian Goldsmid's Somerhill, near Tonbridge, recorded her experiences in her journal. Goldsmid, whose family had emigrated from Poland to Friesland in the sixteenth century and then to London in the early nineteenth, was a banker with a Portuguese title – Baron de Goldsmid de Palmeira – and was also made a Privy Councillor before his death in 1896. Eight Goldsmid daughters were born in eleven years: 'The Goldsmids are much to be pitied,' Lady Monkswell observed. 'They have £100,000 a year and everything you can think of – except one, a son.' Somerhill had more of the attributes of a village than a house and footmen would usher guests into 'the longest room in Kent' after their collection from the station by an impressive range of carriages and flunkeys.

'The house is simply gigantic', Lady Monkswell found in October 1883. And the entertainment? 'We had a good deal of bad singing from Lady Goldsmid, and a very little good singing from Mrs Underdown.' The hostess 'besides being an Italian [actually a Dutch Jewess brought up in Florence] wears, *en grande toilette*, rather fewer clothes than decency commands, so she is naturally rather cold'. Lady Monkswell, by contrast, nearly fainted with the heat – though not the following year when she was lodged in the new wing, next to the stables, where 'the cold was something arctic' and it was ninety yards to the dining-room.[33]

Country houses were often without basic comforts. When a rich American took Killeen, country home of the Fingall family, he burnt a ton of coal a day heating it. Originally an old Norman castle, it had been rebuilt in imitation of Windsor. Lady Fingall found it, at least in the beginning, 'monstrously ugly in its furnishing and extraordinarily uncomfortable'.[34] Luxury and comfort looked less like synonyms in the Edwardian age than any other. Even the American ambassador, secure in progressive London, had to write home in 1913: 'They don't really like bathrooms yet. . . . The telephone – Lord deliver us! – I've given it up.'[35] Neither bathrooms nor telephones were part of the exacting traditions of rural England.

Some of the new rich did not get much further than the suburbs in their pursuit of a gentlemanly existence: from among the department-store owners, William Edgar, founder of Swan & Edgar, bought Eagle House, Clapham Common; James Marshall of Marshall & Snelgrove acquired Goldbeater Farm, Mill Hill; the second Peter Robinson built Brookleigh at Esher. (What is suburban society, Carlyle had asked, but 'retired wholesalers looking down upon retired retailers'?)[36] Alfred Beit's Tewin Water had 700 acres attached, but it was only twenty miles from London and it may well have been doctor's advice that led him to purchase it four years before his death. Lionel Phillips, back from South Africa as a partner in Wernher, Beit & Co., made more of Tylney Hall, Hampshire. He said he found a variety of useful and interesting occupations 'in connection with county matters and the investigation of traditional customs of the country-side, some

Sir Joseph B. Robinson

Barney Barnato

The Louis XIV-style Sitting Room at No 146 Piccadilly, home of
Sir Sigismund Neumann, late 1890s

of a very feudal type, arising from the pronounced conservatism of the people.' He even won 'the ancient office of High Sheriff' of the county: but he was back in South Africa within nine years.[37]

There was an element of sham in all this. Colonel North, who had made a fortune in South America, was never happier than when playing the role of the country squire down at Eltham. The journalist Sir Henry Lucy lunched with him there eight days before his sudden death in 1896, North dressed 'in what I fancy he regarded as the best style of a country gentleman – light trousers and coat, with white waistcoat and a flowered silk necktie' – and carrying an umbrella, 'though a cloudless sunlit sky hung over Avery Hill'. In his £180,000 house he indicated with some satisfaction the empty champagne bottles which had been used, with meats from his estate, to feast 350 railwaymen the previous night.[38] Retainers for a new age, we might think.

Plutocracy in the countryside had its most grotesque consequences when the loyalties of the new rich were torn between the desire to place their own rise to power within the ruling tradition and the knowledge that their world, the world they were creating, was based on rather different principles. The architectural results – the mansions they built – were appalling. They are not only seen in cartoons (a client in 1890 wanted something 'nice and baronial, Queen Anne and Elizabethan, and all that; kind of quaint and Nurembergy, you know – regular Old English, with French windows opening to the lawn, and Venetian blinds, and sort of Swiss balconies, and a loggia').[39] Nor merely in literature (that product of Hilaire Belloc's imagination, Mr Clutterbuck's 'The Plas' – with its peacock-room, Japanese and Indian rooms, Henri Quatre Alcove and Jacobean snuggery – was the expression of the maxim that 'a large part of every important income must of necessity be expended in luxury').[40] Nothing in fiction would be adequate preparation for sight of Castle Drogo, begun in 1911 900 feet above sea level, on the edge of a gorge, 200 feet above the Devon River Teign.

In March 1885 Julius Drewe formed the Home and Colonial Trading Association, which he controlled and of which he was the main shareholder. The development of the chain of stores that followed was a story in itself, but within a few years Mr Drewe withdrew from management to expend his energies on the reconstruction of a dubious family pedigree. He claimed to be descended from the twelfth-century Devon figure Drogo de Teynton, from whose family Drewsteignton (Dru-his-town-on-the-Teign) received its name.

In the winter of 1909–10 Mr Drewe approached Edwin Lutyens with the idea of building in local granite 'such a home as Drogo de Teynton might have had'. 'I do wish he didn't want a Castle,' Lutyens wrote to his wife in August 1910, 'but just a delicious loveable house with plenty of good large rooms in it.' But the grandeur of Lutyens' own designs were appropriate for the last great age of private splendour: after the First World War the scale demanded public finance; before it Lutyens became the willing architectural exponent of the plutocratic parade.

Appropriately, it was on his way to South Africa that he worked on the plans for Drogo. Julius Wernher and Alfred Beit's brother had suggested that he should be involved in developing ideas for Cape Town University, to which they ultimately contributed half a million pounds. Drogo was never completed – that added to its dramatic eccentricity – mainly because of Drewe's decision to double the thickness of the walls: thereby doubling the cost. Many of the forty great granite-walled rooms were hung with tapestries; dimly lit through mullioned windows, they had beamed ceilings – the massiveness of the whole distracting attention from the fine detail of everything down to the specially designed door latches.

A castle, with a portcullis, in the twentieth century! It all took twenty years; and in those twenty years the dreams of Edwardian England faded for ever.[41]

Equipped with social recognition that appeared to go with ostentatious luxury and country-house living, the plutocrats next found a more obvious way of making their mark. The Emperor Napoleon was once asked what was the more important thing, war or money? He said money. The next most important thing? More money. And most important of all? Most money. William Lever quoted this anecdote approvingly; nowhere in the Bible, he pointed out, did it say that money was the root of all evil – rather, it was the love of money, holding to it, hugging it to the heart, that was wrong.[42] Money, once made, could be given away. According to *Truth*, in the first year of Edward VII's reign, titled millionaires tended to spend their money on themselves or their families, while generous acts towards others almost all came from men 'who have sprung from the people'.[43]

Of course this proved nothing in itself, and there were other sources to state the opposite view, such as the Edwardian essay 'On Money'.[44] An analysis of all those people who had bequeathed more than £100,000 to charity between 1881 and 1914 nevertheless revealed only two from landed society – the Earl of Moray and Lady Forester; the balance was made up of bankers and financiers, manufacturers and department-store owners.[45] Andrew Carnegie explained: 'The ambition to found a family, and the maintenance of an aristocratic class by means of primogeniture and entail, tend to divert fortunes from this nobler path into the meaner end of elevating a name on the social scale.'[46] If this was meant to imply that the plutocracy of a Republican America in the same period were all philanthropists, it was nonsense. But it had some force in an English context.

The motives of plutocratic philanthropists were often questioned. There was, indeed, something very self-conscious about the Rothschild Lady Battersea's diary note of her 'Rescue Work' among poor Jews in 1885: 'Have started a Home, furnished it and engaged Superintendent and working Matron. . . . Care less for society than I did formerly, far more for works which show some result.'[47] *Truth* satirized the whole Society attitude to the poor in inventing an East End Ladies Association: its purpose to clothe the half-naked West End

ladies who had to attend social entertainments and the
theatre, and to enlighten the fashionable as to the insanitary
conditions of the life they led. With Mrs Bill Sikes in the
chair at the inaugural meeting at Spitalfields, the labouring
classes pledged themselves to make every effort, whatever the
cost or sacrifice, 'to improve the moral and physical conditions
of life amongst the upper criminal classes'.[48]

When Belgravia and Mayfair took over St George's-in-the-
East in slumland, 'good works' tended to dissolve into 'smart
functions'. Competition seemed to be the rule not only in
industry, but in the organization of charities: the biggest
donors received the biggest prestige. The large-scale contri-
butions to King Edward's Hospital Fund came from familiar
names: Wernher (£390,000), Carnegie (£100,000), Cassel
(£66,000).[49] Even relatively small amounts were brought to the
notice of readers of *The Times* – in January 1912, for example:
'Sir Ernest Cassel has sent a special donation of £700 to the
Prince of Wales's General Hospital, Tottenham, this sum
being in addition to a grant of £800 allocated from the recent
gift of Sir Ernest to the King Edward Hospital Fund.'[50] In
1914, after Wernher's death, George V included a special
message in the annual report of the fund, recording his
'splendid example', which will 'long be remembered by all
interested in hospital work'.[51]

Bernard Shaw interpreted all this as part of the plutocratic
desire for power. 'When Mr Carnegie rattled his millions in his
pockets', he wrote, 'all England became one rapacious
cringe.'[52] Not surprisingly, perhaps, Marie Corelli also saw
philanthropy as another example of 'the flagrant assertion
of money-dominance over every other good'. She was not
ready to support Carnegie, for ever 'strewing Free Libraries
over the surface of the country, as if these institutions were so
many lollipops thrown out of a school-boy's satchel'.[53] It was
true that, if the sums involved were often large, they were
not on the whole used in a novel way; the personal considerations of the donor, rather than cost–benefit analysis, came out
on top. Hospitals, libraries, museums were the main objects:

all built in a style that reaffirmed the principles of conspicuous waste rather than public benefit – a typical building, in Veblen's description, 'faced with some aesthetically objectionable, but expensive stone, covered with grotesque and incongruous details', designed with 'battlemented walls and turrets and . . . massive portals'.[54]

Whether the progress of science was in the long term more beneficial than direct humanitarian aid is an open question, but it was apparently an important consideration for the philanthropists.[55] Otto Beit left £215,000 to found thirty research fellowships at London University in memory of his brother, Alfred. Cassel provided £200,000 for Edward VII to found a sanatorium for consumptives (and was somewhat inappropriately photographed in ancient baronial costume when *The Tatler* reported the donation in the middle of January 1902). Cynics might suggest that such gifts were a reminder that even plutocrats were not immortal. As an aged, ailing Sir Thomas Lipton wrote from his country home in July 1931, 'what is a man's wealth when he has not the good health to attend to his duties?'[56]

When the plutocrats spent their money ostentatiously, whether on themselves or – through philanthropy – on others, they found their most potent ally at the very top of the social hierarchy. According to the Vienna journalist, Sigmund Münz, the Kaiser Wilhelm II referred to his Uncle Edward – Prince of Wales and heir to Queen Victoria's throne – as a 'stockbroker' who borrowed money from Sir Thomas Lipton and depended financially on such Jewish bankers as Maurice de Hirsch and Sir Ernest Cassel. His succession in 1901 – at least in the eyes of one contemporary – was to confirm the social sovereignty of wealth throughout his realm.[57]

At first sight royalty and plutocracy made strange bedfellows. It was not that Edward was a radical in the political sense; on the contrary, he believed in the continuation of the hereditary principle in the House of Lords, and expressed 'a strong dislike' for the 1909 budget, which contained proposals against the interests of landed society. Still less can he be associated with social informality. Sir Lionel Cust, who was keeper of the royal art collections, recalled that 'King Edward . . . had an innate love of Court pomp and ceremony, and was a ruthless stickler for correctness of deportment and organization, even to a button on a uniform or the exact position of a decoration on the breast of its wearer.' Typical was the occasion when Sir Henry Howard dined at Windsor Castle after his appointment as Ambassador to the Holy See and his elevation as a GCB, and the King drew him aside to tell him that he had the ribbon of his order in the wrong position.[58]

The single most important influence in shaping Edward VII's life-style was the court of his long-lived and melancholy mother, Queen Victoria. Depression, dowdiness and decay were the Victorian keynotes for nearly forty years after the death of Prince Albert, the husband to whom the Queen had been devoted. Her favoured present for one of her daughters was once a 'mounted enamelled photograph of our dear mausoleum', and that was not a misleading indication of her taste.[59] 'Mama is dreadfully sad . . . and she cries a lot', another daughter wrote; 'then there is always the empty room, the empty bed, and she always sleeps with Papa's coat over her.'[60] Clare Sheridan, a niece of Lady Randolph Churchill, associated the Queen with all that was dull and grim and mournful after seeing her when she was a child: 'A wind was blowing, the Queen had opened a black umbrella and held it firmly against the side on which we were, and that was all we saw after our long standing wait.'[61] Not a Queen who wanted to make herself known to her young subjects, she surrounded herself with austere dowagers or frightening figures like Lady Ponsonby, who praised the court for providing 'the discipline of an almost religious rule in everyday life'.[62]

One can imagine a typical dinner, the restraint involved – 'The dinner was very whispery', Lady Wolseley wrote from Windsor Castle to her husband.[63] The frugality – Disraeli, who once dined on successive nights with the Queen and then with the household, thought the latter enjoyed a banquet in comparison with the former. And the strict etiquette, which left all but a few, a very few, ill at ease. Even the environment: Rosebery said he thought the drawing-room at Osborne House the ugliest in the world – until he saw the drawing-room at Balmoral. How uninviting it all was!

The consequence was that there was no court for much of the year. Yet, as Bagehot observed, 'The queen bee was taken away, but the hive went on.'[64] Society life in the second half of Queen Victoria's reign revolved to a large extent around the Prince of Wales's London and country homes, Marlborough House and Sandringham. In the early days, it was the wildest of the young patricians who were asked to leave their visitors' cards in the salver that lay between the paws of the stuffed baboon in the entrance hall at Sandringham; as the years passed, the dominance of sheer money became more and more noticeable. The closest companions of the heir to the throne had never before been chosen from men whose birth, social position and achievements recommended themselves so little to the established order.[65] The last Tsar, shortly before he succeeded his father in 1894, wrote a perplexed letter to his mother, the Tsarina Marie, from Sandringham: the house-party was 'rather strange. Most of them were horse dealers, amongst others a Baron Hirsch!'[66] The house-party on the weekend of 10–12 July 1895 showed the social net spread even wider to include not only William Waldorf Astor, millionaire expatriate scion of the American Astor family, but two men so patently *arriviste* that their presence sent a wide section of old England into a state of shock: Colonel North, the 'Nitrate King' of South America, and J. B. Robinson, fresh from the South African gold-fields.[67]

In part, Edward's association with the millionaires had a more positive origin than a mere reaction against his parents' existence. *The Times* was probably right: 'If he had been born in a humbler station, he might have become a successful business man.'[68] It was not simply a question of ability allowing for exaggeration, as Asquith said, 'In this great

business community there was no better man of business'[69] –
but of interest too: the manufacturer Sir Charles W. Macara,
proudly spending 'A Day with King Edward at Windsor', was
struck by the evident knowledge of the work of the International Cotton Federation displayed by the Court.[70] There
were also more pressing reasons for interest in money. In his
chapter on 'The Prince's "Debts" ', the very laudatory
biographer Edward Legge – writing in 1912 – could only say
that he 'knew how to make a thousand pounds go about as
far as most people'.[71] Right from the beginning his income
never matched his tastes and his expenditure; those who
could provide the best of everything were therefore natural
friends. What happened was clear: the costs of the Prince's
pursuit of pleasure escalated at precisely the time when the
landed classes were hit by the changing economy.

The results were seen to the full when Edward at last
became king. Queen Victoria had died in the early evening of
22 January 1901 and an immediate move to change the
atmosphere of the royal household symbolized what was to
come. 'His Majesty the King', declared the first issue of *The
Tatler*, 'finds time among his many serious occupations to set
his houses in order for future residence.'[72] *Truth*, less rever-
ently, explained that the so-called service room at Balmoral,
for many years a private chapel, was to be converted into a
billiard room.[73] The Windsor Castle State Apartments were
hopelessly antiquated and, as Sir Lionel Cust observed, were
lacking in quite ordinary comforts, despite their use as
lodgings for royalty.[74] Buckingham Palace, described by
Edward as the 'Sepulchre', was given electric light, new
bathrooms, a telephone switchboard; and the suite occupied
by Prince Albert was refurbished for the first time in four
decades. One of the Queen's favourite homes was dispensed
with altogether: 'I have finished with Osborne House,'
Edward said. 'As a private residence, it is utterly unattractive
to me.'[75] The King's millionaires would not fit easily into the
old Queen's environment.

The coronation, postponed once because the King was

seriously ill, set the tone for the reign. The Rothschild Lady Battersea was held 'enthralled through eye, ear and heart'.[76] The middle classes and the new rich were fascinated by minor points of procedure: 'As to widows of Peers who have remarried with a Peer of lower degree, their precedence, according to precedent, is that of their last husbands.'[77] *Truth* reported that an American was having a diadem made in Paris for £250,000 and that tickets were being sold in New York to the highest bidder.[78]

The expense of it all seemed to be the most noticeable feature: 'The King's Coronation', a volume from the Goldsmiths' and Silversmiths' Companies, showed colour sketches of the aristocracy's coronets, with details of the cost; no longer could this be thought tasteless, it was said, for 'now that some of our oldest and best families are very poor, while millionaires are running up the prices of everything, the Goldsmiths have every justification for announcing that they can manufacture the necessary coronets at moderate prices.'[79] *The Tatler* itemized the bills involved in attending, down to the £2 2s for lunch and £5 5s for a chair in Westminster Abbey (though the latter could be sold for profit).[80] A few hints alone suggested some uneasiness at the display: Lady Warwick came up the aisle without any diamonds, serene 'in the absolute perfection of her beauty', and it made everyone else (with some reason) feel vulgarly ostentatious, 'as if we were a lot of American or South Africa millionairesses vying with each other in the weight of our money-bags'.[81]

The image of luxury and ostentation which is associated with the Edwardian age was, in a literal sense, related to Edward VII himself: to be an Edwardian meant to be a member of the society which acquired its style and its meaning from Edward himself. It was not difficult to see why the plutocrats should seek to have 'free and easy familiarities with "Bertie" . . . and "Alex"', as Marie Corelli disapprovingly put it.[82] And what Edward liked was exactly what the millionaires could provide: travelling and racing and shooting and yachting; good food, good wine, good company. E. T.

Raymond pictured the King having his revenge: at the beginning of the eighteenth century the aristocrats had destroyed the power of the monarchy; at the beginning of the twentieth the King destroyed the aristocracy.[83] There were strict political limitations on the monarch's powers, but he was socially absolute – the old order could either pay up, and thereby be rapidly impoverished in trying to match plutocratic riches, or go to the backwoods, away from the social centre.

Not since a mullet had been bought at the price of a province in Roman times, had the cost of entertaining a crowned head stood so high as it did in the England of Edward VII. One of the Tudor kings prosecuted the Earl of Oxford for having transgressed the monarch's own sumptuary laws in entertaining him. Now, however, riches were to the fore. One of Edward's contemporaries observed: 'Today Royalty's reception means, from roof to basement, from cornice to floor, from the entrance hall to the park lodge at the end of the avenue, a transfiguring and recreating'; the old country house had become like 'some Hotel Metropole, specially affected by Israelites and stockbrokers', or 'some annexe of Messrs. Maple's warehouse'.[84]

Edward VII was an itinerant king. If he came to stay you would need supplies of his favourite aubergines, ginger biscuits from Biarritz, bath salts, and cigars.[85] Even the Duke of Devonshire entertained him not so much because he was one of the greatest nobles, but in his role as one of Edward's wealthiest subjects.[86] Each time a room would have to be converted into a private postal telegraph office; at Glenquoich, in 1906, lines were brought twenty-six miles for the occasion; at Tulchan Lodge, taken by the millionaire Arthur Sassoon, they had come across the River Spey from Advie post office. There were equerries, valet, secretary, perhaps grooms, loaders, horses, dogs to be accommodated. There had to be sporting opportunities of an active kind, for Edward was too impatient to appreciate to the full the delights of the dozen miles of salmon fishing at Balmoral.[87]

Money did not always ensure that the shooting went

smoothly. All went well enough with the great nobles and what were described as 'the more or less patrician plutocrats', to both of whom pleasure or duty suggested a visit.[88] But there were others who would do more or less anything to secure his presence. Sigismund Neumann, created baronet in 1912, held the tenancy of Invercauld, near Balmoral, and invited Edward to a deer drive in 1898. Neumann was one of the new South African rich, who had retired relatively early from day-to-day management to pursue a social career. Pioneer conditions in Africa do not seem to have been his ideal: the day his gold-knobbed walking stick gave him a black eye when the springless mule cart in which he was travelling hit a bump, seems a typical enough occasion, if we judge from his contemporaries' anecdotes. But the large amount of money he made was not in doubt.

The animals of the South African bush were at least less perverse than the deer that refused to be driven in the proper direction at Invercauld: in a two-hour drive no one managed a shot. Luncheon would have acted as a restorative, but a half-hour walk to Neumann's chosen spot failed to find the food. According to Sir Frederick Ponsonby, Neumann looked about and 'like a hound who is trying to pick up the scent, he circled round and round but with no success'. Edward began to mutter 'about rich men undertaking things they know nothing about and ended by shouting suggestions to the wretched Neumann, who was still scouring the country-side at a trot'. Much consulting of maps indicated a confusion of two places with similar names, five miles apart: 'H.R.H. . . . called Neumann every synonym for an idiot.'[89] There was no time for another drive that day, though Neumann's persistence produced better results in later years at his sporting estate of Raynham, between Sandringham and Cromer. In the 1910 season a single day produced a thousand pheasants and 870 ducks, and the King was said to have made special inquiries concerning the methods that produced such good sport.[90]

Shooting represented excitement bought expensively:

horse-racing came into the same category. The American Price Collier remarked in 1909 that 'smart' Society in England centred on the King and the horse.[91] The juxtaposition of royalty and animal was not insulting: Edward loved horse-racing as much as he loved yachting – an owner from 1871, he won the Derby twice and in 1909, with Minoru, became the first reigning monarch to do so.

The connection between Edward, his plutocratic friends and racing was close. It was, to begin with, a gambling one. Daisy, Princess of Pless, lunched at Newmarket in November 1905 with the King, his mistress Alice Keppel, the courtier Horace Farquhar . . . and Arthur Sassoon, 'the Jew page boy' 'who gets up after each course to make bets for the King and the others while they are at lunch'.[92] The largest amount Edward ever lost on a single horse was the £600 he had placed on Maurice de Hirsch's Matchbox, favourite for the Paris Grand Prix in June 1894; the results were not always so disastrous – Hirsch's La Flèche, bought at Edward's suggestion, won three classics (the Thousand Guineas, the Oaks and the St Leger) and the Cambridgeshire in 1892. The plutocrats had no worries about money, but they did need Edward's social blessing. Sir Blundell Maple, who initially raced pseudonymously as 'Mr Childwick' and in 1901 alone won fifty-eight races and £21,364, finally secured election to the exclusive Jockey Club a few months before he died in 1903. He had been a Derby winner, but in the Jockey Club he had few friends. A mere 'retail tradesman' could not expect a welcome from that august body and Edward had been forced to use all his influence to obtain his election to the club.[93]

The criticisms made of the King because of his association with the plutocracy were encouraged by the financial scandals in which his friends were involved. Horace Farquhar, who later became a Viscount and Earl, was a banker before he took up his position in the royal household, and remained a director of Parr's Bank until 1915. In early 1907 Lord Carrington recorded in his diary how shares in a Siberian gold-mining company had risen rapidly to £16; now they were down 'with a rattle, and Horace Farquhar is said to have netted £70,000'.[94] Farquhar, it was rumoured, had secured several well-known names, including the King's private secretary, Francis Knollys, to sit on the board. And Farquhar, according to an article in *Mayfair* in 1910, was 'the only peer who was elevated to the Upper Chamber at the direct request of the late King'.[95]

Other courtiers lost money in Ernest Hooley's 'Hydraulic Joint' scheme, notably Sir Jacob Wilson, of the Board of Agriculture, who was instrumental in introducing Edward, as Prince of Wales, to Hooley. According to Hooley's own account, he had purchased 2,000 acres adjoining Sandringham in 1896, which the Prince's land agent had not expected to reach its reserve price; it was subsequently arranged that, taking into account Hooley's improvements, the estate should be sold to the Prince at cost – some £29,200. Hooley's notoriety was matched only by that of Whitaker Wright, who committed suicide at the law courts in 1903 after his sentence for frauds involving the collapse of the London and Globe Society; and Wright's fall involved Lord Dufferin, former Viceroy of India, and the Duke of Connaught, one of Edward's younger brothers.

The fact that mention was made in such circumstances of the name of a highly respected courtier like Viscount Knollys, whose ancestor had been Usher of the Chamber to a Tudor king 400 years before, indicated the dominating spirit of Edward's entourage. Some contemporaries lamented the declining influence of men like Sir Nigel Kingscote or Sir Dighton Probyn – country gentlemen with estates, not necessarily sizeable, that had been in their family's hands for generations.[96] The old families still obtained the honorary offices, but that was not a true sign of continuity with the past. Edward's grandson, briefly king as Edward VIII, defined what happened: 'Although I was too young to realise it, I was seeing the birth of a new era. . . . High office or ancient lineage were no longer the sole criteria of status. Beauty, wit, wealth, sophistication – these had now become valid passports to the Sovereign's intimate circle.'[97] And of these wealth came first.

What did it all amount to, this plutocratic assault on society? *The Times* looked at the changes of the previous thirty years in January 1912.[98] There seemed to be two vital facts: 'more people, rich people, as well as poor people, in the world'; and 'the restlessness produced by perpetual locomotion', which had wrecked the system by undermining the stability of the London Season. The sad conclusion was that the conditions which once 'made the inner circles of London society rather better worth living in, and rather better worth writing about, than they are at present, or seem likely to be in the future' had long gone. In the 1870s and 1880s 'London society was still manageable and still discriminating. The hereditary aristocracy, which was the nucleus and centre of the whole, had not then been swollen by an influx of wealthy financial and provincial mediocrities.' Exclusivity in social life had degenerated into 'promiscuous gatherings, to which everybody goes and where nobody counts'.

By this time, indeed, the plutocrats – described by *The Times* as 'the possessors of authentic millions' – could almost be given equal status with 'the owners of historic millions': at least by comparison with the gaggle of nonentities who were also finding their way into social life. Their success, we shall now see, was a measure of an application to the pursuit of power which went far beyond obeisance to social pleasantries.

Chapter 7

In at Last: Public Life Succumbs

Luxury and philanthropy, the pleasures of society and the company of the King of England – these were nice, very nice for those with traditions of the ghetto or the grey reaches of lower-middle-class land. But there were more direct means used by the plutocrats in the pursuit of power, both in the localities and on a national level. Social prestige, once achieved, was used as a means of entry to the institutions of government and influence; and entry was the first step to dominance.

'An old form of government which has served us for five centuries and more, is breaking up . . .', wrote F. W. Maitland in *The Reflector* in February 1888. 'Hitherto such government as our counties have had, has been government by justices of the peace – government, that is, by country gentlemen, appointed by the Lord Chancellor in the Queen's name, on the recommendation of the Lord Lieutenant of the county, legally dismissible at a moment's notice; but practically holding the offices for life.'[1]

It was actually the Tory President of the Local Government Board who took the really important step in 1888, but this Tory – Charles Thompson Ritchie – was the son of a Scottish businessman. 'Squire' Chaplin, who had declined the presidency because it carried no place in the Cabinet, was happy that it did not fall on him to introduce the bill: 'he should have felt compunction in putting an extinguisher upon too many of the class with which he had associated himself – the country gentlemen of England.'[2] The Local Government Act at last created elective county councils, and sixty large towns were given the status of county boroughs, emancipating them from rural control. Not all prophecies were as doom-laden as that of Chaplin, but even the Prime Minister, Lord Salisbury, declared that country gentlemen 'probably will be less prominent . . . in attending to public affairs' in the future.[3]

The Times, in a leader on the prospects for the new county councils, seemed most concerned – in its inimitable fashion – to throw light on 'why it is that lunatics – especially pauper lunatics – are so very apt to tumble into over-heated baths', but it did also suggest that the councils would provide vehicles for manufacturers to press their interests: the decline in landed power would not mean the end of rule by the rich.[4] A number of working-class men were elected in January 1889, though only a tiny proportion; nobility and gentry filled almost all the posts of chairmen of the county councils. The key point is missed, if the focus of these events is seen as the apparent survival of landed influence, or if note is taken of isolated cases such as that of the Earl of Northesk who retired because it had 'come to his notice' that the tenant farmers in his part of Hampshire wished to be represented by one of themselves.[5] The most important social fact in local government was the intrusion of businessmen, of the plutoc-racy, into a traditionally landed preserve. In Cheshire, by the 1880s and before the 1888 Act, all the large industrialists were already sitting on the magistrates bench. Typical was Duncan Graham, the Chairman of the County Council, and head of a Liverpool firm of merchants trading with South America, who moved to the village of Willaston about 1860 and made substantial financial gifts to the local community for use in education and by the church.[6]

The process of making local government dependent on

popular election was completed by the Act of 1894 which set up nearly 7,000 parish councils. It too was passed only after controversy; the Commons spent thirty-eight days in debate; 619 amendments were put forward; and Knatchbull-Hugessen was not strictly accurate in feeling himself 'the only Tory left in the House' to vote against what was seen as a revolutionary measure.[7] Contemporaries of many shades of opinion agreed that the gentry had been thrust 'like a nameless element into a democracy which will henceforward control their destinies';[8] other legislation followed which seemed to take even more power from landed society – for example, the abolition in 1906 of financial and residential qualifications for JPs. But all this was to have its impact over a long period. If the gentry had an immediate threat to face, it was the transference of their authority in the localities to rich men of another kind. In the past the gentry would have absorbed the plutocracy; now the relationship was merely one of alliance. Social standing remained the most important criterion in local government until the First World War, but only because of the reluctant coming together of the old order and the new to perpetuate the old system in the interests of both.

This process of power-sharing was equally apparent in the central bastion of landed privilege, the House of Lords. There also the underlying theme was one of attack by the forces of democracy, temporarily warded off by allowing entry to plutocracy.

If landed and aristocratic influence in politics was a long time dying, it was not always because the class concerned pursued their interests energetically – on a day-to-day basis, when Bagehot was writing in 1867, one might have found ten peers in the Lords, possibly only six: three was thought of as quorum for transacting business. The days of landed dominance were numbered, but the Lords could sometimes count on stronger support from the rising working and middle classes than from their own number: for someone whose new horizons included the possibility of social enhancement,

inequality suddenly became attractive. 'Demos himself', wrote
Ramsay Muir in a polemic of 1910, 'though now legally
enthroned . . . preferred to be ruled by Gentlemen.'[9]

The House of Lords had long since become the second house
in importance. Bernal Osborne, the great wit and MP,
lamented Disraeli's creation as Earl of Beaconsfield in 1876:
'With all his genius, Dizzy loves tinsel!' he wrote. 'I cannot
help looking upon this elevation as a *fall* to such a man!'[10] Most
important bills were introduced in the Commons and limits
on the Lords' power in connection with financial legislation
dated from as far back as the seventeenth century. But the
peers remained, as Bagehot noted, 'a hidden but potent
influence' in the Commons; as late as 1880 170 MPs were the
sons of peers or baronets, and the importance of local personalities in elections continued, in many cases, to be decisive.
John Buchan, in a little remembered period of his life, when
he wrote for the *Scottish Review*, suggested that it was safer to
keep the 'great landowners and rich men' in the Lords, 'rather
than turn them loose with their great power of influence and
wealth to dictate many of the elections to the popular
Chamber'.[11]

The situation was frustrating to radicals, but it looked very
different through the eyes of the landed aristocrat. He had to
listen to L. G. Chiozza Money – author of *Riches and Poverty*
(1905) – insistently telling him that 'the land is now probably
at bed-rock price', providing the opportunity for national-
ization 'at an absurdly low price' and the means 'to recreate
our social structure'.[12] The financial plight that went with
agricultural depression was worsened by a whole series of new
or increased taxes. At no time during the nineteenth century
did direct taxes bring in more than half the Exchequer
revenue. As late as 1904 the Chancellor of the Exchequer
expressed hopes of reduction in income tax, but it was clear
by then that the tax had become a permanent part of life;
and even more ominously, the Liberal budget of 1907 introduced a distinction between earned and unearned income.[13]

Businessmen could, by and large, afford to pay their taxes;

hard-pressed landowners felt that they could not. Death duties did not look like a terrible burden from the figures quoted by Chiozza Money – in 1894–5 estates worth nearly 200 million pounds brought in less than 11 million; in 1908–9 estates worth nearly 300 million brought in just over 18 million. But Queen Victoria said of Harcourt, who had introduced the duties in 1894, that he was 'actuated by spite to, and a wish to injure, the landed proprietors'. (Natural justice being what it is, Harcourt himself had death-duty difficulties from his brother's estate, and the funds from the sale of the London family home all went in duties.)[14] The Dowager Duchess of Chevron, in Vita Sackville-West's novel *The Edwardians*, never quite recovered from her experience in protesting to the Chancellor about the Harcourt duties; to be told, politely, that no exception could be made in individual cases was something she had never experienced before. A higher rate was introduced in 1907 and much larger increases were proposed in Lloyd George's much-celebrated budget two years later. The American George W. Smalley pointed out that the latter was 'the logical and inevitable sequel' of Harcourt's measures, which marked the dividing line between 'the Old and the New': 'taxing Capital instead of Income'. Harcourt 'had adopted the doctrine of ransom which Mr Chamberlain had first proclaimed' – a reference to Chamberlain's famous attack on the Lords and landowners in the 1880s.[15]

The 1909 budget brought the clash between the landed Lords and the Liberal government to a head. Its terms, which included a super tax on incomes of more than £5,000 a year and several land taxes, were a response to the previous year's deficit, itself the result of increased expenditure on the navy and, in particular, the introduction of old age pensions. The Lords had become more obstructive as their interests were threatened, and the attacks upon them became more common. Howard Evans, the author of *Our Old Nobility*, described the sort of England that would have survived if the peers had had their way: not one man in forty would have the vote; no Jew or Catholic or agnostic would sit in Parliament; towns would be governed by closed corporations, counties by the great landlords; trade unions would be unlawful, newspapers would be taxed. The record of the Lords from the time it rejected the first Reform Bill in 1831 by a majority of forty-one to its 1906 mutilation of the Tenants Right Bill had been one of unrelenting reaction.[16]

Ironically, no one better described why the powers of the Lords had to be curtailed than Lord Willoughby de Broke, one of the leaders of the Die-Hard Conservatives when battle finally commenced. In 1908 the Lords rejected the Licensing Bill, which was primarily designed to reduce the number of licences for liquor. The Liberal government, elected in 1906 by a landslide majority and equipped thereby with a full mandate for its reforms, was thwarted by the decision of a group of Tory noblemen, summoned to a meeting in the drawing-room of Lord Lansdowne's London home. The conversation was said to be 'great fun' and some who had never been consulted on a national issue 'met each other fresh from the hunting field, and were able to compare notes about the past season and to discuss the possible winners of the spring handicaps'. Those who had breakfasted at cock-crow to catch the early train were in no mood to listen to any arguments for tampering with the liquor trade. Once attitudes had been made clear at this meeting, the huge Tory majority in the Lords made the vote a formality.[17]

Political considerations did usually allow the Tory leader, Balfour, to tell Lansdowne, who led the party in the Lords, how to vote – a pleasant reversal of their roles at Eton, where Balfour had fagged for Lansdowne. Nevertheless, the very fact that the Tories had been so heavily defeated in the January 1906 election focussed attention on their numbers in the Lords; and the overt consciousness that this was – as John Buchan put it – 'a house of landlords fighting for what it regards as its own' developed rapidly on both sides.[18] The constitutional crisis that followed the Lords' rejection of the budget in 1909 – the first such rejection in two centuries – was long drawn out, and its details have often been recounted.

The peers, Lord Willoughby de Broke recalled, came as near to cheering as peers can when the result became known. The decision was not electorally popular, as the elections of January and December 1910 indicated; but the issue was clearly put by the Fabian Beatrice Webb when she said that the Lords had to throw out the budget if they did not want to admit that they were powerless to fulfil their main function – the protection of property and the *status quo*.[19]

The novelist Mrs Humphry Ward, whose son stood in West Herts in January 1910, specifically rejected any notion that the Lords and the rich should not bear the main burden of taxation; what was intolerable was the singling out of 'a particular kind of rich person – the owners of land – and piling an unfair proportion of the new taxes on them'.[20] Lord Charles Beresford, campaigning in Portsmouth, argued that high taxation was acceptable only if it was spent on defence 'instead of being wasted on Socialist experiments', and if it was levied on income rather than capital.[21] Vigorous defences of the hereditary principle were made in Lords' debates: sternly by Curzon – 'It has saved this country from the danger of plutocracy or an upper class of professional politicians'; wittily by Willoughby de Broke – 'He had been brought up in the midst of fox-breeding all his life, and he was prepared to defend the hereditary principle in that or any other animal.'[22]

The passage of the Parliament Bill in 1911, which imposed important limitations on the power of the Lords, had much symbolic significance in the story of the decline of landed society: it was the last link in a chain of actions and circumstances working to curtail the economic and political power of the 'natural rulers'. Regular meetings of Die-Hards took place from June 1911 at the London home of the octogenarian Lord Halsbury, involving many of the great Dukes – Somerset, Sutherland, Bedford – and such other patricians as Lord Salisbury. The King's willingness to swamp the Tory majority in the Lords by creating new peers was made officially known to Balfour and Lansdowne the following month, and interestingly the list would have included Sir Thomas Lipton.

When the final vote was taken in August Curzon actually voted with the 'traitors' – 'He could not bear to have his Order contaminated with the new creations', Wilfrid Scawen Blunt recorded in his diary.[23] But there were few patricians on the victorious government side; and the unpleasant scenes at the Carlton Club following the division, when the Die-Hards expressed their anger at those who had voted for the bill, argued for a bitter legacy.

The image of the landowning aristocracy's last stand may be the most important feature of a situation which was in fact singularly confused. To begin with, there was by no means unanimity in the Lords about rejection of reforms; *Punch*, on 30 March 1910, showed 'The Problem Picture' in the Selecting Committee's Room at the Peers' Royal Academy, symbolizing the various schemes for change:

> Rosebery approvingly: 'That's mine. Pretty good, eh?'
> Lansdowne: 'H'm, I can't say I quite – '
> Curzon: 'I'm sure I could improve it.'
> Halsbury: 'Take it away!'[24]

In practice most of the country found radical measures such as Arthur Ponsonby's bill to end hereditary titles – 'the main cause of the quite unfathomable snobbishness, obsequiousness, sycophancy, and flunkeyism' in British social life – as extravagant as the Die-Hards' behaviour. As long before as 1888, the radical Labouchere had risen in the House of Commons to move the motion:

> That, in the opinion of this House, it is contrary to the true principles of representative government and injurious to their efficiency that any person should be a Member of one House of the Legislature by right of birth, and it is, therefore, desirable to put an end to any such existing rights.

But it was not merely left to that stern traditionalist, Curzon, to retort that Labouchere was 'a man of facetious and fanciful temperament, and no institution was safe from his quips or his satires'; it was W. H. Smith, owner of the chain of newsagents' shops, who expressed the mood accurately when he spoke of the general desire in the House to bring the debate to an end.[25]

In the years that followed, the Die-Hards became less and less typical of Lords' membership. When *The Standard* analysed the membership of the House on 22 November 1909, it counted 147 landowners, but 39 Captains of Industry, 35 Bankers and 35 Railways Directors too. As Ramsay Muir observed in 1910, since 1886 the Lords had been the citadel of the united wealthy classes – and its power had been vastly greater as a consequence.[26] Other radicals portrayed a Lords swarming with directors, largely South African, connected with as many as twenty companies: the archetype of grasping and greedy capitalism.[27] The first half of 1910 saw the creation of five great businessmen as Lords, among them Sir Weetman Pearson, the public-works contractor, as Lord Cowdray, and Hudson Ewbank Kearley, the store-owner, as Lord Devonport. Hilaire Belloc went so far – he always went further than most – as to describe the Lords as 'a committee for the protection of the Anglo-Judaic plutocracy'.[28]

Important businessmen met in June 1909 under the chairmanship of Lord Rothschild to consider action against the new tax proposals, and Northcliffe's *Daily Mail* pointed out that the strength of the Budget Protest League lay in the City. Lloyd George himself said that Britain was not going to have its politics 'dictated by great financiers'; William Waldorf Astor reacted accordingly by remitting one and a half million pounds to New York which would otherwise have been invested in his adopted home of England. What had happened to enable mere businessmen to ally themselves with a House of Lords that had landed traditions going back hundreds of years?

In a society with a long, relatively stable, history, ancestry was bound to be important – wherever it led. The Guinness family privately published a family tree showing the descent of 454 of them from Richard Guinness, born *c.* 1690 in Co. Kildare and father of the founder of the famous brewery.[29] What practical social purpose it all served depended on a number of factors: Sir Edward Guinness – created Lord Iveagh – was the owner of a newly acquired East Anglian estate, but his Irish ancestors had their own traditions. He had an easy insolence, one of his contemporaries noted, unlike the crude swagger of the mere plutocrat. His pretensions were supported above all by the award of his title and, with some, enabled him to pass as 'one of nature's noblemen'.[30]

Lady Colin Campbell, in her *Etiquette of Good Society*, noted the trade in crests and family trees; in this brazen age anything could be bought.[31] As Lord Iveagh had discovered, the most visible means of buying status was to acquire a title or other honours. Herbert Gladstone calculated that more than a fifth of his father's letters to Queen Victoria were concerned with honours.[32] *Punch* poured scorn on all the new decorations in reporting the *Newcastle Daily Journal*'s announcement of the grant of an earldom to 'Field-Marshal the Viscount Kitchener of Khartoum, P.G.C., B.O.M.G.C., S.I.G.C.M., G.G.C.I.E.'[33] Army men and diplomats apart, it was the plutocrats that benefited most from these developments. The Clerk to the Privy Council noted with distaste the swearing in of 'Sir E. Speyer, a most characteristic little Jew,' who 'was apparently quite ready to take the oath on the Testament, so long as he could do it with the rest; but I kept him to the Pentateuch and thus saved the Gospels from outrage.'[34] Speyer was the man largely responsible for the electrification of the London Underground.

The honours tout began to make a shadowy appearance, apparently encouraged by the needy political parties. Sir William Marriott QC, MP for Brighton from 1880–93, obtained Ernest Hooley's admission to the Carlton Club and offered a bribe on his behalf to Middleton, the Tory Principal Agent.[35] For £50,000 Hooley expected to become a baronet in Queen Victoria's Diamond Jubilee honours. He also established a 'Jubilee Charity Fund' and told the *Pall Mall Gazette* in

January 1897 that 'I have devoted a sum of £400,000 to capitalize it.'[36] The amount was absurdly exaggerated, and the Tories decided that this time – and with this particularly disreputable figure – they were not going to be bought. Hooley himself later claimed: 'I made a certain noble viscount a present of £35,000 to save him from going into the Bankruptcy Court, in return for which I was to have a title of my own.' Just before his financial empire crashed, he received an invitation, addressed to Sir E. T. Hooley, Bart., to the service in St Paul's for Queen Victoria's 1897 Jubilee; little comfort, perhaps, that his fall at least saved him from receiving the infamous title of 'the bankrupt baronet'.[37]

In July 1907 Hugh Lea MP, frustrated in the Commons by the Speaker, who refused to allow a question concerning the award of an honour on the grounds that it would interfere with the royal prerogative, wrote to *The Times* claiming that honours were being sold in return for donations to party funds. Much fuss followed, and Lord Robert Cecil argued that the letter was a breach of Commons privilege; but neither of the party leaders specifically denied that the sale of honours took place. Some years later, when Lord Riddell discussed the question with three leading politicians, all of them vigorously denied that honours were sold. But Riddell's talks elsewhere did not support this conclusion, and the Liberals, evidently, were as much involved as the Tories.[38] The issue took its most important form over the sale of peerages, as it became more and more apparent that a whole new class of Lords was being created without much regard for the merit of the men concerned.

More than three-quarters of the new peerages conferred between 1833 and the fall of Gladstone's second ministry in 1885 went to politicians.[39] Nothing really changed until 1886. Between then and 1914 246 new peers were created, probably only a quarter of them from the inheritors of landed estates.[40] In a sense, this figure was a remarkable testimony to the survival of landed influence in an increasingly industrial country, but the contrast with the past remains striking.

After Salisbury's ministry of 1885–6, the percentage of new peers with important industrial and commercial connections never fell below twenty; it was forty in the Liberal years of 1905–11.[41] Henry Allsopp, Lord Hindlip, the Burton brewer, began the process in 1886; and it was fitting that the Prime Minister responsible was the patrician Salisbury. The radical Arthur Ponsonby explained: 'It was not until the last decade or so of the century that the possession of money, pure and unadulterated by merit, became in itself a sufficient qualification for admission to the peerage and through it to the aristocracy.'[42]

Price Collier made a lengthy, revealing and seemingly interminable list of some of those whose position had been gained through 'force of long purses gained in trade': 'Ashburton, Carrington, Belper, Overstone, Mount Stephen, Hindlip, Burton, Battersea, Glenesk, Aldenham, Lister, Avebury, Burnham, Biddulph, Northcliffe, Nunburnholme, Winterstoke, Rothschild, Brassey, Revelstoke, Strathcona and Mount Royal, Michelham, and others, too many to mention'.[43]

The origins of some of these men tell their own story. Mount Stephen (George Stephen) and Strathcona and Mount Royal (Donald Smith) were both Scottish emigrants to Canada. Strathcona's wife was the first Red Indian peeress.[44] The 'beerage', among them Hindlip and Burton, figured prominently, as did other figures from commerce and industry. Lord Allerton – one of a range of names not on Collier's list – became Chairman of the Great Northern Railway in the early 1890s after spending his early life in the tanning and leather industry. 'He was essentially a self-made man, overcoming all the obstacles to success, and gradually rising step by step by sheer ability and tact', said his obituary in *The Times*.[45] Significantly, the same paper noted of his son that he did not inherit his father's interest in business or politics, and preferred to live on his property, occupying himself with country pursuits.[46] Collier, unlike most Americans, was sufficiently impressed to assert that social origins counted for nothing in the matter-of-fact land of England, where riches and power passed automatically to the successful.[47]

Awarding titles to prosperous and useful members of the community could not be thought too objectionable. But there was more to it than that. The Labour MP Ramsay MacDonald made a speech in June 1910 after the creation of seven new Liberal peers. 'If he was going to have an aristocrat,' he said, 'he wanted a genuine aristocrat and not merely a plutocrat.' He had no wish for a reformed House of Lords – even with curtailed authority – to be made up of 'men who had bought their way into the Upper Chamber by liberally subscribing to party funds'.[48] Yet the honours lists, according to the *Candid Quarterly Review of Public Affairs* in 1914, 'contain many names of men who have never attained any eminence or shown ability of any kind or been known to do any public service of any kind, such as gives any claim to the bestowal of honours'. It was easy to see that these were the rich men on the list.[49]

Some of the objections were simply radical comments on upper-class rule of any kind. Howard Evans, who had attacked the landed Lords, agreed that Guinness sold good stout, Bass and Allsopp good ale, but that was no reason 'why Lords Ardilaun and Iveagh and Burton and Hindlip and their successors for all time should have the right to sit in judgment over the legislative work of the representatives of the people of the United Kingdom'.[50] Labouchere also joined the chorus of protest against the 'beerage': 'Why were brewers selected as peers? Simply because they, of late, had accumulated very large fortunes by the sale of intoxicating liquors, and for no other reason . . . who ever heard of them as politicians?'[51]

Radical objections were easily overruled. The major political parties needed money and support, and that, as much as a deliberate broadening of social origins or a recognition of political necessity, was what made the change possible. The newspaper peerages conferred on Lords Glenesk, Burnham, and Northcliffe were said to be mere party payments for unsavoury services rendered.[52] The Liberals were in special need of aid in the Lords after many of their number were lost in the Home Rule split of 1886; when the second Home Rule Bill came before the Lords in 1893 only 41 could be found to support the Liberal government, with 419 against. The Irish Home Rule question had many effects on the course of British history; one of them, as the Liberal Prime Minister Rosebery said, was to 'throw the great mass of Liberal peers into the arms of the Conservative majority'.[53] Thus by the time the President of Harvard wrote his celebrated study of *The Government of England* in 1908, the House of Lords was overwhelmingly Conservative.[54] The Home Rule defectors took with them not only their vote, but – in the case of the old Whig families – their money; and it was no surprise that Francis Schnadhorst, the Liberal party organizer, listened sympathetically in the 1890s when he heard that two rich men were thought to be willing to buy peerages.[55]

The first was James Williamson, Lord Ashton or – as others called him – 'Lord Linoleum'. He was hardly known at all outside Lancashire, or even Lancaster, for which he became MP in 1886. When Gladstone retired in 1894, he left a request with his successor, Rosebery, to proceed with the peerage, which was finally included in the new Prime Minister's own resignation honours in July 1895. Despite much local philanthropy Ashton was driven away from his home district by the attacks on him.

Sidney Stern, who was the second figure to cause something of a scandal, had been a Liberal candidate through the 1880s and had only become an MP in a by-election in 1891; he was raised to the peerage as Lord Wandsworth. A decade later, when Herbert Stern became Lord Michelham shortly after becoming a baronet, the *Saturday Review* asked:

What services, in court or camp, in public or in private have the Sterns rendered to the British Empire that two Prime Ministers of opposite parties in the State should vie with one another in inviting them to take a seat amongst . . . 'the

best, the bravest, the noblest' ... that England can produce.
Do Lord Wandsworth and Sir Herbert Stern answer that
description of aristocrats. Obviously not: then why have
they been made peers? The answer is, Money.

The *Saturday Review* was making a broader attack on 'The
Adulteration of the Peerage'. In the past, the one 'constant
and indispensable qualification for admission to the chamber
of nobles' had been 'the continuous and meritorious performance of some public duty or national service'; now a man
might be given 'the right to sit and vote amongst the hereditary aristocracy of Great Britain' merely because he was very
rich. Mr Zangwill and his friends – the Zionists looking for a
Jewish homeland beyond the seas – would be glad to abandon
their dreams if the furious ennoblement of mere financiers
continued: the House of Lords would have superior attractions.'[56] The magazine's conservatism cannot hide the real
corruption of the period. Lord Suffield, who was offered a
quarter of a million pounds by one man for a peerage, was
one of many who was propositioned with bribes, one of the
few who refused them.[57]

The tittle-tattle of titles talk had become a serious political
issue by 1914. In February of that year a whole day of
parliamentary debate produced an admission from Lord
Willoughby de Broke that he had offered to attempt to obtain
a baronetcy in return for a contribution to a particular cause,
and a judgment from Lord Milner that the practice was
growing fast.[58] Those, like Lord Ribblesdale, who argued that
much complaint was being made to very little purpose, were
criticized both in and outside Parliament. The *Candid
Quarterly Review of Public Affairs* suggested that he was
effectively saying: 'Are not plutocrats after all "a very nice
body of men?" The more money there is the better the Party
Government will be.' The magazine put the rates – depending
on the wealth of the aspirant, his skill in bargaining and party
needs – at £1,250–£4,000 for a knighthood, £6,000–£25,000

for a baronetcy, £40,000–£50,000 for a peerage. Their lordships, it commented, were well placed to discuss the subject; many of them knew by recent experience the market price of a peerage.[59]

The practical advantages of being a peer seemed few; he had the doubtful benefit of being entitled to a silk rope if condemned to death, but such ancient survivals of privilege were scarcely a major attraction.[60] The political advantages were non-existent. Three young men, Curzon, Brodrick and Woolmer, even tried to introduce a bill in 1894 to prevent their inheritances from depriving them of their seats in the Commons.

Matthew Arnold, visiting Andrew Carnegie in 1887, explained the real motives of those who bought titles: 'a duke is always a personage with us, always a personage, independent of brains or conduct', he said. 'We are all snobs. Hundreds of years have made us so, all snobs. We can't help it. It is in the blood.' (Arnold himself, when in New York, wanted especially to see Cornelius Vanderbilt. It was Carnegie who told him that there was nothing special about the millionaire. 'No', Arnold replied, 'but it is something to know the richest man in the world.' A self-made man was more interesting than a lord who merely inherited rank from others.)[61] Carnegie's attitude was more straightforward: 'Fine fellow, Rosebery,' he remarked, 'only he was handicapped by being born a peer.' On one occasion Carnegie's forcibly, if playfully, expressed views on the upper clases drove the Earl of Southesk from his Scottish castle in (temporary) fury.[62]

Carnegie's career was too much of an American success story for him to enthuse about feudal relics, but others realized the truth of his distinguished fellow-countryman's analysis: 'The personal influence of the Lords', wrote Lawrence Lowell, 'is far greater than their collective authority. With the waning of the landed gentry the respect for the old territorial aristocracy has been replaced by a veneration for titles, and this has inured to the benefit of the peerage.' Peers enjoyed popular confidence. Free from the temptations of the ordinary working man, they exercised power not by means of political privileges but through their social lustre.[63]

Truth's columnist Marmaduke satirically suggested, at the beginning of Edward VII's reign, that Lord Salisbury was secretly engaged in a scheme for flooding Britain with gold by giving every Englishman a peerage, thus enabling him to marry an American heiress: the millennium by a short cut. The same week the *Spectator* discussed the social and pecuniary advantages of peerage ; the rank which peers gave to their brides was worth millions of pounds a year to them. Such comments provoked fury from some quarters – the *Englishman* of Calcutta, for example: the English in India were far more English than the English in England. But nearer home *Truth* correctly registered 'the fascination which the Peerage exercises over the millionaire class'. 'And', the paper asked, 'is it not the millionaire class that rules the world?'[64]

No answer was necessary.

That same millionaire class was shrewd enough to appreciate that their attentions should not be confined to the prestigious corridors of the House of Lords. If the House of Commons ruled the nation, then the House of Commons must be won for plutocracy. As with everything else, it was the last three or four decades of the nineteenth century that provided the decisive changes. In his introduction to the second edition of *The English Constitution* (1872), Bagehot recognized that the House of Commons had become more plutocratic than aristocratic, its more prominent members connected with 'the new trading wealth'.[65] This was an exaggeration, but it became more and more accurate as the years passed. Andrew Carnegie, writing in the *North American Review* in January 1886, asserted that the old-fashioned squire had been displaced by barristers, merchants and employers. A Liberal manager had told him that he had on his list thirteen titled gentlemen for whom no satisfactory constituencies could be found: their titles were actually a weakness 'before the new voters'.[66]

The fascination of the period comes from the impact of the new order on the surprisingly resilient old. The authors of *The Great Governing Families of England* in 1885 were clear that in the most radical borough in the most radical county of England 'the chance of the eldest son of a great landed proprietor is, *ceteris paribus*, better than that of any conceivable opponent, except a recognized statesman or orator of the very first stamp'.[67] It is easy to imagine the scene in 1910 when a local landowner's agent, accompanied by supporting farmers, stood in the schoolyard outside the polling booth, while 'one of the checkers at the door was a carpenter employed on the estate, and seated at the table in the booth was Sir D. Broughton's chief clerk, Mr Cope'.[68] But this sort of influence was no longer accepted everywhere, as may be judged from the protests that followed Colonel Egerton-Warburton's decision to give one of his tenants notice to quit in 1893; the Colonel's demand that all his farmers should be Conservative, Church of England and volunteers for the yeomanry cavalry seemed to belong to another age.[69]

The mixture of past and future could be seen in the composition of the Commons after the Liberal landslide in 1906: nearly half the members connected with finance or insurance, but landowners still a fifth of the whole and Old Etonians alone comprising a sixth. Aristocracy survived longest in the Cabinet, though here too new faces began to be seen from the 1880s, above all Joseph Chamberlain.[70] The Conservative Prime Minister, Arthur Balfour, had a view of businessmen which was seen in his description of his successor as Irish Chief Secretary as 'that *rara avis*, a successful manufacturer who is fit for something besides manufacturing'.[71] But even he bowed to progress when he became the first Prime Minister to go to Buckingham Palace in a car. Herbert Asquith, who held that office from 1908, was the son of a Yorkshire woollen manufacturer, though it was left to the Tories – fighting over the succession after Balfour's fall in 1911 – to show the true power of business.

The Savoy, awaiting a private dinner party in 1895

The South Drawing-Room at Halton. Alfred de Rothschild completed the house in 1886

The possible candidates were Walter Long, with a long landed ancestry; Austen Chamberlain, Joseph's son; and Bonar Law – Canadian son of a Presbyterian minister, Glasgow businessman, dour, teetotal, bored by society: just the man to seize the opportunity when the others looked as if they might tear the party apart.[72] Max Aitken, the brilliant Canadian businessman who was later to rival Northcliffe's press power as Lord Beaverbrook, helped Bonar Law's finances – perhaps to the extent of £10,000 a year, free of tax.[73] He organized his friend's successful campaign, held him firm; no wonder the new Tory leader spoke highly of Aitken's ability 'as a man of business' when he lunched with Lord Riddell – at Aitken's invitation – in 1913.[74]

The political inheritors of the aristocratic world were more plutocratic than democratic, in France and America, no less than in Britain. Robert de Jouvenal's famous essay, published in Paris in 1914, described France as *La république des camarades* – a republic of plundering, capitalist comrades; and if Carl Hovey's 1912 life of Pierpont Morgan proved anything, it was that the socialist prophecy of the supremacy of the proletariat had been delayed: 'the millionaire had arrived, and his conquest is already assured'.[75]

Politics had always been for the rich: now the choice – in Britain, at least – lay between two types of rich, aristocratic and plutocratic. As Emerson put it: 'Piracy and war gave place to trade, politics and letters; the war-lord to the law-lord; the law-lord to the merchant and the mill-owner': the important point was that 'the privilege was kept'.[76] The reactionary Lord Edenborough was relieved to note, in the first elections after the 1867 Reform Bill had widened the franchise, that 'As yet no roughs have presented themselves' as candidates, though he was not sanguine about future chances.[77] Mesmerized by statute – by the Reform Bills of 1832, 1867 and 1884 – contemporaries often failed to notice that it was a funny sort of democracy in which perhaps a quarter or more of the seats remained uncontested: 243 in 1900, 163 in December 1910. Forty per cent of the adult male population remained unregistered to vote in 1911; plural voting survived: 'Is the man who is too illiterate to read his ballot paper, who is too imprudent to support his children, to be placed on the same footing as the man who by industry and capacity has acquired a substantial interest in more than one constituency?' The question was asked by Sir William Anson in the Commons in 1912. The answer provided by the House of Lords, which killed Plural Voting Bills in 1906, 1913 and 1914, was unequivocal. It remained theoretically possible for one London property-owner to have a vote in thirty-seven constituencies.[78]

Political divisions were not yet reflected in social distinctions; there were Tory families and Liberal families, but in active politics they were almost all rich men's families. By 1914, it is true, there were forty-two Labour MPs and an appropriately named survey of *Gentlemen of the House of Commons*, published in 1902, admitted that the Commons was now familiar with 'a class of member more distinctly novel than appeared during the early portion of the nineteenth century'; but even 'the Labour representatives', with 'their exemplary course and bearing', looked as if they had been absorbed into the system.[79] Mr Snowden MP gave some readers of *The Times* a fit of apoplexy when they read of his talk on 'The Abolition of the Idle Rich',[80] but radical opinion failed to seize the initiative at any time up to the First World War. 'Blessed indeed are the Rich, for theirs is the governance of the realm, theirs is the Kingdom' – Chiozza Money's unsubtly accurate polemic was not a political programme.[81] More to the point, and more witty, was the observation that 'Liberty flourishes in Regent Street' – Arthur Liberty had founded his famous shop in 1875 – 'but Fraternity and Equality have gone under.'[82]

Money was a key influence in politics as in all else in the era of the plutocrats. British public office, observed (accurately) from America, was rarely, if ever, used as a means of acquiring wealth – but wealth was used freely to procure office.[83] This did not necessarily imply corruption, but the impact of riches was very visible. The Rothschilds colonized Buckinghamshire; Buckinghamshire returned a Rothschild in every election from 1865 to 1923.[84] The biggest employers in Reading were the biscuit manufacturers, Huntley and Palmer: the Liberal G. W. Palmer, won the seat in 1892 and – said the *Reading Mercury* – 'Not a few Conservatives either absented themselves from the poll, or actually supported Mr Palmer from purely local ties and associations.' Nothing in politics was entirely predictable and Palmer lost in 1895: but he won again in 1898 and 1900.[85] Money and local power were bound to be important electoral influences while few issues of great relevance to the mass of the population divided the parties.

In Stephen McKenna's novel *Sonia* George Oakleigh went in search of a Liberal seat with nothing more than a note to party headquarters from his uncle. The key question was 'how much I was prepared to put down'. A large sum would give him a safe seat in a mining area; the party would pay expenses only if he was willing to tackle a 5,000 Tory majority.[86] In another novel of the period, Hilaire Belloc's Mr Clutterbuck discovered 'that he was expected, to his own advantage, to subscribe a sum of money; that he was expected to subscribe it to a political party; that a man called Bozzy, who was also called Delacourt, was in the inner ring of such affairs, and that of the two Parties it would best suit a merchant of his standing to tender such financial support, through the said Bozzy, to the Party in power'. Mr Clutterbuck, once elected, immediately dispatched a further £1,000 to party funds, and though his election was eventually declared invalid, he ultimately had the satisfaction of receiving a knighthood for services to the (as yet non-existent) Caterham Valley Institute.[87]

Sir Henry Lucy, in September 1909, recorded in his diary that he had seen the cash account kept by an MP – £747 spent that year so far on chapel subscriptions, church funds, sports clubs, help to constituents.[88] There were no salaries for MPs until 1911 and Curzon had for once not been wholly alone in opposing payment on the grounds that it would let into the House careerists, determined to make 'a business of the duties and obligations of government'.[89] The *Fortnightly Review* had observed the effect more than twenty-five years before; to refuse to pay members was to limit the choice of the electorate to the rich; and while rich MPs might mean well, they took a rich man's view of all major issues.[90]

Elections could cost each candidate £1,000 in the early years of the century – many times the annual wage of a skilled worker. The *Newcastle Weekly Chronicle* confidently asserted that 'constituencies are not now debauched; voters are seldom either bribed or brow-beaten':[91] some tribute, perhaps, to the effects of the 1883 Corrupt Practices Act, which had attempted to reduce election expenditure. But what legislation could prevent an Ilkeston colliery and ironworks manager from going to the local parliamentary candidate – it was Ernest Hooley – and telling him that he had no money to pay the week's wages? 400 men, 400 votes: Hooley offered to buy 20,000 tons of pig-iron for £40,000 – and lost nothing, since all the local manufacturers, in panic fear of dumping, helped the man in trouble.

Colonel North, the 'Nitrate King', was said to have been so worried by the Corrupt Practices Act when he fought Herbert Gladstone at Leeds that his aides sewed up his pockets every morning before he left his hotel to stop him displaying 'that natural benevolence and patriotic generosity which might be mistaken for deliberate bribery'. North claimed to be sound about 'Home Rule and all the other things' but was sure his audience was more interested in government contracts for Leeds.[92] He failed, just, to get elected; but many others like him were successful.

The electorate, after the third Reform Bill of 1884, might not have been as broadly based as it should have been, but there were still five million electors in 1885 compared with the three million registered in 1880. The party organizations needed money in order to cope effectively: hence the Conservative party fund, as little as £20,000 in 1874, had quadrupled by the 1890s, while the Liberals, at a very low ebb in

1886, had accumulated £700,000 by 1901.[93] Moreover, much of the power in the modern party machines that developed as a result, passed to manufacturers, businessmen and financiers – at least on a local level. Critics of the caucus – like Lord Sandon – saw it as a 'dark monster . . . sitting monstrous and supreme'. They were bound to think of it as 'the creature of tyrannical oligarchy' – Lord John Manners's phrase – because it took power from their hands.[94] The store-owning Debenham family were described in 1904 as the political house of their guild – the commercial equivalent of the Cecils or Cavendishes, and the arbiters of admission to the political set of trading society, perhaps to elections too.[95] For many Victorians, influenced by decades of apparent, if hypocritical, public probity, none of this improved the moral climate of politics; instead it was said to have encouraged 'the dirty work of the handful who pull the strings': money foully gained would be foully spent.[96]

The attractions of a seat in the House of Commons were diverse for the businessman. The casual style of the 'natural rulers' was much admired: Viscount Grey remembered that news of an important crisis in Egypt and the Sudan in March 1895 reached him at his cottage in Hampshire, where he had gone to prune his roses.[97] So long as government was a matter of country-house or clubland decision by gentlemen, the social importance of a political career would continue. Lord Esher recorded in his journals in June 1908 how the Prime Minister's party had left for Huntercombe by motor for the inevitable golf after luncheon: golf and bridge in combination would doubtless ensure an easy surrender to the Germans when the time came, he commented tartly.[98] Even fifty years later, a cabinet minister, Richard Crossman, was to note in his diaries how the Tories benefited from 'those great country-house parties': 'How much we in the Labour Party miss the country houses which we don't have!'[99]

Politics and fashionable society remained linked well into the twentieth century, in town and country. Parliament, as

the President of Harvard observed, sat during the high
Season in the capital of the Empire, where Society from the
whole British Isles met – and where 'everything of moment in
the world passes under review'.[100] When the Duchess of
Marlborough died in 1899 a large chunk of London Society
was plunged into mourning; but it was not only the Season
that suffered – her daughter, Lady Tweedmouth, closed
Brook House and the Liberals consequently lost their most
important political salon.[101] Sir Ernest Cassel, who acquired
the house, won a property with a political as well as a social
aura: the two could barely be distinguished.

The death of the political salon was constantly predicted,
while nostalgic memories were paraded of Lord Randolph
Churchill's use of Lady Dorothy Nevill's luncheon table, or
Lady Stanhope's (Conservative) evenings at Grosvenor
Place. But its revival received equal attention at frequent
intervals; and Ladies Lansdowne, Wimborne and Tweedmouth, were only the chief among the political hostesses in
1904.

And in the country? In the country there was 'The Thanks-
giving of the Small Country MP's wife', which 'she offereth
week-end-ly':

I acknowledge Thy mercy and goodness in permitting that
for the moderate cost of Two Thousand Pounds and
upwards, – a sum not greatly in excess of my dressmaker's
annual bill, – I may set my foot on the two dumb and
prostrate Letters of the Alphabet now attached to my said
Husband's new calling and Election, and may mount
thereon to those heights of County Society where, ever
since I was born I have eagerly thirsted to be. . . . Dedicated
to Thee, O Bland and Blessed Deity of Surplus Cash and
Social Advancement.[102]

The government of an industrial country, however, was
bound to become more technical, more concerned with
regulating industry. The businessman, with his special

interests – and special talents – could help to control this process. Classical metaphors still figured strongly in parliamentary speeches, but a new world had dawned when an MP would be heard to compare the mind of an opponent to a series of condensing chambers; or when, on 17 June 1895, at 10.15 pm, the Prime Minister could telephone the Chief Whip for news of developments in the Commons.[103] Thus after the founder of the International Stores, Hudson Ewbank Kearley, later Lord Devonport, became Secretary to the Board of Trade in December 1905, Lloyd George wrote to his brother: 'A first-rate businessman, but a poor speaker. Just the man for me.'[104]

Kearley had first come into Parliament in the old casual way – his business situation was satisfactory enough for him 'to indulge his fancy'. A March 1890 meeting with Harcourt, 'a very tall and suave young gentleman', at the National Liberal Federation offices; and another the following August with Francis Schnadhorst, discussing constituencies through a formidable ear-trumpet – these were the undemanding preliminaries.[105] Nevertheless, Devonport was to hold a number of key posts in the years that followed, including the running of the ministry of food – if not with complete success – in the First World War.

Parliamentary influence could be directly helpful. W. H. Wills, of the giant tobacco firm, was MP for Coventry in the first half of the 1880s and for Bristol East between 1895 and 1900 – he became a tobacco lord, a variation on the 'beerage', as Lord Winterstoke in 1906. In 1899, when he talked to Sir Michael Hicks-Beach, Chancellor of the Exchequer, he was told: 'Well, if you can show me that I shall be about straight next year, I'll face the matter and stick to present Duty.'[106] It was not just that an increase in tobacco duty was costly, but that any change involved expensive alterations to price or the quality of the product; and political lobbying could, and did, aid big business in this instance.

When Campbell-Bannerman became Prime Minister in 1905 he ordered ministers to give up directorships in limited companies, though even then exceptions were made in the case of Kearley and Thomas Lough, the latter also being the chairman of a grocery group.[107] The problem was not entirely new – thirty-seven out of fifty merchants in the Commons in 1760 had had business dealings with the government. But it had not seemed so serious a few years before. There were protests when Cecil Rhodes, as Prime Minister of Cape Colony, remained head of the British South Africa Company in the 1890s, but when the Home Secretary in 1898, Sir Matthew White Ridley, retained his seat on the board of the North-Eastern Railway, no one thought it was extraordinary.[108] Few people had yet focussed on the possibilities of corruption for those with both political and business responsibilities.

Financial scandals in politics were a prominent feature of the western world in the last twenty-five years before the First World War, as antiquated institutions struggled to cope with new conditions. Tammany Hall in America and the Panama Canal affair in France were important in persuading the great political scientist Ostrogorsky that democracy could be equated with plutocracy.[109] Hilaire Belloc reached very much the same conclusion in *The Party System*; and Belloc, through the paper he founded – the *Eye-Witness* – was to be the most violent critic of the system in the biggest scandal in British politics of the period.

Guglielmo Marconi's inventions in the field of wireless telegraphy had brought him comparatively little reward until Godfrey Isaacs had suggested to the government that the British Empire could be linked by a chain of wireless stations. It was recommended that six stations should be built initially, at a cost of £60,000 each. Marconi shares rose from 6s 3d in 1908 to nearly thirty times that in 1912.[110] Rumour had it that a number of leading politicians – including the Postmaster-General, Sir Herbert Samuel, the Chancellor of the Exchequer, Lloyd George, the Attorney-General, Sir Rufus Isaacs, and a Liberal whip, the Master of Elibank – were corruptly involved in Marconi share speculation.

Rufus Isaacs was Godfrey's brother, the son of a fruit-broker; he had spent a wild youth running away to sea, being hammered on the Stock Exchange, trying to emigrate to Panama – and eventually reading for the bar. A brilliant success in his legal career, probably earning more than any other barrister of the time, he entered Parliament in 1904 (taking Palmer's Reading seat), became Solicitor-General in 1910 and the first Attorney-General to sit in the Cabinet in 1912. He was also a Jew; and while Belloc denied anti-semitism ('anybody less Jewish than the Chancellor of the Exchequer I cannot conceive'), he outlined the dangers stemming from the power exercised by cosmopolitan finance – in which 'the racial Jewish element' was a large one.[111] Belloc made this claim during the course of a successful libel action brought by Godfrey Isaacs against the editor of the *Eye-Witness,* Cecil Chesterton; and it was an interesting comment on the critic's attitude to progress that many years before the scandal arose, Cecil's brother, G. K. Chesterton, had fulminated against 'combinations and centralizations and steamboats and Marconi wires'.[112]

A Select Committee cleared Samuel, and both Lloyd George and Isaacs received no worse than a judgment of serious impropriety in their conduct from the Tory minority. The Master of Elibank had purchased for the Liberal party, with Liberal funds, 3,000 American Marconi shares for more than £9,000; but no record of these securities appeared on the list passed to his successor as Chief Whip, Percy Illingworth, in August 1912. Not the least sign of censure was forthcoming from Illingworth, who explained: 'the finances of the Party are, as they ought to be, in the uncontrolled discretion of the Chief Whip. They are now at this moment in my own; I consult nobody; it is my own business.'[113]

C. F. G. Masterman claimed that Isaacs and Lloyd George would have resigned if the Committee's report had been unfavourable.[114] As it was, the former became the first Jewish Lord Chief Justice in 1913, successively a baron, a viscount, an earl, a marquis – and Viceroy of India. Small penalty for being the object of Kipling's poem of hate, *Gehazi*. Lloyd George continued as Chancellor and later became Prime Minister; Herbert Samuel was made Home Secretary in 1916. Today, it has reasonably been asserted, they would all have been hounded out of politics.

Of Rufus Isaacs's financial ability there could be no doubt – his marvellous, clear-headed analysis of Ernest Hooley's affairs at his trial had been one proof of that. But Lloyd George was bored by financial technicalities and detail; he preferred grand designs: once on Sir Thomas Lipton's yacht, he was said to have 'talked like a man hypnotized by the facility with which things could be nationalized'.[115] *The Times* pointed to an important lesson of the Marconi Affair: if a man steps into a puddle that might easily have been avoided that is his fault; if he says he did not know a puddle was there, 'we say he ought to know better'.[116] The most successful businessmen made unsuccessful politicians; the most successful politicians made poor businessmen: a dilemma that no twentieth-century government has yet solved.

'My father and grandfather were brought up among City people and I am proud of it', recalled Margot Asquith, wife of one of the longest-serving prime ministers in English history. But 'it is folly to suppose that starting and developing a great business is the same as initiating and conducting a great policy, or running a big Government Department . . . the qualities that go to make a businessman are grotesquely unlike those which make a statesman.'[117] In part this was romantic nonsense, but no one could deny that, for example, Lord Randolph Churchill had an appeal that 'bourgeois nonentities' like W. H. Smith could not match.[118] Churchill could write off Smith as one of 'the Lords of suburban villas, the owners of pineries and vineries'; his aristocratic style matched against Smith's plodding conscientiousness was unbeatable.[119] And when 'Squire' Chaplin told 'the Right Honourable Gentlemen opposite' that 'I assert, I aver, I go so far as to say that I asseverate', how could someone whose life had been spent in the pursuit of money – not the skills of

oratory or the excitement of ideas or the sensitivities of wit –
conceivably know how to react?[120]

Business efficiency could help a man into Parliament. Max
Aitken organized card indices for all voters and involved a
corps of assistants to canvass when he first tried (unsuccessfully) to win a seat. But the two activities remained, at least to
some extent, mutually exclusive. At the end of the day, 'My
interest in politics is not as great as my interest in business',
Aitken wrote to Lord Elcho in 1911.[121] Besides, there were
other ways of achieving power than through Parliament –
Aitken himself first put money into the *Daily Express* in 1912
on the condition that the paper would print favourable items
about him which could be quoted elsewhere. Despite the fact
that daily newspapers still only reached about twenty per
cent of the working population in 1910, their influence in the
era before radio and television was unsurpassed.

The plutocrats explored all the roads to power and finally
settled for those they understood best. There was more to
politics than a seat in the Houses of Parliament. When war
came in 1914, the Labour MP Philip Snowden was just one of
many who saw it as 'the result of secret diplomacy carried on
by diplomatists who had conducted foreign policy in the
interests of militarists and financiers': international finance
was described as a bloated spider sitting in the middle of a
web of intrigue and chicanery.[122]

The unsubtlety of such socialist interpretations cannot
undermine the obvious connections between trade and
political power, a point that was dramatized over and over
again in the race for empire in the second half of the nineteenth
century. *Truth* exploded in May 1896:

What a comment on our morality has been our action during
the last few months! We quarrelled with the Americans
about Venezuela about a bog in which we fancied there
might be gold; we remain in Egypt because we are looking
after the interest on Egyptian bonds, and finding salaries
for a herd of English employees; we are engaged in the

Soudan expedition because Dongola is fertile, and its possession will afford a plea to us to violate our pledges to leave Egypt; we are disputing with President Kruger because he has fallen out with a crew of company mongers; we are backing up a company in Rhodesia because its shares have been put up to a high premium on the Stock Exchange.[123]

The plutocrats' influence on national policy was more difficult to prove because it was carried on behind the scenes. But added to their influence in local government and the Houses of Parliament, it helped to confirm their stranglehold on many of the avenues to power in their society.

Chapter 8

Through Contemporary Eyes: the Plutocrat in Fact and Fiction

The rise of the plutocrats was a phenomenon widely noted by their contemporaries. At Scarborough in January 1901 Sir Osbert Sitwell listened to the tolling of bells that announced the death of Queen Victoria: the prelude to what he called 'the Rich Man's Banquet' – a decade-long feast in which the greediest won all the prizes.[1] As the son of a squire who had experienced the great agricultural depression in the second half of the nineteenth century, Sir Osbert was not an unbiased observer of his childhood society, but there were others – more admired, if more eccentric – who came to the same conclusion.

Marie Corelli, obsessively wrestling (like St Paul) against 'the rulers of the darkness of this world, against spiritual wickedness in high places'[2] has not (yet) endeared herself to a modern audience, but she was much celebrated in her own time. Though she had turned to writing after a 'psychical experience' in 1885, there was no gainsaying her huge popularity: the author of no less than twenty-eight novels, whose publisher, Sir William Robertson Nicoll, told Lord Riddell in January 1909 that his firm had practically agreed to pay her £7,500 for her new book – the previous one having sold 180,000 copies.[3]

The Corelli analysis was singlemindedly simple in its concentration on 'The Vulgarity of Wealth'. 'Our evil star, the evil star of all Empires, has long soared above the eastern edge; fully declared, it floods our heaven with such lurid brilliance, that we can scarce perceive any other luminary.' The name of that star was Mammon.[4]

The Sitwell and the Corelli judgments had considerable significance in their very different ways. Both were the work of writers; and connections between life and literature are of course revealing when they can be unravelled. It was no accident that Vita Sackville-West's *The Edwardians*, actually published in 1930, carried the statement, 'No character in this book is wholly fictitious'; in it the Duchess of Chevron's home was in fact the country-house of Knole.[5] Similarly, Harold Frederics wrote *The Market Place* for the Drury Lane stage as 'the epic of Hooleyism', though his central character, Thorpe, was deliberately made not to resemble Ernest Hooley.[6]

Also adopted by a writer was Baron Albert Grant, a German Jew whose real name may have been Gottheimer: company promoter and Member of Parliament, he was the object of the taunt:

> Kings may a title give
> Honour they can't –
> Title without Honour
> Is a barren grant!

He strongly resembled Augustus Melmotte, central figure of Anthony Trollope's most emotional novel, *The Way We Are Now* (1875), in which the desire to make money or win social position was the central preoccupation of the society described. Trollope reacted strongly against men like Grant, whose aim (he thought) was to destroy rural England in the pursuit of wealth.[7]

In the early days of the plutocrats, their portrayal came close to caricature – literally so in George du Maurier's drawings in *Punch*. The magazine itself provoked many imitations but as late as the mid-1880s, when it was discussed by T. H. S. Escott in the latest edition of *Society in London*, it remained the most important medium of social satire.[8] The Du Maurier cartoons of Sir Gorgius Midas produced the complete indentikit plutocrat.[9] Sir Gorgius, we learn in 1862, lived at Midas Towers, 'our place in Surrey': 'be it ever so 'umble, Jones, there's no place like home', the millionaire told the Reverend Lazarus Jones in 1878. At the time he was surrounded by no less than seven footmen, and footmen – the visible indication of wealth – were clearly of the greatest importance to him; as he arrived at his London mansion some time after two o'clock early one morning in 1880, his diamond studs sparkling, he was annoyed to find that only four of the dandified robots were still awake: why, ' . . . if I'd a' 'appened to brought home a friend, there'd a' only been you four to let us hin, hay!'

Vulgarity was the obvious sign of Midas's behaviour; and usually naive vulgarity (one wonders how he had the ability to acquire his fortune in the first place): when, in 1883, Lord Reginald Sansdenier expressed surprise that Sir Gorgius was not robbed of the £20,000 worth of plate on his dinner table, back came the reply: 'Good 'eavens, I'm sure yer Lordship's too honnerable heven to *think* of sich a thing!' Accent was an important preoccupation of a class-conscious, but highly mobile society; Disraeli, to the general amusement, had once accused Peel of managing his elocution like his temper: neither was originally good.[10]

Sir Gorgius's other activities were also meant to be characteristic of his type. He travelled around the 'Continong', dispensing champagne to his younger son 'enry (in 1881). He sought, at first in vain, a peerage, and was comforted in 1880 by Mrs Ponsonby de Tompkyns: 'No man of your stamp need ever despair of a peerage' – 'And Mrs P. de T. is, as usual, quite right'. He was mean, a man who locked up his decanters after the gentlemen joined the ladies to prevent the servants from taking a quiet drink; one night in 1881, indeed, he forgot the stoppers, only to have the butler bring them to Lady Midas on a platter: 'And before his Grace, too, who has at last been induced to accept an invitation!' Midas was in fact 'a successful *sausage-maker*' – so we learn in 1882 from the Duchess of Cadbury, unhappy to find herself (at Mrs P. de T.'s) in the company of the millionaire's wife.

Lady Midas was treated roughly. In 1881, she sat for her portrait by the fashionable artist, Mr E. R. Sopely; as 'a mere work of art' the result surpassed everything she (Mrs P. de T.) had seen by Titian, Rembrandt or Velasquez; as a likeness of 'my dearest Lady Midas', however, it was quite simply 'a libel!' None the less, Lady Midas liked to visit Mrs P. de T., at least in preference to Lady Oscar Talbot: in 1879 she might receive a worse snub at the former, but 'who cares . . . so long as she's clever enough to get the right people!' Four years later we find at her dinner table: the Marquess and Marchioness of Chepe, the Viscount and Viscountess Silverlacke, the Hon. and Lady Margarine Delarde, Sir Pullman and Lady Carr, and the Cholmondeley-Mainwaring-Carshaltons. Her son, just back in 1880 from a week at the Duke of Stilton's place – where he was most unhappy at the lack of attention paid to him – was much sleeker than Sir Gorgius himself: equally vulgar, but, with his tiny, neat moustache, rather like a confidence-trickster.

The Midas's had one great advantage by the time 'enry came of age: the landed aristocracy whose company they coveted had hit hard times. It was no surprise to discover, in 1884, that Lady Matcham de Ryde and her Diana had been in competition with Lady Catcham de Wyde and her Constantia for 'enry's hand in marriage. Fifteen years later the results of landed economic decline were fully visible in E. F. Benson's appropriately titled novel *Mammon & Co*, in which the penniless Lord Conybeare, who had sold or mortgaged all he could, still contrived to entertain princes at the best balls in London. For him, 'Money is the most interesting thing in the world and the most desirable': 'I often wish', he added, 'that I saw more of it.'

His wife Kit (who had the endearing habit of getting to sleep by mouthing her dislikes, 'a long and remarkably varied list beginning "Marie Corelli, parsnips"') was cynical in a more demonstrative fashion: we find her first dressing in four tints of orange chiffon – *Dante, faisan doré, Vésuve* and *pomme d'or* – blazed together; over the whole 'a fine net of pale mandarin yellow, to which was tacked a cusped acanthus pattern of sequins'. As for jewels, her maid's suggestion that pearls and pearls alone (*pas un diamant*) would be consummately chic, was not accepted. To be chic was a luxury she could no longer afford: the rubies, and the rubies alone, were necessary 'to hit 'em in the eye'. (For both good and ill, the rubies, being entailed, could not be sold to repair the Conybeare fortunes.)

The purpose of these preparations was not Lord and Lady Conybeare's impending presence at dinner with the King – though the dress had been purchased for that event – but a meeting with a floater of gold-mines and his City friends. Frank Alington was the perfect wicked financier: he cheated at baccarat; he kept a special source of money ready to purchase a baronetcy; he was a man who knew no God but Mammon and who trampled on the bodies of those who aided his career without compunction.[11] And real life? It is interesting to note that the compilers of *The Hooley Book* (1904), a vigorous attack on Ernest Hooley, reasserted the supremacy of fact over fiction by dismissing Benson's Mr Alington as 'absolutely unlike any promoter who ever lived'.[12] If that was so, many other novelists paid no attention. Mrs H. de Vere Stacpole's Archdale in *London 1913* was 'London, business London, the concretion of all its wealth and power and dominance and trickery and the deceit that knows not friend from foe'; everyone could applaud when his life ended with a dose of chloral.[13]

The special wrath of writers and social commentators was reserved for financiers of non-British origin: Alington and Archdale were, at root, weak, pathetic figures – not so Sir Adolf Erckmann, in Stephen McKenna's *Sonia* (1917), whose career bore many superficial resemblances to those of real-life plutocrats: Julius Wernher, perhaps, certainly Sir Edgar Speyer, and, above all, Sir Ernest Cassel. McKenna, who held important administrative posts in both the First and Second World Wars, was a young man in the period he described. He introduced Erckmann first at the Eclectic Club in 1905: 'the most medieval club in the world' had in effect been forced to recognize his importance by electing him, though an efficient use of the blackball was to prevent him from taking it over completely in the years that followed.

By 1905 you might already have heard of Erckmann and his many activities: for City men, there was Erckmann Brothers of Frankfurt, London and New York; in the rubber market you would encounter Erckmann Irmaos, and if you had anything to do with the South American chemical trade, you would look to Erckmann Hermanos of Valparaiso. Real estate, diamonds, timber, furs – it was difficult to avoid Erckmann or his court, the sycophants who provided a bored and boring accompaniment to his lavish entertainments. Already worth more than a million pounds, he increased his wealth from then on by geometrical progression.

Once his business needed less attention, he turned his energies towards Society. His knighthood came in 1911, his baronetcy a few years later. He captured London Society, modernized it, and left it dominated by the loudest and richest. Only the electors of Grindlesham were wise enough to accept his bribes but reject him, twice in 1910 and once in a by-election three years later. Young men-about-town could get rich from Erckmann's advice: '"You wand a good dime, hein?" he would say invitingly. "You gome with me, my vriend." And they came.' Always he would use social position to pursue some end of his own; if he lunched at the Eclectic Club the champagne and Corona cigars suggested that business was in train, and the result was an issue of new companies with some such name as Sir Roger Dainton, Bart, MP, on the prospectus. 'Ve vos all chentlemens here, yes, no', he claimed after a disagreeable bout of apparent cheating at baccarat: the portrayal was unremittingly vituperative, not merely censorious.[14]

There is no need to accept the identity of real and fictional life to ask why the plutocrats should have provoked such bitterness. McKenna was writing in the hysterically anti-German atmosphere of the First World War, in which Speyer and Cassel, both Privy Councillors, were by no means the only German-born financiers to face difficulties. But McKenna was only one voice among many that castigated the wicked plutocrat in a way that argued for something rather deeper than a simple objection to what, in recent times, has been called 'the unacceptable face of capitalism'. What sort of society was it that could get so upset about its most successful businessmen?

The answers to this question – and there are a variety of them – are a roll-call of the preoccupations of British Society in the period. Political objection to a system which (Price Collier noted) concentrated 'even the money power in a few hands',[15] was an obvious motivation for anyone with radical leanings. It has been suggested that the distribution of income in Edwardian England was as unequal as it has been anywhere and at any time in the history of the world.[16] The rise in working-class living standards, which had helped businessmen make their fortunes from consumer industries, came to an end towards the end of the nineteenth century; and the workers' economic decline coincided with the energetic display of riches by those same businessmen and the other rich sections of the community in the last twenty-five years before the First World War.[17] In the last year before the war the working classes found themselves paying twenty per cent more in taxes than they received in benefits.

The figures in L. G. Chiozza Money's *Riches and Poverty*, first published in 1905, needed qualification, but nothing could alter the broad conclusions to be drawn from them: 'more than one-third of the entire income of the United Kingdom is enjoyed by less than one-thirtieth of its people'.

The trend, moreover, was to increase the divisions between 'the Rich Classes', 'the Comfortable Classes' and 'the Poor Classes': a point noted by Chiozza Money in 1910, when revising his statistics for a new edition.[18] To be a millionaire in a society with poverty under control was scarcely worthy of comment; to be Barney Barnato, earning £5 a minute throughout the working day in the world of 1895, or Andrew Carnegie, selling his steel works to Pierpont Morgan and securing a yearly income from this source alone of more than £3,000,000 was an assault on the imagination – and the conscience.[19]

The consequence was that money itself, rather than the social conditions that led to inequality, became the main object of radical attack. This was a society which rested not on the birthdays of Saints but on what it called 'Bank' holidays. 'The closing of our banks is the one signal that for twenty-four hours we are free,' Arthur Ponsonby, first a Liberal, later (from 1922) a Labour MP, commented sourly; no real escape from 'the unqualified belief in money as a means, money as an end, aim, object, ideal; money as representing the method of securing a greater deal of physical wellbeing, money as power, money as pleasure, money, therefore, as happiness'. Ponsonby ascribed most of the blame to the plutocrats.[20]

The best-known Liberal critic of *The Condition of England*, C. F. G. Masterman, was MP for North-West Ham in 1909 when he presented 'the astonishing facts of "super-wealth"' accumulated in the previous thirty years. Both the rate of accumulation and the amount of expenditure, he argued, were quite without parallel. Extravagance coincided with what he called 'a strange mediocrity': this was an England of great country houses engaged in 'lavish hospitality' while rural life crumbled into ruin; of vast hotels, machines to exhibit 'a combination of maximum expenditure and display with a minimum return on enjoyment'; a country that had 'annexed whole regions abroad' – Biarritz and the Riviera coast, Austria and the German watering-places – merely to find any distraction that will 'forbid the pain of thinking'; and that plunged into gambles for fresh wealth anywhere in the world where the reward would be 'the conversion of the one pound into the ten'. A nation of conquerors had become a nation of the comfortable; and perhaps the most important part of the process was the weakening of the 'aristocratic caste' as it merged itself into 'a wealthy class'.[21]

As a description of a decadent society, all this had some force; as a basis for a political programme it was negative and unhelpful. Even when Ramsay MacDonald – one day to become England's first Labour Prime Minister – attacked 'the scum of the earth which possessed itself of gold in the Johannesburg market place',[22] he was only offering a variation on Marie Corelli's assumption that a man who had no other claim upon society than that of mere wealth, was 'a kind of monstrosity and deformity in the general equality and equilibrium of Nature'.[23] The strange result was that radical politicians and conservative critics of contemporary morality engaged in an obsessive and empty concentration on the evils of modern society. The tirades of Mrs Desmond Humphreys ('Rita'), Father Bernard Vaughan, the Revd. F. B. Meyer and T. W. H. Crosland, were all in this vein.[24]

Crosland defined 'The Wicked Life' as 'the life led by most commercial people' – a judgment that was bound to lead to disapproval of a country that was, in all essentials, a modern commercial society. The son of a merchant or stockjobber 'knows nothing about noblesse oblige, having no noblesse to oblige; he has money without position; lands without ancestry; servants without authority; lust without discrimination; ice in his champagne; college colours on his hand-bags [the ultimate ungentlemanly trait].' At least the wicked men and women of the past – Nero and Cleopatra and Burke (Burke?) – had 'a certain brilliancy of execution which is entirely lacking in the practitioners of our own dull but not less wicked time', the people who scrape and scratch and cheat for money, making the West End 'a hell by night'.

The fact that Crosland's 'Jerimiadical diatribes' – his own

description of Rita's attacks on the 'smart set' – may have an unintentionally humorous impact cannot hide their deeply deferential undertones. Crosland's respect for the establishment – any establishment – was much deeper than that of Marie Corelli. It enabled him to decide that the very rich had no incentive to be wicked because 'they have wealth and position, and consequently all the virtues'; by this standard the millionaires, no less than the dukes, could be judged 'men of austere and virtuous life'. It was 'the middlings' who were the guilty ones – 'the successful traders, the stockbrokers, the company promoters, the usurers and financiers, snobbish doctors and solicitors, strutting actors and music-hall agents, and retired brewers and tailors.'[25]

Though Crosland was unusual in excluding the millionaires from the catalogue of disapproval, his attitudes had the same basic roots as the whole range of social critics of his time. These roots came together in hostility to what the creation and expenditure of wealth was doing to traditional society. Mr Gladstone, looking back and looking forward at the time of Queen Victoria's Golden Jubilee, warned the country: 'Let us beware of that imitative luxury, which is tempting all of us to ape our betters . . . let us be jealous of plutocracy, and of its tendency to infect aristocracy, its elder and nobler sister; and learn, if we can, to hold by or get back to some regard for simplicity of life. Let us respect the ancient manners.'[26] The dilemma was a real one for proud Victorians like Gladstone or Lecky, the historian, who believed in moral progress, and associated industrial civilization with 'the moral value of thrift, steady industry . . . constant forethought with a view to providing for the contingencies of the future.' They did not disapprove of wealth, but of wealth without responsibility – the fortunes made by manipulating pieces of paper, involving no landlord duty to tenants or factory-owner duty to workers. In Lecky's view, 'Such fortunes give unrivalled opportunities of luxurious idleness, and as in themselves they bring little or no social influence or position, those who possess them are peculiarly tempted to seek such a position by an ostentation of wealth and luxury which has a profoundly vulgarising and demoralising influence upon society.'[27] As the German economist, Werner Sombart, pointed out, the values of modern life were those of a child: delight in physical size, in quick movement, in novelty and in a sense of power. For those who did not understand the way their society was changing, this sort of analysis was bound to be attractive.[28]

No one formulated an effective political programme to curb the power of the plutocrats, or change the system that concentrated wealth in their hands, for one simple reason: an inability to come to terms with the fact that twentieth-century urban civilization had arrived. Nostalgia was a large element in much of the social criticism of the plutocrats. George du Maurier's Sir Gorgius Midas, for example, was a brilliant portrayal of the way the *nouveaux riches* sought to acquire respectability: to their money they added as much that was visible as possible – houses, footmen, carriages, horses, clothes. But Du Maurier's cartoons were based on a highly romantic view of the aristocracy. Born in Paris in 1834, he was himself the grandson of émigrés who had left France during the Terror and then returned; his mother was the daughter of Mary Ann Clarke, once a mistress of the Duke of York.[29] Du Maurier's book about his craft and his predecessors in *Punch*, John Leech and Charles Keene, indicated that his cartoons strongly reflected his own view of society. He mourned the passing of the splendid old grandees of high rank:

> Sir Gorgius Midas has beaten the dukes in mere gorgeousness, flunkies and all – burlesqued the vulgar side of them, and unconsciously shamed it out of existence; made swagger and ostentation unpopular by his own evil example – actually improved the manners of the great by sheer mimicry of their defects . . . He has married his sons and his daughters to them and spoiled the noble curve of those lovely noses that Leech drew so well.[30]

The naivety of this description – the eighteenth-century

aristocracy were masters of cultured ruthlessness – was in some ways less significant than its emphasis on vulgarity. Snobbery, a confused and confusing element in English history, fuelled the nostalgia which produced hostility to the plutocrats. William Makepeace Thackeray actually compiled a *Book of Snobs*, which first appeared in the columns of *Punch*. (G. K. Chesterton, who introduced a new edition in 1911, pointed out that *Punch* was a radical paper in Thackeray's day, but now – nearly sixty years after his death – was in danger of being 'a book by snobs'; still, he was happy to be given the chance to show how Thackeray's 'ephemeral journalism' 'proves to us how eternal journalism can be'.)

The basic proposition was straightforward: 'It is impossible for *any* Briton, perhaps, not to be a Snob in some degree.'

Mr Snob was therefore by no means the only exponent of the vice from which he took his name. His hilarious visit to Major Ponto in Mangelwurzelshire was suitably revealing:

'We are distantly related, MR Snob,' said she, shaking her melancholy head. 'Poor dear LORD RUBADUB!'

'Oh,' said I, not knowing what the deuce MRS MAJOR PONTO meant.

'MAJOR PONTO told me that you were of the Leicestershire Snobs: a very old family, and related to LORD SNOBBINGTON, who married LAURA RUBADUB, who is a cousin of mine, as was her poor dear father, for whom we are mourning. What a seizure! Only sixty-three, and apoplexy quite unknown until now in our family! In life we are in death MR SNOB. Does LADY SNOBBINGTON bear the deprivation well?'

Mr Snob confessed that he didn't know . . . but noticed on the drawing-room table 'the inevitable, abominable, maniacal, absurd, disgusting "Peerage" . . . interleaved with annotations, and open at the article "SNOBBINGTON".' During dinner Mrs P's questions continued in profusion; she wanted to know:

'When LADY ANGELINA SKEGGS would come out; and if the

countess her mamma' (this was said with much archness
and he-he-ing) 'still wore that extraordinary purple hair
dye?'. . . 'Whether my LORD GUTTLEBURY kept, besides his
French chef, and an English cordon-bleu for the roasts, an
Italian for the confectionery?' . . . [and] 'who attended at
LADY CLAPPERCLAW's *conversazioni*?'

The company would not have been complete without 'the two
tall and scraggy MISS PONTOS' (and their governess, Miss
Wirt), and Wellesley Ponto, the Major's son in the 120th
Hussars, whose misfortune it was to discover that his
'wedgement's so *doothid* exthpenthif'.

After forty-five columns in *Punch* Thackeray felt that
'The word Snob has taken a place in our honest English
vocabulary. . . .' Snobbery could always be recognized, even
if, like wit, or humour, or humbug, it could not be defined.
The purpose was not entirely frivolous, for Thackeray was
effectively castigating the invention of a concept of 'gentility'
which killed 'natural kindliness and honest friendship'.[31]
When Hippolyte Taine was compiling his *Notes sur L'Angle-
terre,* which first appeared in English translation in the *Daily
News* in the 1870s, he talked to Thackeray, who confirmed
everything that he had written about the snobbish spirit.[32]
Interestingly, Lord Esher was to write to his son in March
1903 that the sort of 'snobism' that Thackeray had mocked
had disappeared, except for traces in Bayswater or country
villages[33] – but, then, he, as Deputy Constable of Windsor
Castle, had seen with mixed feelings the influence of Sir
Ernest Cassel and other non-patricians on Edward VII.
Patrick Balfour, Lord Kinross, was more perceptive in
recalling, in 1933, that the opening of Society to a much wider
range of people did not mean the end of snobbery: snobbery
of birth and breeding was merely replaced by a range of other
snobberies.[34] In the first decade of the twentieth century, there
were, perhaps, 800,000 people with incomes between £150 and
the solidly comfortable level of £700 a year:[35] still enough to
aspire to a servant or two, or a social pretension or three.

For many centuries all notions of social superiority had
been summed up by referring to 'the gentleman'. When
Curzon, as Chancellor of Oxford University, was shown the
menu for entertaining the King at Balliol, he said only that
'No gentleman has soup at luncheon'; he did not say 'No
monarch', 'No marquis': he appealed, as Evelyn Waugh said
in recounting the story, 'to the most elusive standard in the
world'.[36] Until the Industrial Revolution brought riches to an
entirely new section of the community it did not matter that
definitions of 'the gentleman' tended to be contradictory:
gentlemen could identify each other well enough without
recourse to intellectual niceties. It was only when businessmen
began to assert their new-found power in great numbers that
definition became of urgent importance. In the first half of
the nineteenth century the obvious solution for those safe-
guarding the traditions of gentlemanly dominance was to
stress the incompatability of trade and the gentleman. 'At
the bottom of their hearts . . .', observed Taine, the English
'believe or are tempted to believe that a manufacturer, a
merchant, a monied man, obliged to think all day about gain
and the details of gain, is not a gentleman.'[37]

So strongly did this idea become entrenched that when,
towards the end of the century, businessmen – by sheer weight
of influence and numbers – began to be accepted in Society,
the pretence was maintained by a tacit acceptance of industrial
and trading wealth, provided it somehow dissociated itself
from money. The fact that money was money had to be
disguised by pretending to avoid the article itself. When
Sonia Keppel, daughter of one of Edward VII's favourite mist-
resses, was married in 1920, 'a fat cheque' arrived from Sir
Ernest Cassel; to her dismay, her mother told her that cheques
were vulgar and she had to content herself with an unwanted
stole and muff of Canadian sables.[38] By and large plutocrats
like Cassel, despite their efforts to adopt the gentlemanly
code, failed to disguise their direct contact with the making of
money. The latter process identified them – and helped to
explain the hostility to them.

The earliest notions of 'the gentleman', associated with knightly ideals, were therefore totally at variance with what developed in the nineteenth century and after. *The Cornhill Magazine* discussed the issues involved in 1862: the gentlemanly qualities were divided into 'artistic', 'moral' and 'intellectual', and no gentleman, therefore, would blow his nose with his fingers, tell gross lies or be unable to read. But by far the most fundamental of the three attributes was the first: a gentleman was above all 'a man socially pleasant'.[39] What emerged, and what was at its height in the years from 1840 to 1914, was a cult of 'respectability' under the pretence of being a cult of the 'gentleman'.[40] To some extent, and to some extent only, the very richest were freed by their riches from caring: Barney Barnato delighted in relating the grim details of his youth as an East End slum kid. His views on society were complex, but he never described himself – as some suggested after his death – as 'the son of a gentleman of Devonshire Terrace'.[41] For him, at least, it was something to have come from the gutter.

Accusations of vulgarity attached to Barnato and other plutocrats had two main roots. The first stems from the fact that the social ideals of any society take a long time to catch up with the economic realities. The French observer, Emile Boutmy, was right to point out in *The English People* that the England of the early twentieth century was 'another country altogether' from the England of a century before, right to single out the progress of material civilization as the key catalyst.[42] The ownership of land was no longer the road to riches, and the death of the old order – social, political, economic – could be safely predicted. But the evolution of society has much to do with individual men and women, reluctantly torn away from cherished and familiar habits of thought in order to come to terms with a new set of circumstances: ultimately a liberating process for some, but usually tardily and painfully undertaken.

The Europe of the last twenty-five years before the First

World War was still a Europe of monarchy and aristocracy. When 1914 came only three European countries were republics.[43] It was the great paradox of the era that what E. F. Benson called 'the fairy-tales of science' turned into 'sober facts of commerce and convenience' while the ideas of a dead age continued to be expressed through the social and political institutions of Europe.[44] No one quite understood how fast industrialization was changing society. Since they did not understand it, they were unwilling to accept its chief protagonists: the plutocrats.

What was not understood was also feared. The second reason for the deep hostility to the plutocrats had nothing to do with nostalgia for a lost world. It followed from an observation of the power they wielded. The stakes were high in one of the strongest countries of a Europe that controlled most of the land surface of the world and all its seas; in a Britain whose social and political ideals and institutions no longer reflected the realities of economic power. Hostility to the plutocrats was much more than moral disapprobation of the worship of wealth; it also indicated a conscious or unconscious terror of the power wealth gave. Everyone could laugh with Lady Priscilla Whopper, Society Star and Belle Dame at the Royal and Imperial Courts of Queen Victoria, King Edward VII and Napoleon III, when she confronted the Silver King, the Gold King, the Nitrate King, the Diamond King, the Pork-pie King (and the Sausage King) that crossed her snob-laden path.[45] But no one liked the idea that in some respects England seemed to be becoming a suburb of Empire and Europe – linked by a bond of money to New York. As Mr Dooley expressed it, when Edward VII was crowned: 'Andhrew Carnaygie lint Wistminsther Abbey, Pierpont Morgan the tapestries for its dicoration, the Frohman Syndicate lint the theatres, and . . . another Syndicate conceded the use of the Thames.'[46]

It was easy to rationalize these fears by basic appeals to the emotions: the need to preserve the nation from outside influences. Many of the plutocrats were aliens: in their country of origin or their religion, or – as was often the case – in both. Sir Almeric Fitzroy expressed the general distaste when he quoted the German-born Jew Sir Edgar Speyer discussing the prospects for a European war in 1912: 'It will be a terrible thing if we English', Speyer said, 'go to war with us Germans'.[47] Wernher, Beit, Cassel, Speyer – they all pointed to the truth of what was called 'the ascendancy of the Teutonic element'. To be German was one thing; to be Jewish as well compounded the disgrace. In 1800 there were perhaps 8,000 Jews in England – hardly enough for anti-Semitism to flourish. In 1900, after a century of arrivals from Germany and Russia and Poland, there were 160,000 in the capital alone. By the time of the First World War England had experienced a Jewish Prime Minister, Lord Chancellor and Lord Chief Justice – and a Jacobson among the bishops of its national church.[48] 'Nowhere does the Jew receive better treatment than in Great Britain,' wrote John Foster Fraser in *The Conquering Jew* (1915); 'There is not a single disability. Anti-semitism does not exist.'[49]

Fraser's comment was less than the whole truth. The very success of the Jews strengthened the hatred of them. They were generally pictured as a totally unscrupulous section of the community, out for what they could get: '"in England [said Elaine, in Saki's *The Unbearable Bassington* (1912)] no one really is anti-semitic." Youghal shook his head. "I know a great many Jews who are."'[50] The Jews were said to have taken over society: an 'Israelitish army', with its encampments in the City extending due west into Mayfair and thence north-west into Bedfordshire and Buckinghamshire. If so, this invading army was unique in its failure to bring destruction and desolation in its wake. According to T. H. S. Escott, the Jews sustained almost on its own English art and music in the capital: they were not so much a materializing as a spiritualizing force in Society.[51]

Sir Edgar Speyer, among the most attacked of all the Jewish-German financiers, had Richard Strauss's opera 'Salome' dedicated to him. Henry James would often dine with the Speyers in their Grosvenor Square London home, accompanied by his young musician friends Percy Grainger and Cyril Scott; Grieg and Debussy might also be met there. Speyer's wife Leonora, daughter of the Silesian Count von Stosch, was a professional violinist, and he was himself the driving force behind the syndicate that ran Queen's Hall and Queen's Hall Orchestra. The conductor, Henry Wood – whose name has passed deep into English consciousness through its association with the Promenade Concerts – was Speyer's own choice.[52] All this said, for many Englishmen, alien cultural dominance was no more palatable than dominance of any other kind. Members of all classes could join in the music-hall castigation of 'the financiers with the Rhine-wine names' as they sang: 'I am the rich Mr Hoggenheimer, I am the beautiful Mr Hoggenheimer, I am Mr Hoggenheimer from Park Lane.'[53]

These then were English society's reactions to the rise of the plutocrats: a mixture of naive contempt, resentment and fear. But it was no real paradox that, in response to the overwhelmingly urban and industrial civilization of the new world, a rather different view slowly, very slowly, developed. The businessman became the new hero of one part of bookland. 'I started life with nothing to depend upon but my own energies': Sir Charles Macara, leader of the cotton industry, had the best inheritance.[54] *The Life of Sir Sidney H. Waterlow Bart. London Apprentice, Lord Mayor, Captain of Industry, and Philanthropist*: George Smalley's 1909 biography of the founder of one of Britain's biggest printing companies was typical. Richard Welford's *Men of Mark 'Twixt Tyne and Tweed* took three volumes in 1895 to praise the men to whom 'we owe – all civilised nations owe – most of the commercial facilities, domestic comforts, and personal conveniences which make life worth living'.

Business increasingly permeated all aspects of life. Women were not immune: *Business Girl*, the official organ of the Institution of Women Shorthand Typists, began in 1912; nor even the staid literary and political journals: 'An article on the present aspect of the financial position has little need to apologize in these days for obtruding itself even into the pages of a monthly magazine,' declared the *Contemporary Review* in July 1896.[55] The Society reference-book found its counterpart in *Men of Note in Finance and Commerce*, 'a biographical business directory, modelled upon an idea which has been developed in many directions from the establishment of Debrett's Peerage in 1713 down to the more modern "Who's Who", but which has not yet been satisfactorily applied to the financial and commercial world'. Plutocrats even had their own hierarchy, every effort being made 'to distinguish between the representative man of commerce and the ephemeral trader; between the representative of la haute finance and the self-styled financier'.[56]

Businessmen took advantage of these changes to the full. Conscious of their power, they used it in such organizations as the French Union of Economic Interests or the German Navy League, or – in less sinister fashion – simply displayed it in their self-confidence. Picture, in 1897, 'the prosperous gentlemen in glossy, silk hats, with high white collars, and deep wristbands, who, having placed a new rose in their button hole, drive high-stepping cobs to their suburban railway station every morning, and who, if a stranger strays into their Stock Exchange, deal with that unfortunate person as an Epsom mob treats a welsher.'[57] Who were the masters now?

Chapter 9

The World Comes to Mayfair

London acted as a magnet for those who had made fortunes overseas. There, in the social capital of the world, South Africans, Americans, even Oriental Jews, were to display their riches with a mixture of pride and arrogance. Of these the diamond and gold men made perhaps the greatest, certainly the most noted, impact on existing institutions. Once the old-time digger had been replaced by the financiers, South Africa had itself developed a brand of provincial high society: the first race meeting was held at Johannesburg in 1886 and the country soon sported its own Turf Club. It was not long, however, before a succession of imperial plutocrats made the lengthy journey to England – with its promise of cosmopolitan excitement in the midst of ancient splendour. In time, they were to turn Park Lane into a colony of their own.

The first shock-waves came in the 1890s – perfectly symbolized by the dinner Barney Barnato's nephew, Woolf Joel, gave in the Savoy in 1896. Woolf had won £16,000 in half an hour at Monte Carlo when recuperating after a hansom accident, and more than thirty guests were invited to commemorate the event at a special dinner. The winning red of the roulette wheel was reflected in an overwhelmingly red décor, seen in everything from the waiters' uniforms to the lighting; the number nine and ace of diamonds were fashioned in the floral decorations.[1] In memoirs and accounts of the period the names, the date, the details become changed and mixed up. But the dinner happened – and like others equally ostentatious, its reverberations reached ominously into the patrician corridors of England's oldest families.

Julius Wernher's wish to live in London was forcibly expressed nearly twenty years before he acquired British citizenship in 1898: 'The trend of things in Germany now and the manner in which liberal development is fettered in every conceivable way is intolerable to anybody who knows English life', he wrote.[2] His activities in London were to make an interesting commentary on this statement, for any attachment to liberalism was bound to be expressed in peculiar fashion by someone worth many times his own weight in gold sovereigns. Physically Wernher was a rather curious figure: over six feet in height, with deep-set eyes a notable feature, he managed to appear both commanding and yet awkward, an impressive, shambling giant. According to H. O'Kelly Webber, who used to lunch at his offices, he looked like a German professor.[3]

As a millionaire he was an obvious object for those concerned with collecting money to improve social conditions of one kind and another, and perhaps the most revealing of his relationships was the result of his careful cultivation by one of the most extraordinary couples of the period – Sidney and Beatrice Webb. The Webbs were satirized by H. G. Wells as 'two active self-centred people, excessively devoted to the public service'. There was something of the miser about them; they gathered and usuriously invested not money, but knowledge of public affairs – obsessionally. Beatrice had a passion for order – the sort of person who found 'trees hopelessly irregular and sea cliffs a great mistake'. She was the daughter of a rich railway magnate and, according to Wells's rather unfair characterization, 'a dealer in Refined Social Reform for the Parlour'.[4] Sidney Webb, in his wife's description, was 'undistinguished and unimpressive in appearance': a funny, overweight little figure, complete with lisp and goatee beard, remote and lacking in casual conversation and intimate friends. The two of them sought out Wernher's company partly out of curiosity, partly because of a growing respect and liking for him, but above all for a practical reason: their connection with him over the Charlottenburg scheme.[5]

Charlottenburg, near Berlin, was the site of the great German *Hochschule*, monument to advanced scientific education. The Webbs' friend, Richard Burton Haldane, the intellectual Liberal politician, persuaded the government to make available land and buildings to form what the Webbs referred to as 'Charlottenburg' – what was in fact to become the Imperial Technical Institute, now the Imperial College of Science and Technology.[6] Though Sidney Webb and Haldane managed to obtain an annual grant from the London County Council, they needed more extensive financial support.

Haldane had made the first approach to Wernher. Some years before the scheme came to fruition he called on the millionaire and found him, with Alfred Beit and the other members of his firm, at their office. An immediate offer of £100,000 was later supplemented by other very large sums.[7] In the end, indeed, Wernher was involved to the extent of half a million pounds: not the only example of philanthropic benefits which included £250,000 to found a university at Groote Schuur, South African home of Cecil Rhodes, £400,000 in gifts and other benefits to King Edward's Hospital Fund, and a further £100,000 in his will to various charities.

A number of strange dinners introduced Wernher to the Webbs' circle. In February 1902 Sidney and Beatrice asked Sir Oliver Lodge, a physicist interested in psychical research, to stay with them. A mixed company dined one evening – among them Wernher. The stage was represented by the Granville-Barkers, the Fabians by Lucy (Lion) Phillimore, the Bertrand Russells by the inimitable couple themselves. Beatrice 'sacrificed myself during some part of dinner to the millionaire' – her unenthusiastic description of Wernher. Arthur Balfour, the Prime Minister and also a guest, evidently concurred, showing an open antipathy to Wernher and to Sir Halford Mackinder, the director of the London School of Economics: 'mere philistine materialist administrators he would feel'. Wernher and Mackinder did not appear to care; they 'chummed up and walked away together'.[8]

Eight months later, Sir Julius was beginning to rise in her estimation – 'a heavy, good-natured, public-spirited and scientific-minded millionaire' – though he was scarcely the star attraction of the party: his broken German no match for George Bernard Shaw's scintillating conversation. Mrs Prothero, Irish wife of the editor of the *Quarterly Review*, was suitably sceptical of the playwright's wit, but Lord Lytton (doubtless not yet dreaming of the day, many years later, when he was to become Viceroy of India) hung on Shaw's words. Still, no one could deny that this was 'a somewhat crooked party' – straightened out 'by sheer energy on my part into a comfortable affair'.[9] Wernher's suspicions of Shaw's dazzling but acid set-speeches may well be imagined.

Wernher himself entertained in rather different style. His London home, Bath House, was originally the site of a mansion built by William Pulteney, Earl of Bath and opponent of Walpole in George II's reign. It was the head of the banking firm of Baring Brothers who was responsible, in the third decade of the nineteenth century, for the Bath House that Wernher knew: as one Edwardian noted, the house 'does but continue a tradition of successful finance'.[10] By Wernher's time it had acquired some celebrity as the gathering place of famous poets, philosophers and scientists, especially through its association with Harriet, wife of the second Lord Ashburton (who was himself a Baring).

Literati and *illuminati* were not so much in evidence one July evening in 1906 when the Webbs came to dine.[11] The company was almost exclusively made up of financial magnates and their hangers-on. The rooms, the flowers, the fruit and wine and music, the pictures and works of art – all were an exaggerated expression of one thing: wealth. In Beatrice's eyes, everyone seemed to be 'living up to it, or bowing down before it'. 'There might just as well have been a Goddess of Gold erected for overt worship', she said – 'the impression in thought, feeling and action could hardly have been stronger.'

Wernher himself was, perhaps, an exception: 'I have no time, even to know that I am wealthy,' he told Beatrice, 'the only result of my millions is to make me dread being introduced to a new person lest they should begin to beg from me. The really happy person is the man with £10,000 a year, reputed to have £2,000.' In a sense, Beatrice concurred: 'What you enjoy is not your wealth but the power it gives you to organize the affairs of the world.' The answer that came back was laboured, weary, wary: 'Yes, perhaps, that is so.'

One is less sure that Wernher's wife would have been so honest: Alice, daughter of James Mankievicz, was 'a hard, vainglorious woman, talkative and badly bred', if 'not otherwise objectionable', according to Beatrice Webb.[12] She was not the only society-loving wife of a withdrawn millionaire in Edwardian times: a millionaire, in this case indeed, who – again like many of the others – seems to have been closer to his mother than to anyone else in his life; 'I am your declared lover', was the message that lady once received from him.

It may have been Alice who persuaded Julius – created baronet two years afterwards – to purchase Luton Hoo, in Hertfordshire, in 1903: 'a very stately place indeed', according to Dr Johnson, who visited it in 1781; 'in the house magnificence is not sacrificed to convenience nor convenience to magnificence.'[13] In the early seventeenth century Robert Sandy built a brick mansion on the site of an existing house; like Wernher, nearly three hundred years later, he entertained the King there.[14] But the real glory of Luton Hoo began in 1763 when Lord Bute commissioned Robert Adam to provide a new house, while 'Capability' Brown created marvellous lawns and a large artificial lake, amidst a remarkable growth of trees, in the 1,600 acre park. Fire damage in 1771 and 1843 was followed by extensive rebuilding, but it is not very likely that the Wernhers cared that the purity of the original had been lost. They made their own alterations: a great staircase, with bronze stair-rail and lined by a collection of Italian Renaissance bronzes by such masters as Andrea Riccio and Giovanni di Bologna, was created for Sir Julius; the main hall, with its spectacular but florid decoration, marble chimneypiece and elaborate candelabra, was unmistakably and extravagantly Edwardian.

In May 1908 Sir Julius wrote to the Webbs offering them the opportunity to stay in 'The Hermitage', a small house in its own grounds but in his park, for as long as they wanted. There, by a grand irony, they composed their famous minority report for the Royal Commission on the Poor Law. Wernher himself was seen at Luton Hoo only during a few months in autumn, or on occasional Sundays. In the meantime, 54 gardeners, 10 electricians, 20–30 house servants and an apparently uncountable number of labourers continued to be employed by him – on a great, ghostly estate, the only sounds coming from the game complacently awaiting the guns of autumn. All this cost £30,000 a year and, Beatrice Webb was quick to point out, made a damning contrast with the slums, poverty and high infant mortality of Luton, the town on the estate's doorstep.[15]

The wealth with which Wernher surrounded himself was used as a shield from the world and his feelings. To make money had certainly been his earliest ambition; to organize the South African gold and diamond industry and further its development through the application of advanced technology became his major occupation.[16] He preferred to use his millions to speak for themselves, rather than to employ them singlemindedly in the pursuit of social ambition. It is said that one of his favourite jokes was that everyone assumed the 'Wernher' of 'Wernher, Beit & Co.' was merely Beit's Christian name: the story is not difficult to believe, for this was a man whose self-effacement – according to the not usually so trenchant *Dictionary of National Biography* – 'amounted almost to a passion'.

None of this minimized the effect of his intrusion into British life: the existence of Bath House and Luton Hoo alone was enough to provide constant material for Society gossip. His partner, Alfred Beit, was considerably more outgoing, though he too was not happy in the full glare of public life. In a sense both men never quite satisfied themselves that their riches were real: the luxury in which they lived provided a message for others which they were unable to absorb themselves. Beit had one advantage – warmth of personality – and he was consequently better liked. At his dinner table were found not only the other millionaires, but Moberley Bell, editor of *The Times*, and, in his last years, such well-known theatre figures as Lena Ashwell and Herbert Beerbohm Tree.[17]

He had first looked for a permanent London home in the late 1880s, when he lived in Ryder Street and began a serious interest in art-collecting. Probably the richest bachelor in the capital, he commissioned Eustace Balfour to build him a house at 26 Park Lane, which he shared after its completion in 1895 with his secretary and his fox terrier. Unlike other houses in this street of millionaires, it had only two storeys: a peculiar mixture, it was said, between a bungalow and a dwarf country mansion. Its Germanic winter garden, perhaps unique in London's West End, provided – at any rate for Frank Harris, who interviewed him there – 'an abode of grateful dim coolness and shuttered silence, silence made noticeable . . . by the vague hum of the outside world'.[18] The dining-room served also as a picture gallery, home for part of a collection which included *Head of a boy* by Frans Hals, two Rembrandts, two Gainsboroughs, two Reynolds's – one of which, *The Cockburn Family*, was left by him to the National Gallery. Beit's feeling for art went far beyond its investment possibilities.

Alfred Beit became a British citizen in 1898, but there is no doubt that his German origins posed a genuine problem for him. His friend, the Berlin art curator Von Bode, told him that the Kaiser was annoyed at his patronage of the National Gallery, and he responded with presentations to the Berlin Museum. But when a message reached him in Hamburg, where he was visiting his mother, that the Kaiser wanted to offer him the Order of the Red Eagle, he pointed out that, as a British subject, he would have to ask permission before receiving a foreign decoration. In England, the situation was reversed. G. K. Chesterton complained: 'to ask us in the name of patriotism to remember that he is of our people is about as accurate as asking us in the name of family feeling to remember that he is our great-aunt.'[19] The editor of the *Cape Times* may have proved he was no poet in contributing an obituary to the *Westminster Gazette* in July 1906, but he caught the essence of the dilemma: 'He worked for England', he wrote, 'to be dubbed "Herr Beit".'

The Anglo-German relationship, in the light of what happened in 1914, was one of the gravest of contemporary political issues. Beit was at least in some position to play a role behind the scenes, especially at the end of 1905, when German fears had been aroused by British support for the French in Morocco. In November, in Paris, he had seen the French Prime Minister, Rouvier, and just after Christmas he had an audience with the Kaiser. The German Chancellor, Von Bülow, received a long letter from Wilhelm the following day, reporting the conversation. Von Bülow, in his memoirs, claimed that 'this original, and, in his way, important man' had been admitted by Edward VII into 'the circle of "his personal friends"'. There is no evidence for the latter statement, though Wilhelm too described Beit as 'the notorious Stock Exchange crony and speculator of H.M. E.VII'.

The Kaiser was told that England wanted nothing of Germany, except that the countries should live on good terms; the only 'black spot' was the Morocco question. Wilhelm reacted by saying that, if France and England threatened Germany, 'What could we do but feel for our revolvers?' Beit interrupted him excitedly, declaring that the British offer to help France would only apply in the case of 'an unjust German attack on France'; there was no question of attacking Germany *à la improviste*; and the whole nation, including the government – many of whose members were his 'personal friends' – wanted peace.

Wilhelm claimed that the English spent 300,000 francs in a single year in the Paris press on anti-German articles. Beit conceded the point, though he said he had not heard the sum mentioned; he even agreed that the English press spread calumny against Germany in anonymous articles by 'Diplomaticus' or 'One Who knows': 'if only one could pin them down – find out whose those scoundrels really are. It has often infuriated me too', he said. His broad message was that government, Stock Exchange, City, businessmen, all wanted to avoid war; only Sir John Fisher, the First Sea Lord, was a hawk, and he need not be taken seriously. There were worries, certainly, that if the French should 'happen to be attacked' in Morocco, they would be compelled to help them, but he would definitely convey the German anxieties to London.[20]

That happened when Lord Esher was asked by Edward VII to visit Beit in January 1906. There was no place for Beit in the index of his copiously indexed diaries, however, and he asserted that the primary purpose of the audience had been connected with Beit's presentation of a Van Dyck to the Berlin Museum the previous year. Indeed, whatever the motive, it is Alfred Beit's philanthropy that has left a more permanent mark than his excursions into diplomacy. His will was especially revealing: nearly two million pounds in charitable bequests, in addition to much more than one million for the Beit trust for Rhodesia. It may not have been an accident that Beit, never very successful at school and unable to afford to go to university, devoted vast sums to education: from £100,000 to establish a university at Hamburg, to endowment of a Chair of Colonial History at Oxford. Lady Sarah Wilson, who travelled out to South Africa with him on the *Tantallon Castle* in December 1895, thought he was 'interesting as the man who had made the most colossal fortune of all the South African magnates', but also noted that he was 'already said to be the most generous of philanthropists and the kindest of friends.'[21] The attributes were not often put together so sympathetically: but a more or less accurate judgment of the man might be assumed from the probability that time after time private requests for help made to the companies with which he was associated were met by Beit after their official rejection.[22]

The same could not be said of J. B. Robinson. Robinson took Dudley House, Park Lane, family home of the Earl that had purchased 'The Star of South Africa'. His sycophantic biographer, Leo Weinthal, asserted: 'The salons were spacious, and decorated in that subdued artistic taste usually associated with the London homes of the British aristocracy.'[23] *Mayfair*, in 1910, was more straightforward in describing 'a veritable palace'. 'The house is famous for its brilliant musical entertainments, although, strange to say, the owner himself suffers from deafness.'[24] Not so strange, in fact: Robinson's aesthetic interests went no deeper than the social profit they were meant to provide. His art collection contained works by Rembrandt and Gainsborough and Romney, Italian Old Masters and the Dutch School in the seventeenth century – the result not of artistic discernment, but of a calculated attempt to show his superiority over his Park Lane fellows, whose cultural interests sometimes did not extend much beyond Ruff's *Guide to the Turf*.[25]

Robinson hated the thought of expenditure which did not contribute to his own ends; the painter P. Tennyson Cole described him as 'A man of many economies' after visiting his huge South African house in the Cape Town suburb of Wynberg. The evening caller would find the great place in darkness, the bell producing a single light and Robinson himself to answer the door. Later, at Dudley House, he came near to tears as he told Cole that the Boer War had decreased his fortune from ten to six million pounds.[26] The *African World Annual*, discussing 'South Africa's first Baronet' in 1908, declared that his heart lay in South Africa. The truth was that Robinson's attempted conquest of London Society failed.[27]

He lacked subtlety – something for which low cunning was no substitute. Margot Asquith met him in January 1896 when she went to dine with Lord and Lady Reay. Almost his first question: are you rich? And he proceeded to tell her how he had made his money. It was typical of him that one of his few recorded acts of generosity was to send some uncut diamonds to the Earl of Rosslyn's daughter as a wedding present; they would have cost so much to cut that they were left by their recipient in their natural state. Robinson never expressed a coherent philosophy – very little existed for him outside himself, his money and his paranoia. His only compensation was the distant acclaim of the magazine article: a hero for the lower-middle-class readers of the first volume of *Pearson's Magazine* in 1896 was found in Mr Joseph Benjamin Robinson with the 'keen business instinct and hard common-sense' that have raised him 'from modest origins to the giddy heights of financial greatness', with the magnificent estate on Cape Peninsula 'whither he sails his own yacht to spend three months in every year away from the English winter' – expensive at the price.

Unlike Robinson, and very unlike the South Africans of German origins, Cecil Rhodes could at least boast an English family and an Oxford classical education. Nevertheless, he faced hostility long before Marie Corelli's attack on the 'almost royal pomp' of his funeral service in St Paul's. In the same month as he was appointed a Privy Councillor, January 1895, he was blackballed by the Travellers' Club. The committee of the Reform said they were prepared to elect him as one of the three eminent persons for whom there need be no ballot. Rhodes replied in April that 'for a non-resident' he had 'clubs enough, as I belong to St James's and Union'. 'I hear they declined to have me at the Travellers': I suppose because I am written about. I was not aware I was up, as I was put down by an old friend, Guy Dawnay, dead these ten years ago, and I had forgotten all about it.'[28] The Prince of Wales, always ready to support the rich, took his name off the Travellers' Club list in response.

Rhodes spent long periods in London, but had no London home; he stayed at the Burlington Hotel in Cork Street instead. Nothing indicates that he enjoyed Society; to Lady Diana Cooper, daughter of the Duke of Rutland, he was 'a thick square man who stared at me and did not know what to say either'.[29] Even when he came to London in 1890 as Prime Minister of Cape Colony and dined at Windsor Castle, it was noted that his manner was extremely brusque.[30] Society chatter exhausted him; he preferred the company of a small group of intimates. Society hangers-on annoyed him; in his aim, subsequently made notorious, for 'equal rights for every civilized man South of the Zambezi', he defined 'civilized man' as someone 'whether white or black who has sufficient education to write his name, has some property or works, in fact is not a loafer'.[31]

Rhodes wanted no distraction from his political ambitions – certainly not from art. Philip Jourdan, writing in 1911, claimed: 'He feared that he would develop a craze for buying pictures, which, he said, he knew would run him into several hundreds of thousands of pounds, and that he could not afford to spend so much money on a fad.'[32] (The exception was the Reynolds portrait of a young married woman that hung in his dining-room at Groote Schuur: the perfect, trouble-free, surrogate wife). *Truth* got it exactly right in 1901: 'he does not seem to pile up his millions for the sake of living in ostentatious luxury, or cutting a figure in London society, or founding a line of hereditary legislators, but because he has political aims and ambitions, and holds that money is power.'[33]

His political intentions apart, Cecil Rhodes was happy to be inscrutable. His most perverse pleasure was the secret provisions of his will. Rosebery remembered him saying in response to a multitude of accusations that he was a money-grubber and disgrace to the name of Britain, 'All this does not worry me in the least. I have my will here' – he gestured, as if he carried it in his pocket – 'I have my will here, and when they abuse me I think of it, and I know they will read it after I am gone and will do me justice after I am dead.'[34]

The story of Cecil Rhodes is not a subject for pathos: the tale of Barney Barnato is. Of course he had come far from the Whitechapel slums when, in November 1895, the Lord Mayor of London gave a Mansion House banquet for him in recognition of the millions of pounds he had poured into the falling market in the previous months. But the Rothschilds would not accept the invitation; and *The Times* sourly remarked that the Mansion House was no place to glorify a man noted only for his manipulations on the Stock Exchange.[35] Barnato loved the publicity that could come from dispensing champagne to the journalists of less august papers, but, given the choice, he preferred to lunch cheaply on porter and chop. He continued to visit his sister in her East End fried-fish shop. Her soul, like his, lay in 'The Lane'; but she chose happiness in preference to diamonds.[36]

Barney, who once went three times round the Palm Court of the Savoy on his hands, found Society demands exacting. The only picture he liked was a *Group of Sheep* by Sydney Cooper; and that 'because one of the blessed sheep looks exactly like me'.[37] He drank more and more and found Spencer House in St James's Square, which he rented in his last years, oppressive. While his wife went to look for expensive furniture and pictures, he would prefer to go to his parents' grave at Willesden Green.

Opposite the drawing-room windows of Lady Llanover's Stanhope Street House, Barney slowly built a splendid new mansion. Born in 1823, Lady Llanover was pictured by the Countess of Fingall sitting in regal (and immovable) state with her two 'ladies-in-waiting' – the poor relations – as the light was gradually blocked from her windows by the building. For her, and her kind, the image presented by Barnato was of unspeakable vulgarity. For Barney, the mansion, like everything else, became an obsession. 'I shall have the finest

entrance-hall, stairs and dining-room in London', he told
Harry Raymond in Johannesburg in the year of his death. 'So
you are really building at last?' 'Building?' he queried
sharply, 'Oh yes, I am building. I must.'[38]

Unlike other millionaire tragedies, this one was openly
visible. His achievements left him in a state of paranoia which
constantly threatened, like the instability of the stock market
itself, to scatter his fortune – as if he could already hear the
laughing taunts of the Society leaders to whom he felt
perpetual need to prove himself. The delirium, in May 1897,
that led him to see banknotes which crumbled to dust between
his fingers as he counted them, and to look for diamonds in
the wall, was followed by his return to England – and what
was probably suicide, when he jumped overboard on the
voyage. He was not yet forty-five.[39] The coroner's jury
recorded a verdict of 'Death by drowning while temporarily
insane'.

He did not live to see the completion of his new home; but
that was not lost to the plutocracy, for it was bought by
Edward Sassoon, who had succeeded to the baronetcy and
chairmanship of his family firm on the death of his father,
Albert, at the end of 1896. On the top of the house, which
stood in Park Lane, were marble statues which formed the
subject of contemporary anecdotes when attempts were made
to identify them: petrified shareholders, the Twelve Apostles
and bookmakers were some of the suggestions. Sir Edward, in
proof of the fact that plutocratic taste was not quite all of a
kind, gave them to Brighton town council for municipal
decoration.

The social career of the Sassoons was in some ways the most
remarkable of all; one generation changed them from Oriental
merchant Jews to westernized leaders of a European king's
social entourage.[40] The schizophrenic effects were made
visible in their coat-of-arms, with motto in Latin and Hebrew
versions: *Candide et constanter, Emeth ve Emunah.* Edward,
Prince of Wales, had first been entertained by the Sassoons

when he visited India in the 1870s; Bombay received from Sir Albert Sassoon the gift of an enormous, double lifesize equestrian statue of the Prince in uniform a few years later. Sir Albert was one of the many sons of the Patriarch David, who had sent the eldest child of his second wife, Sassoon David Sassoon, to England in 1858 to start an English branch of the family cotton manufacturing and trading firm. Sassoon David died less than a decade after, but not before he had taken the 200-acre estate of Ashley Park in Surrey, with a ballroom that had once been used by the court of Henry VIII from nearby Hampton Court. Other brothers followed him to England – in the end, eight of them – and the consequences made a remarkable story.

Arthur had actually been in London in 1855, when he was taught by the son of the Chief Rabbi before gaining business experience in India and China. He married into a Jewish Italian family and his wife's sister married, in January 1881, Leopold de Rothschild. This last event was important because of the presence of the Prince of Wales in the synagogue, and at the wedding breakfast provided by the Arthur Sassoons. The balding, dusky, thoroughly un-English figure of Arthur, who had changed his name from Abraham Shalom, contrasted not only with most members of English society, but with his delicate wife Eugénie Louise, who proved to be the most brilliant of hostesses and the pacemaker of his social acceptance. Arthur kept to his religion, even when Edward VII was his guest: in Scotland, on the day of Atonement, fasting and the substitution of black clothes and prayer shawl for country tweeds, were a bizarre experience, even if watched from afar, for a pleasure-loving king.

Reuben settled in England in 1867 and, though he had little to do with the business, he exuded an aura of money and what it would buy. When Sir Almeric Fitzroy was lunching at Hampden House in March 1904, the game was Cabinet-making for the King; and if Lord Esher was the obvious Prime Minister, Reuben was first choice for Chancellor of the Exchequer.[41] He was, indeed, able to occupy the unofficial office of keeper of Edward's turf account, keeping track of his purchases and winnings. It would not have been surprising if people thought first of Reuben as a dark-skinned Oriental: he had only adopted Western ways, and Western dress, as an adult and had married into a Baghdadi-Jewish family living in Poona. 'The papers think it funny to call us Othello and Desdemona,' said Mrs Langtry, 'since I've got a very swarthy complexion'.[42]

His ostentatious display of gold and jewelled cuff-links and rings and shirt-studs was not much liked in English society, though his habit of having his beard and moustache trimmed in the manner of Edward VII gave him, in the eyes of the Duke of Manchester, 'a certain resemblance' to the King.[43] He was exotic, certainly, but his exoticism was supported by formidable wealth. On the Prince of Wales's birthday in November 1887, when he was staying at Sandringham, he took a childlike delight in recording that Edward – in receipt of six cigarette cases among his presents – preferred the rarest (and most expensive): the gift, of course, of Reuben Sassoon.[44]

Albert was less close to Edward than Arthur and Reuben; when he came to London permanently in the mid-1870s, his wife remained in India, where the climate was more attractive, and more familiar. Nevertheless, as early as 1873 he became the first Jew to receive the Freedom of the City of London: the opening of the Suez Canal made him, as head of the firm and perhaps the most important businessman in India, a key figure for City bankers and traders – a fact recognized in the knighthood he received from Queen Victoria in 1872. His son, the most significant English member of the next generation of Sassoons, was named Edward Albert after the Prince of Wales, and this was back in 1856, long before he met Victoria's heir.

In 1887, Edward married Aline, 'the noblest of the Rothschilds' – the description of the art historian Bernard Berenson, who advised Lady Sassoon on the purchase of the Hainauer Collection in which she was interested. Aline, daughter of

Baron Gustave de Rothschild of Paris, was beautiful, but brilliant too: it was rather inappropriate that the Prince of Wales should name one of his yachts after her. No one, perhaps, was able to record the extraordinary qualities she possessed; even John Singer Sargent, most esteemed of all Society painters, whose picture of her was the star item in the Royal Academy exhibition of 1907, found it impossible to please her admirers and her family. When Sir Edgar Speyer's wife arrived for her own sitting, the short-tempered artist exploded: 'It seems there is a little something wrong with the mouth! Of course there is something wrong with the mouth! A portrait is a painting with a little something wrong about the mouth!'[45]

Albert Sassoon had one advantage over British-born rivals for power and influence. The opening up of the world brought some strange people, with strange traditions, to London. When the Duke of Portland entertained King Chulalonkorn of Siam in 1897, everyone was taken aback by the loudness of the royal visitor's speech: asked 'whether he would take port, sherry, claret or madeira, he disconcerted the butler exceedingly by shouting "PORT!" at the top of his voice.' It was the custom, evidently, for those of the highest rank to make the most noise.[46]

Who better to cope with such situations than the Sassoons? The Shah of Persia was cordially disliked in British royal and diplomatic circles. (Opinion was divided when he said he wanted to buy Lady Londonderry.) Queen Victoria ('my auspicious sister of sublime nature') was absent from the State Ball given in his honour at Buckingham Palace in 1873; but the Shah met the Prince of Wales, and Albert Sassoon was there to speak Persian to him.[47] The Prince's Equerry, Sir Seymour Fortescue, strongly disapproved of another visit in 1889, when the Shah was visibly bored by the assembly of the fleet at Spithead; for him some of the Shah's retinue were nothing but 'scallawags'.[48] The Shah had come to England for a good reason – the British were worried about Russian strategic designs. But what was to be done with a man who spat his cherry stones on the carpet at a Windsor Castle banquet? Alfred and Ferdinand de Rothschild helped by entertaining him; and Albert Sassoon took over the Empire Theatre to provide a sumptuous ballet and supper until the early hours for several hundred guests: thence to his Brighton home for the weekend. Albert received a baronetcy; Britain obtained mineral concessions. (The Shah, alas, was assassinated shortly after in the Mosque of Shah Abdul Azim, near Tehran: a hard fate for someone who rarely went near a mosque if he could help it.)

All the Sassoons surrounded themselves with ostentatious signposts of their wealth. Reuben managed to have stables at the *top* of one of his houses in Belgrave Square – horses and carriages were conveyed up by lift. Albert, at 25 Kensington Gore, showed where his allegiances lay with the tapestry portrait of Queen Victoria that hung over his fireplace: his arrival to take up residence in London had been marked in a scurrilous rhyme which began:

> Sir Albert Abdullah Sassoon
> That Indian auriferous coon . . .[49]

– but anyone who could hold a ball with the Prince of Wales as guest-of-honour, as he did in 1880, could safely ignore Society gossip. Arthur, at Albert Gate, provided hardly a hint of Eastern origins in his equally sumptuous décor: the tone, set by his wife, was thoroughly European – the best from the most fashionable in style.

It was not in London at all, but in Brighton – 'a sea-coast town, three miles long and three yards broad, with a Sassoon at each end and one in the middle', in Labouchere's description[50] – that the Sassoons most frequently entertained Edward VII. *Vanity Fair* even thought it worth commenting when, in 1908, the King stayed for the first time in his reign with the Duke of Fife at Brighton: the Duke was married to his daughter; the Sassoons were his friends.[51] Reuben's annual party for the Brighton races was described as 'ten days packed from morning to night with entertainment and delightfully amusing people',[52] though it was with 'dear Arthur' that Edward generally stayed: at the end of 1908, for example, to convalesce after illness and in February 1910, in pain and irritable, less than three months before he died. Walking arm-in-arm with the Arthur Sassoons along the promenade, he helped to take the monarchy still further away from aristocratic seclusion into the solidly middle-class institution that it is today. The Sassoon houses were ostentatiously furnished inside, but hardly palaces for a king: Sir Frederick Ponsonby and Sir George Holford had to live in a mere hotel when Edward visited in September 1907 (a hotel from which, moreover, they were locked out after arriving back from a late-night bridge party).[53]

The transformation from Eastern merchant Jew to English country gentleman was completed at Tulchan Lodge in Scotland, 'that delightful lodge and moor in Speyside, that was so long tenanted by the late Mr Arthur Sassoon and his charming wife'.[54] Twice before his accession, and four times after, Edward stayed for a week after the Doncaster races. There was no forest, so no stalking, but the grouse were good – Arthur Sassoon gave a brace to each guest's servants and to anyone who wanted to send them to friends. Driven grouse are difficult to kill, but Edward bagged close on a hundred one day, thirty-five at a single drive. If his host's strict adherence to the demands of the Jewish Day of Atonement seemed tedious, he could always visit the Duke of Richmond at Gordon Castle, forty miles away.[55] But not for preference. What a triumph for a family of trading Jews – none of whom had so much as set foot in Edward's kingdom more than fifty years before.

It was more predictable, but no less significant that the 'aliens' in Edwardian society also included what T. H. S. Escott called the 'trans-Atlantic Midases'. It seems strange now to recall the American reaction to the much more highly developed England in the first half of the nineteenth century.

Emerson, who was last in England in 1847, found that 'There is no country in which so absolute a homage is paid to wealth. In America, there is a touch of shame when a man exhibits the evidence of large property. . . . But the Englishman has pure pride in his wealth, and esteems it a final certificate.'[56] This situation was soon to change for ever, especially on the American side of the Atlantic.

Most of the American millionaires in the Gilded Age that followed had started, Andrew Carnegie observed, 'as poor boys and were trained in the sternest but most efficient of all schools – poverty': sons of poor farmers, like Jay Gould, or, in the case of John D. Rockefeller, of a travelling patent medicine salesman.[57] New York, in the anonymous *Our Best Society* (1905), became the Mecca of the conquerors in life, the rich and successful who contended there for the loudest applause. 'There are just two good things in life . . .', said Mrs Eustace at dinner with the railroad-owning Van Zandts, 'They are love and money' – love was the great illusion; money was the great reality; and permanent comfort came only from reality.[58]

The 'reality' was of a rather peculiar kind at the North Carolina ball given by Pembroke Jones in which a midget negro piccaninny emerged from a giant papier-mâché watermelon to dispense gold cigarette cases and enamel watches to the assembled company.[59] C. F. G. Masterman commented on the waste and extravagance of a plutocracy whose second generation 'pursues its existence through an unreal, fantastic world, in a luxurious expenditure as fantastic as a veritable "Dance of Death"': a world of ice-skating in August, tablecloths of woven roses, of 'one dreadful personage in Boston who wears each costume once, and then has it solemnly cremated by her butler'.[60] None of this implied a society without snobbery; on the contrary the penalty of making one's way in a society without deference was a reinforcement of a multitude of snobberies. Edward VII found it difficult to understand why the Vanderbilts were not fully received in New York Society until Consuelo Vanderbilt married the

Duke of Marlborough.[61] Rich New York businessmen like William Waldorf Astor, who banded together in Tuxedo Park, surrounded themselves by wire fences and sentries to keep outsiders away.

Lord Bryce, who was British ambassador in the United States from 1907–12, went to the heart of the matter when he wrote in *The American Commonwealth*:

> It may seem a paradox to observe that a millionaire has a better and easier social career open to him in England than in America. . . . In America, if his private character be bad, if he be mean or openly immoral, or personally vulgar, or dishonest, the best society may keep its doors closed against him. In England great wealth, skilfully employed, will more readily force these doors open. For in England great wealth can, by using the appropriate methods, practically buy rank from those who bestow it. . . . The existence of a system of artificial rank enables a stamp to be given to base metal in Europe which cannot be given in a thoroughly republican country.[62]

By the late nineteenth century, as England's economic progress began to seem sluggish in comparison with America's the attractions of English Society life became more apparent for men of the New World. Andrew Carnegie found a mood entirely changed from the 'quick pace' Emerson had encountered forty years before. In America, he said, 'Ambition spurs us all on, from him who handles the spade to him who employs thousands. We know no rest.' Britain could teach the Americans 'not to lay up our treasures, but to enjoy them day by day': not for him the sadness of being 'an elderly man occupying his last years grasping for more dollars'.[63] The result was that a number of successful American businessmen made their impact on British society: Albert Stanley, for example, actually a Derby-born emigrant who had started work as a Detroit office boy in 1889. He returned to Britain and a career which eventually took him to the Presidency of the Board of Trade and to a peerage as Lord Ashfield. On the way, he found friendship with 'Tom Tea' (Sir Thomas Lipton) and 'Tom Whisky' (Sir Thomas Dewar).

Predictably, the American wives became a driving force in society. 'We are nothing if not American these days', observed *The Onlooker* in 1913; 'It is the American hostesses who take the lead in anything novel.' The 'Surprise Party' in the American style to be given by the Duchess of Manchester in the March of that year was indeed a 'surprise' in the event, because the Duchess fell ill and could not be there; but it was 'one of the successes of the early season' and those present included not only Vita Sackville-West (in 'the gorgeous costume of an ancestor'), the Duchess of Rutland and Mrs George Keppel (in black: 'nothing suits her so well'), but also Princess San Faustino, 'a more or less new star in the social firmament, and an American to boot'.[64]

Inevitably Marie Corelli, employing an unrecognizably fine distinction in her hierarchy of condemnation, thought the worst sort of plutocratic bounder was 'the starred-and-striped Bounding Millionaire', who had usually made his money by 'sweating' labour or fooling shareholders in trust companies, and who came to Britain 'with the fixed impression that everything in the "darned old place" can be bought for money'. ('Unfortunately', she added, 'he is often right.')[65] Mrs William B. Leeds (whose dress allowance alone was $40,000 a year) was persuaded to pay the entire cost – $80,000 – of the Shakespeare Society Ball held on the occasion of George V's coronation. Elizabeth Drexel Lehr, unhappy wife of Harry Lehr, American 'Society's Jester', explained: 'She loved England. When her husband died she took a house in Grosvenor Square, entertaining royally.' But her money was not enough: ostentation was the word applied to her generosity, accusations of vulgarity the consequence of her extroverted exuberance.[66]

The mixing of the wealth from the visible symbols of the American dream come true with a society whose values contradicted those of that same dream was bound to have uncomfortable results. In some ways, however, the most bizarre case was that of a man whose own fortune had not been made by the application of risk capital and entrepreneurial energy to the developing American economy. The Astor family, owners of large tracts of New York, ranging from part of Fifth Avenue to slum tenements, could simply watch their fortune grow before their eyes; and William Waldorf Astor could turn his attention to other things, chiefly his annoyance that his aunt was able to assert the right to be called *the* Mrs Astor in preference to his wife Mary (Mamie): 'It is not that he wanted her to be *the* Mrs Astor so much as that he wanted to be *the* Mr Astor.'[67] Within seven months of his father's death he had left for England, leaving behind him the possibly apocryphal, but not out of character comment, 'America is not a fit place for a gentleman to live.'

As Margot Asquith observed, 'Rich men's houses are seldom beautiful, rarely comfortable, and never original.'[68] The comment was itself not very original, but interesting in coming from someone who must have seen all the great London houses of the plutocracy. But it was the aristocracy who had started the process by building and developing in what H. G. Wells called 'the Great-House region': Mayfair and St James's, passing south-west to Belgravia, becoming diffused and sporadic westward, its 'last systematic outbreak' round and about Regent's Park.[69] The plutocrats usually began by renting a house with historic associations, as Astor did when he took Lansdowne House in Berkeley Square. When asked why the Astors had become tenants of what the American George W. Smalley called 'a palace rather than a house', Mrs Astor replied that it was 'the only one which gave us the two things we most wanted; perfect cleanliness and good nurseries'.[70] Later they moved to Carlton House Terrace, where an enormous house was used only for a few select dinners in each Season, usually followed by concerts in which Paderewski might be found performing.

After a rather tedious dinner there, the Countess of Warwick discovered to her surprise that her host would leave shortly after her: he preferred to sleep in his estate office on Victoria Embankment, for 'There, at least,' he said, 'I am safe.'[71] H. G. Wells actually called the office 'Astor's strongbox' in *Tono-Bungay*; when 'Daisy' Warwick visited it she was shown the strongroom, which included a row of bags stuffed with sovereigns. Set back from the road and the river, the building had stained-glass mullioned windows and a great 70-foot baronial hall, with beams and rafters carved in Spanish mahogany, and portraits of Astor and his ancestors on the cedar walls. The bedroom contained a François Premier bed, too large for the room, and too small for the tall Astor, whose feet dangled in the fireplace. 'He built it', said Smalley, 'to please himself.'[72]

Inside he could feel safe not only because of the security it provided for some of his most treasured possessions, but also because of the sense of protection it gave him from the attacks that surrounded his Society activities. He brought himself ridicule when he made an announcement in the *Pall Mall Gazette* after a concert in July 1900 that Sir Berkeley Milne had attended without an invitation. Milne, a former commander of the royal yacht *Osborne*, had accompanied the Countess of Orford to the concert at her invitation. The Prince of Wales, who had helped Astor by securing his election to the Carlton Club, immediately invited Milne to join him at the theatre in the royal box the following evening. Astor fled to Marienbad and the cure, pursued by the anger of the *Saturday Review* and the rest of the Conservative press.[73]

For those whose fortunes depended on paper financial transactions rather than the building of giant combines, social recognition was bound to be important in the process of self-justification. 'I don't like your English aristocracy. . . . They are not educated, they are not serious,' Astor said; 'but', he added, 'they do interest me.' Astor quizzed the Countess of Warwick endlessly about aristocratic people, politics, stories.[74] When his first wife died in 1894 he wanted very much to marry Lady Randolph Churchill, partly perhaps for romantic reasons, but also to aid his social acceptance. From 1911, he called himself 'The Honourable', and that was something more than a reminder that he had once been a member of the American Senate. But he quickly discovered that status did not imply popularity: the Milne incident was only one example of his social ineptness. Increasingly Astor turned his energies to compiling a doubtful genealogy, connecting him to the Franco-Spanish nobility.

'I am glad that my Great Grandfather was a successful trader,' he claimed in autobiographical notes, 'because in all ages Trade has led the way of Civilisation.' But this trading family had developed a tradition to which he, in aristocratic fashion, was heir: 'In boyhood I was taught that I and the Estate would some day be one and that my life would be judged by my success or failure in its control.'[75] When he renounced American citizenship he published in his own *Pall Mall Gazette* a table purporting to show his descent from the Counts of Astorga, while his angry former fellow-countrymen tried to show how the family tree was bogus. Astor's ward, John Armstrong Chanler-Chaloner, indicated that a butcher's block with cleaver might be appropriate for his coat-of-arms, in view of John Jacob Astor's humble German origins, and that was gleefully seized upon by William Waldorf's many enemies.[76]

In the circumstances, Astor opted to explore his social fantasies in a curious sort of privacy. High walls, topped with glass, surrounded his 300-acre Cliveden estate. The Duke of Westminster's Cliveden had many historical associations – George III's father had used the house on the site as a summer residence. Astor's tenure began with a row with the Duke over the ownership of the visitor's book, which he claimed was part of the contents. He tried, and failed, to enlarge the boundaries of the estate by purchases from a neighbour: 'There are men to whom money is not everything, nor even the first thing', George W. Smalley commented. 'Cliveden as the Duke sold it was a beautiful thing; Barry's façade looking down on the gentle Thames from its lofty terrace, amid woods and over fields of a soft multi-coloured greenness only to be seen in perfection in England.'[77] Astor transformed the interior with a Louis XIV drawing-room, dining-room taken from a French château, hall which became a gallery of art treasures. 'The place is splendid', Lady Randolph Churchill wrote to her son Jack; 'Mr Astor has a great deal of taste.'[78] If so, it was all very studied, a fitting background for his rigidly formal weekend parties which were planned to the last detail months ahead.

He also bought Hever Castle, in Kent, before giving Cliveden to his son. Outside the castle – which had moat, portcullis, drawbridge and battlements – he built a village in Tudor style for guests, and altogether occupied 800 workmen for five years in making changes. He was disappointed that the Society for Psychical Research was unable to find signs of the ghost of Anne Boleyn there; some said that his modernizations had driven her out of her birthplace. But at night, with his drawbridge up, secure in his fortress, he might wander from room to room, past the Holbein portraits of Anne and Henry VIII, the Titian of Philip II of Spain, the armour worn by Francis I and Henry II of France and the bedroom slippers of Elizabeth I.

Astor's most public attempts to win influence were never very successful. He eschewed politics, for his defeat in the American Senate elections of 1881 had made him certain that democracy was not for him. His most energetic attempt to further his interests was through the press: if he paid all the bills at the *Pall Mall Gazette* he expected to be able to direct the policy. In this at least he shared a belief with the other great American millionaire of the period who was attracted to life in Britain – Andrew Carnegie. 'I do not think I would care much to enter Parliament even if I were a British citizen', Carnegie wrote in 1885. 'The press is the true source of power in Britain as in America. The time of Parliament is consumed discussing trifling affairs.'[79]

Carnegie used the newspapers he owned with the radical MP for Newcastle, Samuel Storey, to attack the House of

Lords, not to make money. But his attack on the perils of hereditary wealth and position was also an elitist defence of the American system – the system intended to provide the opportunity for anyone who worked hard to achieve riches and power beyond all dreams. He had himself come from the poorest of Dunfermline homes: an emigrant to America in 1848, where he began life as a messenger boy but enjoyed a rapid rise through the hierarchy of Pennsylvania railroads in the next two decades. As the man who subsequently built up the largest steel company in the world, his forthright conclusion was that the suppression of energy and ability was a far more serious danger than plutocracy could ever be.[80]

The idea that the fittest, having survived, should reap the rewards, was common to many businessmen. Carnegie was not preaching a doctrine of equality when he wrote: 'The best king or family of kings in the world is not worth one drop of an honest man's blood.'[81] It was clear that meritocracy in a world which still found an important place for elitist ideas and institutions spelt plutocracy. When Carnegie compiled his list of the twenty greatest men in the history of the world, his preferences were readily apparent: Bessemer, Watt, Stephenson, Bell, Franklin (for 'discovering' electricity), Neilson (for his role in improving iron manufacturing) were all included. 'All these began as manual workers,' said Carnegie. 'There is not one rich nor titled leader in the whole list. All were compelled to earn their bread.' Their merit was not hereditary; it lay in their massive ability to create wealth. Accordingly, they were to enjoy the benefits that accrued.*[82]

Those benefits were typically plutocratic. Andrew Carnegie

---

* The *Review of Reviews* circulated Carnegie's list to 'the ten greatest living men' – most of whom 'were too busy to reply' – and also to a hundred other eminent figures, in order to make comparisons. The ex-German Chancellor, Prince Von Bülow, indicated the priorities of the class of European statesmen who were to start the First World War when he chose Caesar, Hannibal, Napoleon and Bismarck. Sir Joseph Lyons, the founder of the catering and restaurant chain, opted for Marconi, Darwin and King Edward. The latter, like Karl Marx, managed only one vote in the entire symposium.

liked the romance of castles; but not without modern comforts. His Skibo, in Scotland, where he spent five months a
year, was to have local stone *and* Pittsburgh steel in its
construction. In New York he was willing to build a house at
Ninety-first Street and Fifth Avenue before the rush of the
aspiring rich and fashionable there; but in Scotland, the
country of his family roots, he wanted to express a pride
which demanded a modern version of baronial splendour.
His friend Sir Charles Macara, the cotton manufacturer, who
had been born nearby, made the point simply: 'The dozen
miles around my native place seem to have been fertile soil for
the production of big men.'[83] Now the 'big men' would return
to claim their heritage – a heritage, in Carnegie's case, which
was sought in the purchase of the ruined castle of Skibo, with
an estate twenty miles across, for £90,000 in 1896.

'Skibo was once old and I believe Mr Carnegie would have
liked to keep it old', George W. Smalley wrote for Sunday
readers of the *New York Tribune*; 'but his architect warned
him there was no compromise between leaving it a ruin and
rebuilding from the foundations. He chose the latter, and the
result is that Skibo is probably the newest old castle in the
world.' The Duke of Sutherland was happy enough: 'He
bought a good deal of my land which I wanted to sell', the
Duke was reported to have said, 'and paid me a good price.'[84]
But the ninety-foot swimming pool was not entirely in the
tradition of the ancient laird. John Morley, the Liberal
politician who befriended Carnegie, surveyed it with his
detective in 1911. It reminded the latter 'of the *parvenooe*'.
'Impudent fellow', said Morley, who evidently agreed.[85]

Woodrow Wilson, who was a visitor before he became
President of the United States, thought that the castle was
'like a luxurious hotel. . . . There was everything to do that
you can think of.'[86] Eighty-five servants; a Scottish piper
outside one's bedroom at eight o'clock; breakfast to a background of organ music; trout and salmon fishing, golf and
shooting (though not with Carnegie for this last activity); and
reading in the 25,000 volume library – titles selected by

Lord Acton.[87] Edward VII, when he drove over to luncheon from Dunrobin, was greeted by the reading of Joaquin Miller's florid poem which began: 'Hail fat Edward'. The observation of the King's physical appearance was accurate enough, but – as George W. Smalley told his American audience – 'it is not the custom to dwell on these matters with royalty'.[88] Sir Thomas Lipton used to tell the story that the King had been met by a dripping wet figure in bathing costume: the organist, rushed from the swimming pool to play 'God Save the King' behind a screen which chose to collapse on Edward's entry.

Carnegie liked to win. 'I am beating my friends at golf so all goes well', he wrote in the late 1890s. 'I played eighteen holes today with Taylor. Beat him! Beat Murray Butler Saturday. Beat Franks the day before.'[89] Skibo, situated in what was for him 'the land of childhood, the fairyland', signified his triumph in the struggle of life. When Edward VII visited it, he was able to show him 'my title to nobility' – a handbill in which an appeal for £300 had been made to defend his Chartist uncle from conspiracy charges.[90] How excited he had been, back in 1881, when he reached Scotland and encountered the seat of the Duke of Buccleuch: 'A real castle at last. . . . You want the moors, the hills and glens, and all the flavour of feudal institutions to give a castle its dignity and impress you with the thoughts of by-gone days.'[91] From childhood he could remember the struggles of Dunfermline people – among them his uncle and grandfather – to win rights to use the Pittencrief estate, on the edge of the town. At the end of 1902, after long-drawn-out discussions, he was able to purchase it for £45,000. 'My new title beats all', he wrote to John Morley. 'I am Laird of Pittencrief. . . . I laugh at the importance of it. It really tickles me.'[92] He had conquered – that had to be registered – but Dunfermline working men could enjoy the inheritance: a public park.

Like most of the other plutocrats, Andrew Carnegie engaged in spectacular philanthropy. Before his essays on 'Wealth' appeared in the *North American Review* in 1889 – they were later republished in book form as *The Gospel of Wealth* – his endowments were sporadic and sentimental in kind: an organ to the church in Allegheny where his family had worshipped in the 1850s, for example. The argument he later presented was that the rich man should spend his fortune in his lifetime to further the social good and social progress. The distribution should take place on a rational, scientific basis. And in practice? Well, the *Literary Digest* listed his benefactions, totalling more than $350,000,000. Relatively little of the residue of his estate – less than a tenth of this – went to relations and friends, for whom, he said, he had already provided a sufficiency.[93] He even offered prizes for the best idea as to how he might give away his fortune: a strange problem this – how to stop his money making more money.

An obituary on his death argued that he would be remembered, if not as the earliest, certainly as 'the most ambitious and energetic of the rich men from the West, who marked the reaction against the selfish, sensational, but commonplace plutocracy of the United States'. No one had mourned Jay Gould when he had died in 1892: with Midases of his kind and with the whole host of Wall Street 'bosses' Carnegie had no commercial practices in common.[94] But it was not quite as simple as that. Carnegie himself explained that steps had to be taken to avoid a 'degrading pampering tendency' on the recipients; those to be helped especially were 'the industrious and the ambitious; not those who need everything done for them' – the local administration or the state should help the latter. Self-improvement was the key factor; and his priorities for funds were universities, libraries, hospitals, parks and public halls for meetings or concerts.[95]

The furtherance of peace had been a preoccupation of his since the late 1880s, and he gave enormous sums as an endowment for International Peace. No one could deny that the design was a grand one; nor – and more to the point – that it brought him much international acclaim. There is no doubt that he took delight in being directly involved with the activities of his philanthropic foundations. *Town Topics* imagined him dying happy in the knowledge of the eternal renown he was to receive, waiting for Charon to ferry him over the Styx. A writer, it was suggested, had cut his throat because Carnegie's free libraries had prevented him from making a proper living. The millionaire was not sympathetic: 'at least I am sure of my fame', he said. Not so, the writer replied – authors are the voice of posterity; 'none but they and those whom they are willing to quote can get a hearing.' At this, it was said, the millionaire was 'so sorry for what he had done that he tried to come back to Skibo to lead a different life'.[96]

It was symptomatic of the dislike aroused by the plutocrats from overseas that there should be this attempt to deny Carnegie the last word his bank balance usually gave him. Carnegie, it seems, grew tired of public derision no less than public praise. Most of all he liked to retreat with his family to a cottage, later a house, on the Skibo estates – without guests or servants: but with many memories. There was the same strange quality surrounding the lives of all the millionaires who arrived in England at the end of the nineteenth century: Astor behind his drawbridge, Wernher and Beit and Robinson and Barnato behind the closed doors of their Mayfair palaces. Often rejected and rebuffed, they sought the comfort of tiny private kingdoms over which they could exercise complete control. Only the Sassoons truly thrived in the land they adopted: a splendid reminder at the very height of the European domination of the world that the East was soon to emerge from its slumbers.

Chapter 10

Finance to the Helm

The City of London was the centre of plutocratic activity: the financiers who ran it were untainted by contact with anything but money. Perhaps for that reason their impact on British society was more straightforward than that of the millionaires from America and the Empire: straightforward, but not necessarily the same in each case. Anyone prepared to probe behind the traditionally inscrutable façade of the financier – inscrutable except for its greed – would find at least three categories of City plutocrat. There were the financial aristocrats, above all the Rothschilds, already well on their way to social respectability; there were the newer Europeans, most magnificently represented in the towering presence of Sir Ernest Cassel; and there were the noisy, noisome figures – the company promoters who, like Ernest Hooley, bounced up and down and back again.

First the froth. Ernest Hooley was systematic in his approach to a career which, in his own unreliable judgment, made him at thirty-six 'twice a millionaire, an acquaintance of the Royal family, and the most-sought-after-man in England'. A newspaper cartoon showed him seated in disdain, while Lord Salisbury – in the presence of the assembled heads of the European states – asked him to buy Crete. The Hon. Helen Henniker introduced him to London Society at a dinner party given specifically 'to meet Mr Hooley',[1] and he took a lease on the Hill Street London house of the dowager Lady Hindlip (herself a representative of the plutocracy through her late husband, the brewery owner).[2] His critics pictured 'a grotesque panorama' there, where 'Real "swells" jostled against shoddy "swells", and very soon the crowd of parasitic hangers-on was swollen by importunate creditors and the inevitable "writters"': altogether a subject for a modern Hogarth – *The Promoter's Progress*.[3]

In the country, finding Risley Hall in Derbyshire too small to satisfy his ambitions, Hooley bought the Papworth Hall estate, Cambridge, from James Masker, founder (with Julius Drewe) of the Home and Colonial Stores. It was sixteen miles in circumference, with a Georgian house adorned by Corinthian pillars, and he spent £250,000 on improvements – plus £40,000 for 'My old friend' Maple to provide furnishings. In Monte Carlo, Hooley bought up a thousand bottles of 1809 cognac from a bankrupt Paris hotel; in his own words, he flung money around to acquire 'a houseful of costly china, pictures, bronzes', everything that 'cultured people are supposed to possess'. Astonishing that this man became High Sheriff of Cambridgeshire and Huntingdonshire and thereby a magistrate and Deputy-Lieutenant of the two counties – how he enjoyed going to meet Mr Justice Matthew, judge on the Assizes circuit, 'in my gorgeous scarlet uniform', in a carriage drawn by four big bay horses!

Even after his bankruptcy, Hooley publicly declared, 'I am living at the rate of £15,000 a year, and shall continue to do so.'[4] The Sunday *Daily Mail* examined 'How Ernest Terah Hooley lives as the Gentleman Farmer and the Lord of the Manor'. 'Officially Mr Hooley is a beggar', the paper said; 'practically he is nothing of the sort, but a very well-to-do country gentleman.'[5] The worst social result of his bankruptcy seemed to be his forced resignation from all the clubs – the Carlton, Badminton and Royal Thames Yacht Club among

Sir Ernest Cassel

Ernest Terah Hooley

The Music Room at William Lever's Thornton Manor 1903

them – to which he had gained entry. But social disapproval from the institutions of Society ended dreams too: he could say goodbye to royalty and all that.

The Rothschilds demand more attention.[6] They did not have quite the same need to force themselves on royalty. The three brothers, Nathaniel, Leopold and Alfred – grandsons of the founder of the English branch of the firm – were all born in the 1840s and all died in the First World War; in their youth they were at Trinity College, Cambridge, with Edward, Prince of Wales. In 1886 *Society in London* described how their generation had been transformed from bankers to 'a race of social potentates', to a large extent by the favour of the Prince of Wales.[7] There were certainly rumours three years later that the unexpected passing over of Lord Cottesloe for Nathaniel as Lord Lieutenant of Buckinghamshire was the result of the Prince's favour.[8]

It was through the Rothschilds that Jews began to be accepted by Society.[9] They recruited their staff from their own race 'as religiously as they keep their firm to their own family', it was said, but 'The modish or well-born Gentiles, who stand well with them, are rewarded with snug director-ships.'[10] Marriage with non-Jews could be especially useful: Hannah, daughter of Baron Mayer de Rothschild and great friend of Mrs Arthur Sassoon, married the future Prime Minister Rosebery – a fair reward for her two-million-pound fortune.

Marriage and the judicious cultivation of Gentiles was one thing. More important was a seat in the House of Lords. It was well into the nineteenth century that a radical pamph-leteer wrote: 'You may knock down Nathan Rothschild, though he is a very rich man . . . and the justices will only charge you a few shillings for the liberty you have taken; but if you knock down a peer, though he is ever so insolent, it is almost as bad as murder.'[11] Long after 1850, Lord Granville wrote in a note to Queen Victoria, 'The notion of a Jew peer is startling' – though, he said, it was possible that republicanism in the City might be discouraged by the creation of a Rothschild peer.[12] The Queen refused, in 1869, to honour Lionel de Rothschild, because he made his money by 'a species of gambling . . . far removed from the legitimate trading which she *delights to honour*, in which men have raised themselves by patient industry and unanswering probity to positions of wealth and influence': manufacturers were one thing, money men another.[13]

Lionel's son, Nathaniel Rothschild, reflecting the changes of the 1880s, became Lord Rothschild in 1885. Nothing indicates that he wanted to use the Lords as a political power base; he remained a loyal Unionist after 1886, but was rarely heard debating. He wanted and obtained recognition of his wealth and position in society by his peerage: the very form of title he chose – plain Lord Rothschild – put the seal on his family's supremacy. In private the House of Lords was the object of his sarcasm,[14] but he had no objections when his relation by marriage, Cyril Flower, abandoned an active Commons career for the Lords. Flower's Rothschild wife Constance had written to her sister when he became a Whip in 1886: 'It means real work and no hunting, no dinners and a great deal of London.'[15] It soon became clear that political life in the Commons meant too many sacrifices: Constance recognized realities in noting later that her husband would never take the same position in the Lords that he had had in the House of Commons;[16] but, as Lady Fanny Marjoribanks made clear at dinner with Sir Algernon West in August 1892: 'Cyril Flower wanted a Peerage.' Another member of the Rothschild clan joined the Lords of the land.[17]

Nathaniel, the first Lord Rothschild, was a sort of unofficial King of the Jews. And yet, while his role in the Royal Commission on Alien Immigration in 1902 may have had tempering consequences on the Act that followed, his family's social activities had ensured that it was English first, Jewish second.[18] He showed sympathy, unlike the other members of the Commission, when interviewing a typical Lithuanian Jew – hungry and bulbous-eyed – but would insist on calling him 'my good fellow'. Why was there a constant flow of Jews into England: well, 'they all expect to be leetle Rothschilds!' Sir Almeric Fitzroy took delight in recording: 'Collapse of the great Rothschild, to the huge merriment of the auditory.'[19]

Lord Rothschild was head of the firm after 1879, and remained much preoccupied with business; he was the quietest, most English member of the family in his generation. Leopold, the youngest of the three brothers, made his impact as a pleasure-loving sportsman: much spoilt as a child, he had been named after Queen Victoria's uncle, the King of the Belgians, and was an altogether more flamboyant figure – one of the first people in England to own a car. His racing activities were pursued with genuine fervour; his great pleasure at his election to the Jockey Club in 1891 was not solely based on the social prestige that went with membership.[20] The Hon. George Lambton thought he was over-proud of his horses: 'Excitable and emotional, with a quick temper, I have known him flare up and attack people sometimes without reason', Lambton commented.

Lambton watched Leopold's St Frusquin ('the horse looking beautiful') and the Prince of Wales's Persimmon ('rather irritable, the sweat running off him, and not looking in the least like a Derby winner') on the Downs before the 1896 Derby. The list of owners in this Derby – like others of the period – made a roll-call of the plutocracy: Leopold with his St Frusquin and Gulistan, Lord Brassey, son of the railway contractor Thomas Brassey, with two horses, Sir Ernest Cassel with his Toussaint. It was later suggested that Leopold had allowed the Prince's horse to win and the following month St Frusquin defeated Persimmon in the Princess of Wales's Stakes at Newmarket:[21] but as a Rothschild he might, perhaps, take comfort in the silver model of his horse commissioned by his wife from the Russian court jeweller, Fabergé.[22]

Alfred de Rothschild was different again: physically, with his light colouring, tan-coloured hair and drooping moustache; and, too, in his great enthusiasm for art.[23] His dilettante's approach to the arts and music and life probably reflected his deep love of luxury – he was the sort of man who would condemn March for being the end of the strawberry season – though chronic indigestion often kept him from food and drink, and chronic hypochondria often took him to the medicine cabinet. The extravagance of a mink foot-warmer was some compensation.[24]

No one quite achieved the style of the Rothschilds, in town or country, in the entertainment of royalty. They had 'practically annexed' part of Buckinghamshire, it was said in 1886, 'though, with characteristic caution, their actual investments in land are much smaller than is generally supposed.'[25] And when, in May 1890, even Queen Victoria made a private visit to see Ferdinand and his sister, royal acceptance of the Jewish bankers had come a very long way indeed. Ferdinand, who was the son of the Viennese Anselm de Rothschild, had long been useful to the Prince of Wales; he was prepared to hold a late-night supper party at Edward's request to enable the Duke of Aumale to meet Sarah Bernhardt.[26] (It was not his fault that none of the English ladies present would speak to the French actress; or that the Duke was deaf). When Ferdinand visited Lodge Hill, near Aylesbury, in the 1870s, there was nothing there but a few cottages; on land purchased from the Duke of Marlborough he built a palace on the bare hill-top, dominating a 3,000-acre park. Nature was changed by the application of money (and imagination); even the old trees, which 'contribute so much to the beauty of the place' (Edward VII's chauffeur observed), had been transplanted, 'a special apparatus having been constructed to bear them to their new resting-places.'[27]

Eustace Balfour, who built Alfred Beit's Park Lane house, thought 'The whole is in wonderfully good taste and the views are magnificent' – an opinion which contrasted sharply with his attitude to Alfred de Rothschild's Halton, where Edward had been at the house-warming: 'I have seldom seen anything more terribly vulgar. . . . Outside it is a combination of a French Château, and a gambling house. Inside it is badly

planned . . . and gaudily decorated. . . . Oh! but the hideous-
ness of everything, the showiness! the sense of lavish wealth
thrust up your nose! the course mouldings; the heavy gilding
always in the wrong place, the colour of the silk hanging!'
Any tea served in Sèvres china, with gold teaspoons, was
bound to be unpleasant.[28]

Sir Algernon West, who stayed there in November 1891,
remembered 'An exaggerated nightmare of gorgeousness and
senseless and ill-applied magnificence'. The place appeared to
grow on him with familiarity – on Christmas Day 1895 it was
'quite tolerable' when 'lighted up and full of well-dressed
people' – but West was too provincially English to enthuse
about dinners at which eight nationalities might be represented, including Austrian (Mrs Sassoon), Portuguese (the
Marquis de Soveral), Indian (Prince Dhuleep Singh), French
(Baron Alphonse de Rothschild), and the Brazilian and
Belgian ambassadors.[29] Cosmopolitan riches displaced but did
not replace rural aristocratic England; and the village, Lady
Battersea noted, was 'an unknown entity to Alfred': 'he never
tried to understand the lives and conditions of the inhabitants'.[30] He saw the country as a rest from the business of the
Rothschild offices at New Court, an opportunity to entertain
more lavishly and for a longer period than in London. Startled
guests would watch him in the middle of his Aubusson-
carpeted private circus ring, cracking his whip while his
white side-whiskers shook and the King sat lazily lolling with
half-closed eyes.[31] How often the ludicrous broke into the
vision of gorgeous majesty!

The plutocrats judged, and were judged, by what could be
seen; and that was usually what could be bought. The obsession with the surface veneer was beautifully symbolized
by the discovery, on Alfred's death, that the drains of his
famous London home, Seamore Place, were dangerously
insanitary. People went there to be entertained in luxurious
surroundings, to forget how the rest of the world lived, to
avoid what existed in themselves, in the souls which were in
constant retreat from the physical pleasures of food and wine.

If you were Miss Rothschild, the Duke of Manchester moodily commented, you could raise the height of your room several feet just because you wanted to. 'A millionaire may have as many whims and fancies as he likes for all I care'; but he ought not to be rude – especially to a duke. The trouble was that he could, and Lord Rothschild was; and the Duke left his supper table in disgust.[32] The message from the 'New Reign' of Edward VII, the King who was the regular guest of the Rothschild Jews, was that 'royalty makes itself sadly cheap nowadays.' And sadly expensive for impoverished dukes like Manchester.[33]

When one of Edward VII's early biographers discussed the late King's greatest friends outside official circles he did not choose the Rothschilds, despite their frequent presence in Edward's party. He singled out instead Sir Ernest Cassel and a 'much maligned, but eminently just and generous person', the Baron Maurice de Hirsch.[34] Hirsch, blackballed in France by the Rue Royale Club, banned from the Austrian court, was an odd friend for a prince who might choose his associates from all the great families of Europe. But no dinner at Marlborough House, Edward's London home before his accession, was right without *Parfait au Hirsch* – according to Henry Labouchere.

Hirsch, who had bought himself a title in 1869, first made contact with the Prince of Wales in the 1880s, apparently through the Crown Prince Rudolf of Austria, to whom he made at the same time a substantial loan. His prodigious working habits continued as his social career developed: exercise at 5 am, followed by black coffee and dry bread and then, on his estates in Moravia, no matter whom he was entertaining, he worked for the first eight hours of the day.[35] Edward stayed with him a number of times, sometimes combining state business with pleasure: thus in October 1891 he took the opportunity to have talks with the Austrian foreign minister and the Russian ambassador in Vienna.

The previous year, after a hectic Season in London (for

which Hirsch had taken what was later to be Julius Wernher's Bath House), the Prince had shocked the Austrian court by lunching the King of Greece and the baron together in a Vienna hotel; thence on a special train to the Hirsch estates for shooting. And such shooting too! The Duke of Portland recorded that some guests would stay for six weeks, shooting every day, including Sundays: moderate shots became good simply from the amount of practice they had.

Jennie, Lady Randolph Churchill, pictured the scene at St Johann, Hirsch's castle on the Hungarian frontier: shortly after breakfast, eight or ten victorias would arrive at the door, the horses in gay harnesses, the postilions in hussar-like blue jackets, Hessian boots and shiny, high-crowned hats. At the agreed meeting-place, everyone would draw up in a line until the sound of a bugle and the cry *Vorwarts!* started a sport which enlisted the aid of six hundred or more beaters. They would cover long distances over sandy plains, searching out the enormous blue hares that hid in the stubble, or the game that took refuge in the rare patches of woodland.[36] Edward was not present during the four weeks Harry Stonor spent there in 1894, but the results were not untypical: six to eight guns shot 22,996 partridges, 11,346 hares, 2,912 pheasants, 23 roe, 357 rabbits and 30 creatures of other kinds.[37]

The lavish scale of Hirsch's entertaining was not the only way in which he made himself agreeable company. At the end of 1889 the British ambassador in Paris had worked hard to suppress rumours that the Prince owed large sums of money in various unsavoury quarters; Hirsch came to his aid.[38] The baron was not always so generous, at any rate according to his enemies: Lady Augusta Fane was dining at the short-lived but famous Amphitryon Club in Albemarle Street in the 1880s when she encountered an elderly lady 'who looked like a German hausfrau', with her husband, who was complaining bitterly over the price on the bill for 'potato chips'; that was Hirsch and his wife – but then, as Lady Augusta observed, it is only the impecunious who never query their bills.[39]

At the back of Hirsch's mind, there was always the unrealistic fear of sliding back to the circumstances out of which he had come. The German diplomat, Baron von Eckhardstein, who watched Hirsch's hand tremble when he held a gold louis at Monte Carlo, noted his worry 'that playing might be the beginning of my going downhill'.[40] On the other hand, money brought power too: the Paris Jockey Club blackballed him, but he could, and did, revenge himself by buying the Club and the site on which it was built. He used money to buy influence, but was resentful that he had to be so free with it: 'London society cares more for money than any other in the world, as I know to my cost!' he once exclaimed. The comment stemmed from his fear that his son Lucien, who 'does not like society, or racing, or any of the things that I care for', would be captured for his money; and yet, as he told Margot Tennant, he had discovered that his ideal candidate, Lady Katie Lambton, later Duchess of Leeds, was not to be bought.[41]

All this put his philanthropic activities – especially his help for the Jews – into some sort of context. In December 1888 Jacob Schiff wrote to Ernest Cassel on a matter 'which lies outside business, but in which you, with your good heart, will be greatly interested'. Would he ask Hirsch to provide a large sum to establish an agricultural bank to help the European Jews who were pouring into America? Cassel agreed, and later Hirsch started a fund to help the Jews: 'I feel quite certain', Schiff told Cassel the following year, 'that your intervention has been the controlling consideration with Baron Hirsch.'[42] Hirsch also devoted his turf winnings to charitable purposes – as much as £30,000 in 1892 when he won the Oaks, St Leger, One Thousand Guineas and Cambridgeshire with a single horse; but he gave eleven million pounds to the Jewish Colonization Association, and perhaps twenty millions to all his philanthropic activities. Twenty millions!

From 1884, Hirsch had begun to be friendly with Cassel, then fast making his remarkable way upwards in international finance; and one of the most important things Hirsch ever did was to introduce his younger companion to the Prince of

Wales. The result was soon reflected in letters such as the one
which came from Sandringham on 27 December 1896:

> General Sir Dighton O'Dwyer, Comptroller of the House-
> hold of the Prince and Princess of Wales, presents his
> compliments to Mr Cassel, and writes by direction of the
> Prince and Princess of Wales to invite him to pay Their
> Royal Highnesses a visit at Sandringham from Saturday
> the 2nd of January, to remain till Monday the 4th.
>
> The best train for Mr Cassel to travel down by will be that
> which leaves St Pancras (on Saturdays) at 3.55 p.m. and
> arrives at Wolferton . . . Station for Sandringham at *6.30*.
>
> Conveyances will be sent to Wolferton to meet all guests,
> servants and luggage coming by that train.[43]

Prince and man of money might well have stared strangely
at each other on their first encounter for, as the years passed
at least, it became quite difficult to tell them apart. Sonia
Keppel, daughter of Edward's last and much-loved mistress,
Alice, would meet both of them, often with Sir Thomas
Lipton, at the home of her parents' neighbours, Lord and
Lady Alington. Like the King, Cassel had a beard, wore
rings and smoked cigars; it was no surprise that he too would
usually receive a curtsy.[44] Sigmund Münz, who lunched with
Cassel at the Waldsmühle restaurant near Marienbad in the
year the King died, was struck by the financier's placid but
penetrating and watchful brown eyes; his shoulders and neck
were heavy, expressing, perhaps, a rigid strength and independence: altogether there was an unusual assurance about
the man, though with it, too, went a clouded brow.[45] Sir Felix
Semon, Edward's doctor and himself a German Jew, thought
him 'of distinctly Jewish type, with an almost bald head,
short full beard, big nose . . . carefully but ostentatiously
dressed, anything but a causeur, usually taciturn, not a public
speaker.'[46]

Always very thick-set, Cassel developed an almost obsessive
fear of the obesity which gradually overtook him; and this

may have helped, with the gout from which he also suffered, to explain his explosive bad temper.[47] The Duchess of Sermonetta, friend of his daughter, came to know only too well the clenching of fists at the dinner table – the signal for some furious outburst to follow.[48] When 'Kingy' came to tea with Mamma, Sonia Keppel played a game in which bread and butter would be pushed, butter-side down, along a royal leg – for penny bets as to which was the most buttery piece. Cassel, by contrast, remained a distant, awesome figure: a sort of 'living form of gilt-edged security, a likeness which was enhanced by his wearing shirts with broad parallel stripes on them, like the bars in front of a cashier's desk'.[49]

Nothing better symbolized his refusal to show his true feelings than his relationship with Chaim Wasserman, who had been born in the same year as him in Cologne and who remained all his life a largely unobserved, covert link with the world into which he had been born. Few of his Society friends even knew of Wasserman's existence.[50] This was a reserved, withdrawn man, indiscreet not in his conversation but in the inarticulate display of wealth with which he surrounded himself; and most at peace, perhaps, away from all that in the silence of snow-covered mountains. He was eventually to acquire a holiday home on the south-east side of the Aletsch Glacier, but the Alps had always appealed to him. In July 1890, at Chamonix in the French Alps with his sister and nephew and Jacob Schiff's family, he saved the life of Schiff's daughter, who had broken her shoulder in slipping over a precipice. 'Say to Mr Cassel he is to me the most lovely man in existence', she told her father two years later.[51]

People were not usually so kind. His lack of warmth made him disliked; his Jewish birth made him distrusted. Cassel's wife, who died after only three years of marriage in 1881, had wanted him to become a Roman Catholic, and, indeed, when he himself finally died his memorial service was held at the Jesuit Church of the Immaculate Conception. But his approach to religion mirrored all else about him: it was unsensual, businesslike, secretive. Sir Almeric Fitzroy, who as Clerk to the Privy Council had to make arrangements for Cassel's acceptance as a councillor in 1902, noted in early September: 'I am still without exact information whether Cassel is a Jew or a Christian: further there are rumours that he may turn out a Roman Catholic.' He discovered from Lord Rothschild a few days later that Cassel had responded to his wife's 'earnest solicitation' on her death-bed.[52] There was a strange repeat of the same situation when Edward's son, George V, was proclaimed king in May 1910. According to the Conservative politician George Wyndham, 'The Jews of the Privy Council took their oaths on the Old Testament and the Catholics separately. Among these last, to the general surprise, Cassel.'[53]

Cassel's attempts to make his way in Society had begun long before he met Edward VII. The Countess of Fingall remembered being introduced by Lord Mayo's brother, the great huntsman Harry Bourke, to 'a stout Teutonic gentleman in a pink coat, looking rather uncomfortable in it and on the horse'; but Cassel, in these early days, had 'kind eyes', 'a rich voice', wit and charm, to make up for his lack of ability in country pursuits.[54] The daughter of the Earl of Rosslyn also encountered him, in the period when he rented Lord Willoughby de Broke's Compton Verney: 'It was because of his indomitable pluck and not because of his full purse, that Sir Ernest Cassel was received in Warwickshire society', she said: he could never ride well, but two or three falls a day and unkind laughter left him undaunted – everything he did, she might have added with greater point, was totally singleminded. Invited to a ball he gave at Dalby in Leicestershire, she was suitably impressed by the solid mass of lilies-of-the-valley that lined the walls of the hall and staircase.[55]

After he acquired Moulton Paddocks, near Newmarket, in 1899, Cassel entertained Edward VII there each year: only the bloater the King had sent over specially from the Jockey Club for breakfast each morning defeated him in supplying every want, however idiosyncratic, of his demanding guest. Other estates were bought by him in the last decade of his life:

Six Mile Bottom and Upper Hare Park, near Cambridge, and Branksome Dene, near Bournemouth. But it was in London, in urban luxury, that he was happier. From 1877 to 1889 he lived in Bayswater; then in Grosvenor Square; and in 1905 he bought Lord Tweedmouth's Brook House in Park Lane, which underwent three years of alterations before it was ready for him.

As King, Edward abandoned his former pattern of dining out in London: he visited the plutocracy at their country seats but rarely at their London palaces.[56] But his presence could be felt in Brook House, where the hall contained his portrait, and that of Cassel, on either side: in the dim light, the Countess of Warwick observed after she had lunched there, it was difficult to judge which was which – though the King was, perhaps, a little darker. She thought that, while Cassel had 'nothing of the Rothschild flair', he had improved the house greatly, especially by transforming Lord Tweedmouth's big billiard-room into a dining-room.[57] This dining-room, indeed, could seat a hundred people. Sir Almeric Fitzroy described it some years later, also after lunching with Cassel: 'a magnificent chamber with arcuated ends, the entrance to which is flanked with Corinthian columns, and the walls hung with four superb Van dykes [sic]', 'It is the great merit of your Jew of taste', he added, 'that he never overloads his walls with pictures: a selection in excellence is his aim.'[58]

The Van Dycks had been found on commission by the great art dealer Joseph Duveen, but it may be that Sir Ernest's interest in art and other treasures was the result of his sense that they were a prerequisite if monarchy or aristocracy were to be entertained. Appropriately, he liked jade, and he bought well-known silver – the Tudor 'Bacon cup', for example. The exterior of the house, like the man, was comparatively neglected; the interior might well be – and probably has been – described as a miracle of exquisite bad taste. Eight hundred tons of marble took a year to obtain from Michelangelo's quarry in Tuscany. The entrance lobby, the hall, the stairway, even the six kitchens were marble lined, some of them with a rare blue variety from Canada; the lobby was also panelled in lapis lazuli, the hall rising to a glass dome four storeys upwards, the Corinthian columns at the entrance to the dining-room twenty feet in height and supporting a gallery.

His granddaughter's friends nicknamed it the 'Giant's Lavatory'.[59]

Cassel was an obvious target for social jibes, some – it is true – not too ill-natured: when he was made a KCMG he asked Marcus Beresford, who looked after the King's horses, whether it was advisable to have the lettering of his new title painted after his name on his private horse-boxes. The advice that came back reflected the fact that Sir Ernest was new to racing, as well as to titles: 'you can put the KCM outside,' Beresford said, 'so long as you put the Gee inside!'[60] There was more bite in the fact that it was only in 1908, thirteen years after the registration of his colours, that he was elected to the exclusive Jockey Club. Despite the scale of his stud and racing stables, he was never very successful: his second in the 1914 Derby with Hapsburg was probably his best achievement. Cassel did not even like racing; but the King did; and Society did. *Town Topics* singled him out in 'Who Goes Racing?' Here was 'one of the richest men in England and one of the most generous', a man whose 'godmother having bestowed on him the fingers of Midas, everything he touched turned to gold': also, rather incidentally, besides his financial status, the 'Owner of Wilfrid, winner of the Great Yorkshire Handicap at Doncaster'.[61]

Cassel's influence over the King was widely resented, especially as honour after honour followed: Queen Victoria had first given him public recognition with the KCMG in 1899; the KCVO and membership of the Privy Council came in 1902, the GCMG in 1905, GCVO in 1906, GCB in 1909. The last seemed especially scandalous, since it had been demanded by Cassel when, the previous year, Sir Edward Grey had asked him to help British interests by loaning the ailing Bank of Morocco £500,000. Edward, too, was distressed by this request, but he complied. He always stood by Cassel and openly demonstrated how he relied on him. Lord Cromer came to Buckingham Palace to receive the Order of Merit in August 1909. 'I am happy to bestow this final honour upon you,' said the King, 'and all the more so because I hear so good an account of your work in Egypt from my friend Sir Ernest Cassel.' Wilfrid Blunt's diary comment was succinctly to the point: 'This raised Cromer's bile.'[62]

There are signs that Edward had become disenchanted with Maurice de Hirsch by the time of the latter's death in April 1896; Hirsch had continually sought to use him for his social ambitions, and Queen Victoria's aloofness presented its own problems. The relationship with Cassel was deeper; when Jacob Schiff passed through London briefly in 1904, no difficulties were put in the way of arranging a presentation at short notice. And long before this the social world had been forced to face the importance of Cassel, pictured at the centre of the gossip page in *The Tatler*, with the inevitable caption: 'Sir Ernest Cassel, with whom the King has been staying lately'.[63]

Cassel's cosmopolitan character was in harmony with the King's needs, especially when, in later years, Edward made a stately itinerary. March and April meant Biarritz – 'that horrid Biarritz', as Alexandra called it, after his last visit there before he died. Asquith had to go all the way from England to kiss hands when he became Prime Minister in April 1908. Cassel, as ever, was useful, lending the Villa Eugénie for the use of the King, Mrs Keppel and her children. Sonia Keppel remembered being conscious that her clothes and those of her sister Violet, were less grand than Cassel's grandchildren's: she suspected Nannie of putting in secret overtime, washing and ironing as if to hide the inferiority of the lace on their knickers. Easter Sunday would bring presents of jewelled Easter eggs from 'Kingy' and Sir Ernest; and enormous picnics, carelessly thought of by the monarch as 'impromptu parties', in fact requiring hours of preparations, with footmen to set out chairs, tables, cloths, plates, glasses, silver, food in inexhaustible variety, iced drinking-cup transported in silver-plated containers.[64] 'I see a good deal of H.M. here,' Winston Churchill wrote to the Prime Minister from Biarritz in 1907, 'for he lunches and dines nearly every day with Cassel.'[65] The Biarritz visits usually lasted two to three weeks and Paris would then be visited on the return journey – Cassel's apartment on the Rue du Cirque serving an almost inevitable role with grand discretion.

Cassel's role in Edward's financial affairs was not confined to free entertainment and lodging, though it can only be pieced together with difficulty: he burned many of Edward's letters and was content to leave all accounts of the King with lacunae that only he could fill. Authorship, he said, was not in his line, and he felt not the least obligation to set the historical record straight for the next generation.[66] (What monstrous, infuriating, fascinating silence!) Like Hirsch, he could afford almost anything; as he said of a man with a mere £200,000 a year, 'I do not call *that* rich.'[67] He could be generous in the right quarters – Margot Tennant, who married the future Prime Minister, Herbert Asquith, received a pair of hunters – but he did not like waste: the butler, it was said, was well advised to be able to produce again the uneaten partridge left over from dinner.

It was his close involvement with Edward's finances, as much as his friendship, that probably first gave him the nickname 'Windsor Cassel'. Wilfrid Blunt's diary reflected the rumours in 1901 on his accession: 'It appears that the King's debts have been paid off privately by his friends, one of whom is said to have lent £100,000, and satisfies himself with £25,000 in repayment plus a Knighthood.'[68] Certainly Cassel, with the help of Lord Esher (Deputy Constable of Windsor Castle), Horace Farquhar (Master of the Royal Household) and Sir Dighton Probyn (Keeper of the Privy Purse), re-organized the administration of the royal household and the civil list; and Probyn was able to report that Edward had come to the throne 'unencumbered by a single penny of debt'.

Cassel, it seems, made sure that losses from royal investments were met, at least in the short term, from his own resources, but such transactions were well hidden even from semi-public view – to the bizarre extent that in October 1903 Cassel was asked to hand Edward the profits inside a copy of *Notes at Newmarket*, at the autumn races.[69] The consequences were symbolized in a much-recorded episode in January 1902 when the King went to the St James's theatre to see Oscar Wilde's *The Importance of Being Earnest*. Edward asked the ubiquitous Portuguese diplomat, the Marquis de Soveral, whether he had seen it, and the reply was wittily to the point: 'No, Sir, but I have seen the importance of being Ernest Cassel.'[70] Cassel's influence was unquestionable; and so was the depth of his relationship with the King.

The country benefited from his riches as much as the King: Cassel received the title 'Prince of Charity' from *The Times*. As the Countess of Warwick noted when she met him in the early days, 'I found him kind-hearted, always eager to help the poor, and lavish in support of hospitals.'[71] The results, in *The Tatler*'s view, were simple: 'Sir Ernest Cassel won his prefix of "Right Hon." by his large gifts to charity, especially his magnificent gift for medical investigations. He was confidently named by the prophets for a peerage, but the political influences were adverse to so large a reward.'[72] Yet once the race for worldly honours was over, when old age pushed thoughts of posterity to the fore, a further impetus was often given to millionaire largesse. Not long before Cassel died of heart failure, Haldane visited him. 'I thought that he looked ill,' Haldane recalled; and then he said unexpectedly 'he wanted to spend a million on bettering the condition of the poor'. The eminently sensible Haldane told him that such a gesture would be meaningless without specific objects in mind; a characteristic thirty-second reflection by Cassel settled the issue – half to go to a mental hospital, half to higher education.[73]

The skill with which Cassel exercised influence in the Edwardian period, however, was seen not so much in the direct use of money, but in spheres where his talent for poker-faced human manipulation could be used to the full. Shortly before Christmas, 1909, Edward VII dropped a casual note to Sir Ernest from Milton Abbey. The King would be very happy to dine with the financier on the nineteenth, but – since he was an old man by now – he added: 'A small party, I hope.' The letter concluded: 'I trust your visits to Berlin and Paris will prove satisfactory.'[74] Behind this informal and incidental remark lies a complex story of international finance and diplomacy, a struggle for power and riches. 'Even now', Sir Felix Semon wrote, 'it is not quite clear to me how he originally managed to gain, not only esteem, but the intimate personal friendship of so many of the most prominent men and women of England, the Continent, and of America.'[75]

Cassel's principal political aim was to prevent conflict between England and Germany, a policy he pursued with the especial help of Alfred de Rothschild and the German shipping magnate Albert Ballin. Edward VII supported Admiral Fisher's programme of 1904–5 for increasing the strength of the British navy, and in August 1908 he wrote to Cassel from Marienbad that 'we must go on building'.[76] But he also encouraged Cassel to consult with Ballin as a first step towards an agreement in the naval arms race, and they had in fact met in June 1908 to this end.[77] According to Ballin, Cassel had at once said that naval competition was only one feature – if the most prominent – of a whole series of struggles for world influence. Both men agreed that a visit by Edward to Berlin would have a calming effect, and this took place in February 1909, though political detente had little place in it. Cassel was in Turkey at the time and when the King wrote to him the following month from Biarritz his predominant tone was gloomy – in some measure a comment on his own health, as much as the political well-being of Europe.[78]

Ballin visited Cassel in London in July 1909 and Sir Ernest apparently took a very firm line: it was now more clearly recognized than it had been the year before that 'England must maintain her supremacy at sea under all circumstances and with complete freedom' since English commerce was in decline and the navy alone could maintain her empire and her position in the world. The Liberal government was the truly guilty party; if it had not 'neglected the Navy for the benefit of its own fantastic ideas and social reform, there would to-day have been no question of a hostile feeling towards Germany'. A much more hopeful suggestion the morning after their first meeting – that there should be a secret conference between England and Germany – was frustrated in the main by the new German Chancellor, Bethmann-Hollweg, who wanted to employ the procedures of formal diplomacy. Not long after Edward VII died the following January, the Prime Minister, Herbert Asquith, claimed that the German government refused to slow down its naval building programme.

But this was not the end of the story. Haldane recalled that Cassel had come back from Berlin in January 1912 with a message from Wilhelm II that he thought the most helpful way of improving relations between the two countries would be that 'the Cabinet of St James's should exchange views directly and personally with the Cabinet of Berlin'.[79] Ballin and Cassel had favoured a meeting between the two naval ministers, Tirpitz and Winston Churchill, but Churchill was distinctly lukewarm. Cassel, on 29 January, was nevertheless able to give Bethmann-Hollweg a document proposing negotiations for a wide-ranging agreement; and Haldane's well-known official mission to Berlin took place in February as a consequence. Cassel remained an unofficial liaison officer, staying at an hotel where Haldane visited him at night. The one overt indication of Cassel's involvement – and this only for those in the know – was a portrait of Haldane that the financier commissioned from Sir Arthur Cope and hung in Brook House.[80]

Not everyone appreciated his efforts. Kiderlen-Wächter, on holiday in Stuttgart when Haldane was in Berlin, was angry that he had not been consulted and seemed to blame that 'busy-body' Cassel. Bethmann-Hollweg was also said by Sir Edward Goschen to have been 'most surprised that Cassel had been chosen by His Majesty's Government as our intermediary in an important matter which concerned the two Governments, and when there was a German Ambassador in London'.[81] The Princess of Pless, sister of George Cornwallis-West, was even more scathing. She had seen Cassel in January 1912 at dinner with Lady Paget and had been infuriated by his reaction when she deferred to him for his opinion on the likelihood of war. Cassel said to the whole company that he felt certain there would be war in April. He told her: 'You seem to have all gone mad in your country'; and received the retort: 'I suppose you mean in your country.' The Princess had adopted Germany by marriage; Cassel had been born there.

The Princess had reported all this to the Kaiser, telling him not to trust Cassel (he said he didn't). Her view was that Cassel's ambition was the root of the trouble, and she had encouraged Wilhelm to give him the Order of the Red Eagle to keep him quiet. All to no avail: when they met again after his return from Berlin, he still maintained that war would come – an opinion which would certainly be taken seriously in London. She smiled, with an effort – but 'I could have thrown a knife at him.'[82]

Cassel's views were indeed taken account of: Lord Fisher was interested to note that Cassel had shown how completely unreliable the Kaiser was on questions of detail. But that did not mean that his efforts were praised. 'Of course he takes the German and Semitic point of view of it all . . .', Esher wrote. 'After all, *we* are fighting for our lives, for Imperial and possibly National existence, which will be at stake ere long. The Cassels are at home in all lands – equally rich, equally composed.'[83]

Such criticism had some force. When Edward VII met the Tsar, at Reval in June 1908, Lord Rothschild asked him to intercede on behalf of the Russian Jews. Cassel's concern was for help in raising a Russian loan and paving the way for his reception at the Russian court. The Kaiser claimed that the meeting had 'all been arranged on a money basis'; Edward had acted as if he was a 'jobber in stocks and shares' and made 'colossal' profits from the affair.[84] Wilhelm was not noted for balance in his judgments, but the comment was not totally without meaning.

Cassel received decorations from France, Germany, Sweden, Japan, Turkey: a recognition of his power in the international community. Not all he did was disinterested – there is more than a hint, for example, that he intrigued in 1902 to remove Lord Cromer from office in Egypt in the hope of taking an even greater control over the Egyptian economy. But he could also be useful. 'The Khedive arrived in London yesterday,' Wilfrid Blunt reported in June 1903, 'and is staying with the King's millionaire, Cassel, in Grosvenor Square.'[85] And he was always there, a powerful presence among those much better known – at the Naval Review at Spithead in July 1912, on the Admiralty yacht *Enchantress*, the inevitable picture was of Winston Churchill, Asquith, Admiral Beatty, General Sir John French . . . and the late King's greatest friend, Sir Ernest Cassel.

The King's death had been a great shock for Cassel. In the spring of 1910 he had been at Algiers, travelling back from Egypt with his daughter, when he received a telegram from the King. Cassel returned in time to visit him on the evening of 6 May; he wrote afterwards that he found 'the King dressed as usual, in his sitting room, rising from his chair to shake hands with me'. 'I wanted to see you', Edward said; 'tell your daughter [Maud too was slowly dying, of tuberculosis] I hope she will be careful and patient so as to recover complete health.'[86]

Edward lost consciousness not long after Cassel left: he died shortly before midnight.

After the Privy Council meeting the following morning, Cassel went to see Margot Asquith, the Prime Minister's wife, and they cried together on the sofa.[87] This death, together with those of his family, were, perhaps, the only events that ever brought him to the display of open grief. His friend, Jacob Schiff – no different in many ways – wrote in inarticulate understatement: 'I can very well imagine that, as you write me, the loss of your good friend, King Edward, is a severe blow to you.'[88] Mechanical matters could continue; Mrs Keppel would get her generous endowment from the King, and Cassel would make the arrangements. He could ignore the gossip ('. . . and people are quite disagreeable about Sir Adam [Vita Sackville-West's not entirely fictional pluto-crat], now that he no longer has the King behind him') and withdraw from a society destined to 'become as dull as ditch-water'.[89]

He went as usual to Marienbad that August: 'The English . . .', one contemporary record noted, 'see in Sir Ernest the King still present in spirit.' He was now 'the centre of Marienbad society. Celebrities from the whole western hemisphere, and even from the East, are staying here: luminaries of statecraft, wealth and beauty. But he attracts more notice than any of the others.'

He walked down the Kreuzbrunnen in the morning at eight o'clock, Edward VII incarnate: 'the same stocky, obese figure, the strong reddish face, framed by a short brown beard tinged with grey' – approached by royalty and aristoc-racy.

He behaved naturally now: 'as if he had always enjoyed by right of birth the position his far-sightedness, intelligence, energy, and tenacity have won for him.'[90]

No foreign-born City businessman had ever enjoyed as much influence on English social, political and economic life as Sir Ernest Cassel. No Jewish family of mere financiers enjoyed so long and so far-reaching a social career as the Rothschilds. No men with so little to be said for them by contemporary standards had come so much before the public eye in High Society as Ernest Hooley and Maurice de Hirsch. They were the special exhibits of a peculiar age: the era of the plutocrats.

Chapter 11

Home-grown Plutocracy

The plutocrats who came from abroad could be clearly identified as an alien influence. Those who worked in the City were also a breed of their own: many of them of Jewish or European origins, the archetypes of cosmopolitan finance. The old society of England, however, was also subject to attack from within, from the successful manufacturers and entrepreneurs who made fortunes in developing the British economy in the second half of the nineteenth century. Most of these men too – outward-looking and internationally minded in their business associations – sought at one time or another to enhance their power and influence within their own society.

The results were remarked upon outside as well as inside the country. The Kaiser Wilhelm II made asides to his friends on that strange phenomenon, the King of England who went boating with 'his grocer'. The 'grocer' was Thomas Lipton, whose life-style in the early 1890s had been no more that of a millionaire than it had been when he opened his first shop. There does not seem to have been a single mention of Lipton in *The Times* up to the end of 1896;[1] thereafter, especially after his company went public, he embarked on a social career of self-advertisement that took him into newspapers and magazines all over the world. His mother – long dead by then – had always mattered most to him: 'all his life', he told Beverley Nichols, 'he had worked for her and her alone, and . . . he had never found any other woman in the world who could make him forget her.'[2] She would be remembered in his success; and that success began not on the fringes of society, but, magnificently, miraculously, with the royal family itself.

In April 1897 Edward VII's wife, Alexandra, launched an appeal to provide meals for the poor. Lipton's gifts made the scheme possible, and he later paid £100,000 for her poor people's restaurant. His knighthood in the New Year's Honours List for 1898 looked as if it had been bought, the *Spectator* and others declared with varying degrees of directness. But Lipton had been launched and Captain Hickey captured the mood with his usual stunning simplism: Edward, 'having read so much about this little Irish Gossoon and his publicity pranks he asked to have Tom Lipton presented at Court'; from then they were often seen together 'and this set the aristocrats of London near crazy. They could not understand how the young Prince of Wales [Edward was in his mid-fifties] would ignore them for that small little tradesman, Tom Lipton, the London Grocer.'[3]

There was no real mystery. Lipton was good company; Sonia Keppel found him 'genial and breezy' and would not have been surprised if he had called in pirate costume, with 'a parrot in a cage and a ring in one ear'.[4] (She may not have known that he obtained a job for her father, in which he was in effect touting for society business by selling everything from cars to coal direct to the customer.) He told stories well, and as the years passed he had some to tell: the night, for example, that Jack Dempsey knocked his opponent out of the ring and into his arms. He was friendly, generous, popular – and rich. Edward was prepared to be influenced; Lipton was infinitely preferable to his noisy nephew, the Kaiser.

Some members of the aristocracy tried to close ranks

against Lipton by blackballing him from what was often called the most exclusive club in the universe, the Royal Yacht Club, and it seems that Edward did not press the issue to the point where some members would resign – which seemed a possibility, according to the *New York Herald*.[5] Lipton became a member only much later, but he was still able to exploit the social advantages of yacht racing. Sir Henry Lucy recorded in his diary in 1909: 'Yesterday cruised around the Isle of Wight, bringing up to anchor off Cowes. Close view of the Yacht Races and arrival of the Czar. The *Shamrock* a near neighbour. Lipton, spying us on deck, sent a boat to take us to dinner on his famous yacht, where we met some pleasant Americans.'[6] Lipton's expenditure on his yachts may have gone over the million-pound mark, but the headlines and publicity helped his business – and pleased him.

He was a new type of English sportsman, who applied business thoroughness in order to win: twenty first prizes in 1908, for example, and six cups at the 1912 regatta for the twenty-fifth anniversary of the Kaiserlich Yacht Club.[7] In discussing the America Cup in 1901, *Truth* observed: 'The aristocratic challengers had not the business spirit. . . . Sir Thomas Lipton, whose success in life has been due to his business instincts, has carried all before him.' (Indeed, the moral was that the business administration of the state was best directed by businessmen and not merely by scions of ancient families.)[8] The America Cup had first been competed for in 1851 when the American yacht *America* began a long tradition of American victories. Lipton tried for it in October 1899, in his specially built *Shamrock*, matched against Pierpont Morgan's £30,000 *Columbia*. An American writer in London guessed that 200,000 people were gathered between Fleet Street and the Thames Embankment at half-past ten because of the race – this at a time when the country was on the verge of war against the Boers.[9] *The Times* even contributed a leader, raising the contest to the level of Anglo-American diplomacy.

The following year, when Lipton was walking with Arbuckle, the American coffee and sugar king, he said that *Shamrock* had been 'hoodooed' by the Americans: 'They put something in the water so that I could not win.' 'What was it?' Arbuckle asked. 'The *Columbia*,' quipped Lipton.[10] He had been defeated in all three races, but in May 1900 the American ambassador presented him with a Loving-Cup 'as a token of good-will from the American people' at a Hotel Cecil banquet.[11]

Further challenges followed. 'I have not got money to burn,' he told the designer of *Shamrock II* (which lost to *Columbia* in 1901), 'but if it is going to make her go one second faster, you can shovel on the £5 notes.' At the launching in April 1901 by the Countess of Dufferin, wife of the Commodore of the Royal Ulster Yacht Club, Lipton was presented with a gold bangle and each of the guests with a wing made of *Shamrock* bronze dipped in gold.[12] Edward VII was nearly killed in this yacht, when the rigging collapsed and crashed down on the deck close to him. Sir Almeric Fitzroy noted in his diary: 'The narrow escape of the King a few days ago, while yachting with Lipton, gave many cause for reflection as to what might have happened had some of the flying blocks taken a different course.'[13] Edward was rather shaken, which may explain why he wrote shortly afterwards to Lady Londonderry: 'I wish Sir T. Lipton would give up all idea of trying to win the America Cup with his present yacht . . . she is an unlucky vessel. He is merely wasting his money. He is besides as well known in America as he is here that he really does not require the race as an advertisement.'[14] As it happened, *Shamrock III* lost to Oliver Iselin's *Reliance* in March 1903, *Shamrock IV* to *Resolute* in 1913.[15] But nothing could take away the attention, on an international scale, that Lipton attracted.

'The most popular man in the States at the present moment', *The Tatler* claimed in October 1901, 'is Sir Thomas Lipton.' The American journalist, Dorothy Dix, discovered that he was 'a fascinating human document' – 'this long-limbed, rugged, handsome Scotch Irishman, with his square head and his keen blue eyes, looked like a three-volume romance bound in yachting flannels.' She listened to Lipton's philosophy, which was that of the American businessman: 'A man may think he can go into society, be out at dinners, or go to theatres or dances every night and be just as good a businessman in the morning. But he isn't. You can't be a society man and a businessman at the same time.' ('Which last-mentioned is excellent philosophy for the general, but obviously does not particularly apply to the strange case of Sir Thomas Lipton, the Tea King': despite his abstinence from tobacco and alcohol.)[16]

Lipton knew and liked America above all: 'So extensive and exact is his knowledge of New World politics and currents of feeling', it was said in 1904, 'that his discriminating Sovereign has promoted him to the unofficial post of Court coach in Anglo-American relations as well as seamanship.'[17] This role was the limit of his political activities. 'My politics', he told an MP, 'are to open a new shop every week.'[18] He disliked the deceits and the circumlocutions that went with a parliamentary career. When, in 1892, another MP was discussing the Home Rule Bill with his constituents, he complained: 'Parliaments will be as common as Lipton's provision stores, and I respectfully submit that they will not be equally as useful.'[19] Lipton would certainly have agreed.

Dorothy Dix also described the interior of his floating palace, the *Erin*: the drawing-room walls hung in pale pink brocade with signed pictures of Queen Victoria, King Edward VII and Queen Alexandra, President McKinley; his room and the guest chamber 'little dens all done in dainty lace and silk like a beauty's boudoir'; the dining-room with massive furnishings and beautiful pieces of plate presented by guests of *Shamrock I*. The visitors' book of the *Erin*, Lipton said, contained, 'the names of practically every Royal personage in Europe': yet 'I was the same, plain Tom Lipton'. His message was that no one should care any more if he had relations with social status: all that mattered was what the individual made of his own life. In America, he said, 'they don't worry overmuch about ancestors – they are all too busy making their own ancestry, and I like them for it!'[20] He was proud of what he had achieved (he had all his cups, plaques and other honours photographed), and he loved the publicity ('I've the largest collection of Press cuttings in the whole world'). He liked to entertain all those who had pulled their weight in the 'Ship of Life', but the more he mixed in Society, the more he delighted in royal company – Prince Henry of Battenberg, Alfonso of Spain, the ex-Empress Eugénie, as well as Edward VII. Their photographs, in large silver frames, surrounded him (generally signed, Beverley Nichols observed, 'in that curious scrawl which denotes either royal origin, success behind the footlights, or delirium tremens').[21]

Later, a rather sad old man, he would have them for memories.

Lipton was not the only British businessman to find a place in Edward VII's entourage. Sir Edward Guinness, later Lord Iveagh, abandoned the everyday management of his family's Dublin brewery a few years after it became a public company in the mid-1880s. His attempts to find a suitable landed estate to suit his social ambitions quickly brought him into conflict with the classic case of a landed family in decline.[22] *Vanity Fair* found Lord Ernest Brudenell-Bruce, third Marquess of Ailesbury, 'a bored, and rather haggard figure – wearing an expression of profound pessimism'. He had succeeded in 1878 an extravagant elder brother and father; his Yorkshire estate, granted to his ancestor by James I, was sold for £310,000 to Samuel Cunliffe-Lister in 1886 (and Cunliffe-Lister, rich wool manufacturer, made Jervaulx Abbey his chief seat). Savernake, in the family for eight hundred years, was thereby saved, but the Marquess died shortly after a last, sad visit to Yorkshire and the Abbey, which, he told his son 'would always be written across his heart, like Calais was to Queen Mary's'.

Ailesbury's heir, Willie, was a fine fellow, described by

Curzon in 1878 as 'that young blackguard Savernake who had been sacked from Eton for twice refusing to take a swishing – in addition to other enormities'.[23] R. D. Blumenfeld found him in Romano's in 1892, talking and dressing like a coster, offering hospitality to all; and a place on the sawdust-covered floor for all those who refused a drink.[24] A perfect prey for that much-loved literary figure, the Jewish moneylender, he was ruined by his mid-twenties. The possibility of salvation lay with the plutocracy alone, for Sir Edward Guinness offered three-quarters of a million pounds for Savernake. But the family closed ranks to prevent the sale and a long complicated legal wrangle followed. Willie, reduced to living in Brixton, died in April 1894, his last thwarted scheme being to cut down the ancient forest of Savernake for timber. The fifth Marquess, Lord Henry, salvaged little more than honour from his victory over Guinness, that 'mere upstart merchant, a nouveau-riche Irishman'. He worked hard to improve his farms, grew trees, restored part of Tottenham House, the family seat. But the 40,000 acres of the nineteenth-century estate had become 6,000 in the 1970s – and the new landlords, the unlikely heirs to a family tradition, were dominated by the Treasury.

In the course of the legal battle over Savernake Guinness had been accused of offering bribes, with the result that he lost his patience and bought a completely different estate to match his new status as friend of the heir to the throne. It aided his transition from a business to an aristocratic way of life, for Elvedon, between Thetford and Bury St Edmunds, had boasted a manor house on its site at the time of the Domesday Book in 1086. In the 1860s it had been bought for the Maharajah Dhuleep Singh of Lahore, heir to the Punjab throne, who reconstructed the interior of the house in the manner of an Indian palace. The marble staircase, with scarlet wrought-iron railing, cost him more than £25 a tread, a price that was said to have sent him into a three-day-long insensate rage.[25]

'The Black Prince' died in 1893, disillusioned by England,

but his successor had a delightful time developing the palace. 'Elvedon is an appallingly luxurious mansion', declared *Mayfair* in 1910 with no hint of criticism, 'and Lord and Lady Iveagh the pleasantest and kindest of hosts.' The magazine described the wonderful 'Indian hall', with its beaten and carved copper dome in the style of the Taj Mahal, walls of rare Carrara marble and pavement inlaid with the same material. Iveagh built a copy of the Maharajah's palace, and then connected the two buildings by a vast central portion, with the marble hall rising to the dome. Carvings from the solid marble, two magnificent Renaissance fire-places, and galleries surrounding the whole added to the splendour.[26] This was not a man to do anything in a half-hearted way – even his fancy for old Irish silver potato rings was indulged with fierce application.[27] At Elvedon there were between twenty and thirty housemaids, who were not allowed to go out alone; each visiting lady's maid was given her own room: a suitable place for the Prince of Wales to stay. Edward was indeed to be seen there: 'a big fat man shaking with laughter', according to Lady Fingall's maid looking down from the gallery.[28]

The Iveagh style was not confined to Elvedon; their house on St Stephen's Green in Dublin, which had belonged to Lord Iveagh's father, had grown enormously, 'like the family's fortunes' (said *Mayfair*). In the ballroom, 70 by 40 feet, it was not surprising to find pure white Carrara marble from floor to ceiling. Not a place to live in, the house was used almost exclusively for entertaining.[29] When Edward and Alexandra visited Ireland in 1904, staying at the Viceregal lodge, the Iveaghs arranged a large house party, and took on fifty extra staff for the occasion. Cassel, one of the guests at St Stephen's Green, conveyed to Lady Fingall 'in his guttural German speech' his deep affection and admiration for the King.[30] Others, pleased to be sharing a house with the King's friend, doubtless conveyed the same sentiment with less sincerity.

The most carefully arranged plans could not always be expected to work: when Iveagh arranged to greet the King with a torch-light procession at Elvedon in January 1908, the news of the royal party's approach was not telegraphed quickly enough, and the cars entered the grounds to find the torch-bearers in disarray, waiting for the order to light up.[31] Still, Edward stayed from Thursday to Wednesday, a point recorded by *Vanity Fair*. The magazine praised the heated and lighted marquees which provided comfort for the luncheons that accompanied the main purpose of the visit: the shooting.[32] One of the gamekeepers at Elvedon, who had started working life driving a cart carrying the Maharajah's cartridges, later said that Edward was bored by the shooting, and often remained irascibly on his shooting stick until the ladies joined the party for luncheon. If so, Iveagh – with seventy men catering for the game, a hundred beaters for perhaps eight guns, two loaders, a cartridge boy and a detective for the King alone – must have been a disappointed man.[33] Even the different coverts were connected by telephone so that instant information could be obtained on where the sport was best.[34]

Elvedon was always news, for this was no farming estate. *Mayfair* explained: 'There are extensive woods and plantations, and a very large number of well-placed coverts, the estate being actually a huge game preserve, for the soil is poor and sterile, and does not repay cultivation.'[35] The *Daily News* interpreted the situation differently when, in February 1909, it attacked the sale of estates to the plutocracy, who caused rural depopulation through sacrificing agriculture to sport. Under the Maharajah the farm-land had deteriorated; Iveagh devoted large acreages to game and as much as 2,000 acres was no longer regularly cultivated by 1902. Iveagh's agent replied to the paper, pointing out that about half the estate was unsuitable for cultivation or grazing, and that its population had considerably increased since the purchase.[36]

The second Lord Iveagh, who succeeded to the title in 1927, developed the farming land by rigorous application of modern scientific techniques. But that was merely the prelude to another age – in which the Earl of the 1970s would return to

Ireland for tax reasons and shut up Elvedon Hall on his 28,000 acre estate.[37] The families of Ailesbury and Iveagh had something in common after all.

The most socially successful of the home-grown plutocrats were those who used their wealth to adopt a life-style in close approximation to that of the old aristocracy. But it was still their wealth that was seen as their distinctive characteristic. The means of attracting the presence of the King and other members of the royal family was simple – at least in the eyes of *The Tatler* commenting in Lady Iveagh's June 1902 ball in Grosvenor Place: 'With enormous wealth and plenty of space at her disposal Lady Iveagh can well maintain her reputation as an excellent and lavish hostess.'[38] The same point was made by *The West-End* in 1899: her suppers at 5 Grosvenor Place (and 80 St Stephen's Green in Dublin) were 'perfect triumphs of *cuisine*, and no money is spared to make the entertainments a great success'; Lord Iveagh was a man of immense wealth, who spent immense sums of money on his houses – there was nothing more informative on which to comment.[39]

It was harder for those who remained in complete control of their business enterprises. *Town Topics* discussed the rise of Sir William Lever in 1912: 'If you are the sole arbiter and dictator of a business with a capital of twenty millions, and the controller of the earthly destinies of a town full of men, women and children, with a debt to nature to pay in the form of a certain number of hours' sleep out of the twenty-four, your time for amusement and political recreation is obviously limited.' Lever's case was of special interest; after all, 'A successful Bolton soap manufacturer with an accent you can cut with a knife ought, if he has the slightest respect for the dramatic proprieties, to be a parvenu.' 'Well,' said *Town Topics*, 'Lever is not a parvenu, and has a knowledge of the beautiful things in life, the pictures, the china . . . the rarities, the fine things which money can only partly pay for.' That was not quite the whole truth, and yet curiously the magazine was exactly correct in speaking of art and business in the same sentence: 'His China collection is a miracle, and so is Port Sunlight.'[40]

Who else could tell his audience – at the Oldham Art Gallery in February 1915 – that the prime rule of success in war and business *and* art was 'thoroughness and efficiency', thoroughness of knowledge and efficiency of method? Silly were the businessmen who 'look on Art as hostile to business, as destructive to the common sense of business, and likely to place them at a disadvantage . . . a monster that would come between them and their business and swallow up the fruits of their industry.'[41] As the Imperial Arts League discovered the following month, while the businessman must not let his imagination run away with him ('refusal to romance in business is the business man's honour'), the artist must not work solely for the market. It was no accident that the Lady Lever Art Gallery, which had its foundation stone laid by George V in 1914, was situated at Port Sunlight: the soap works educated the masses in the best business principles, the gallery educated them in the best art.

For Lever great art was a triumph of craftsmanship, just as a great business was a triumph of an allied skill. But it was also a silent refuge for a man deeply hurt by social snobbery: 'A beautiful picture never lectures us – it never humiliates us; it tells us its lesson, and it appeals to us and raises and ennobles us without raising in us any kind of resentment.'[42] Nothing else could elevate without 'humiliating'.

Perhaps through an extension of this argument, Lever had himself painted in great style by such Society artists as Sir Luke Fildes, though the theory that a painting cannot 'humiliate' came badly unstuck in his experience with Augustus John ('I'm not a fashionable portrait painter', the painter once told John Freeman). When the commissioned picture arrived, Lever was shocked by the cruelty of the portrayal: corrupt visage, with hard, unfeeling mouth, and grasping hands. This may have been his soul; it was not his physical appearance, least of all his self-image. By mistake, the portrait was returned to John – but without the head. 'The

William Lever, later first
Viscount Leverhulme

Sir Thomas Lipton by the
Queen's photographer,
Walery of Regent Street

One of the early Lipton shops

canvas', the painter recalled, 'was still fixed in its packing-case from which it had clearly never been removed.' Lever's explanation was that, finding the picture too large for his safe, he had cut off 'what he considered to be the most important part, that is the head' and put it in the safe, while the rest had been sent back in error. 'I was urgently requested to keep the matter dark,' wrote John, 'and invited to dinner at Hampstead' (after living for a few years in a house in Norfolk Street, overlooking Park Lane, in the 1890s, Lever had eventually bought The Hill, on Hampstead Heath). John's answer was to give the story to the press, with speedy consequences. London art students, on a march to Hyde Park, carried 'a gigantic replica of the celebrated soap-boiler's torso, the head being absent'; and in Italy, during a twenty-four hour strike, an effigy of 'Il Le-ver-hul-me' – made out of soap and tallow – graced the streets of Florence before being burnt in the Piazza dei Signori.[43]

More bad publicity attended Lever's other activities. In private Lord Riddell, who came into contact with him over Lever's proposed purchase of Stafford House for the nation, was impressed by this 'public spirited person'.[44] The not unsympathetic *Town Topics*, however, used the headline: 'The Soap King and the House that was built for Royalty'. Built by a royal prince, sold unfinished to a duke, completed by his successor, immortalized by Disraeli, the centre of the most brilliant social gatherings in London, Stafford House had even been envied by a queen – 'I am coming from my house to your palace', Queen Victoria had written. Now it had been absorbed into Port Sunlight. After its greatest days, brilliantly described by Disraeli in *Lothair*, it – and its owners – continued to fascinate.[45] Andrew Carnegie met the Marquis of Stafford 'by appointment' in 1881:

I don't suppose any one ever has expected to see such a staircase as enchants him upon entering Stafford House. This is the most magnificent residence any of us has ever seen. I will not trust myself to speak of its beauties, nor of the treasures it contains. One begins to understand to what the Marquis of Stafford is born. The Sutherland family has a million two hundred thousand acres in Britain; no other family in the world compares with it as landowner. It is positively startling to think of it.[46]

By the time Queen Victoria died, other plutocrats had penetrated the house – *The Tatler* reported the fête held there in July 1901 in aid of the Lifeboat Saturday fund: 'Coronets shone on many a stately head. . . . With the aristocracy were mixed other classes. The new-made millionaires and their magnificently dressed wives readily gave three guineas for fête and concert in the palace of the Duke of Sutherland.'[47] But for a mere soap manufacturer actually to purchase the place – even if he proposed to let ownership revert to the nation after twenty-eight years – Society was not ready. *The Times* quoted Lever on his return from the Congo in March 1913, complaining of 'insinuations and innuendoes' in the Commons 'to the effect that I had been actuated by mercenary and improper motives in the offer I made to present to the nation my ownership of the lease of Stafford House'.[48] In the end the house, renamed Lancaster House on Lever's insistence, was opened to the public in 1914; but not before further bitterness had been aroused by the plan not to present Lever to the King at the opening.

Lever's excursions into political life, like his social activities, demonstrated that his true talents lay in business alone. There was little doubt where his own priorities lay – at least, after he had fought five times as a Liberal before winning a seat, and then experienced the frustrations of parliamentary life. His influence as an employer to some extent proved helpful. In 1895 a mass meeting was held at Port Sunlight by the workers to protest at attacks made on him; and he did do rather well that year, and previously in 1892 and 1894, in the Tory constituency of Birkenhead. He used Parliament to express his capitalist philosophy: when the Pilgrim Fathers had gone to America they had remained poor, wretched, ill-clothed, ill-fed, miserable so long as they clung to the socialist idea of holding land in common; but by adopting 'what we call the individualistic system, the system of private enterprise, they have become the richest country in the world to-day and the country that has the most uniform distribution of wealth in the world'.[49] Even when he pushed motions on the payment of MPs and on the introduction of Old Age Pensions – which, it is true, were by no means popular in a country with profoundly conservative institutions – he was careful not to encourage what he would have seen as the decadence of comfortable living.

Lever sat in the Commons from 1906 to 1909, retiring in the end through pressure of work. His parting gesture came the following year, when he fought the hopeless Ormskirk seat in Lancashire: dominated by the Stanley Earls of Derby and a reminder of a world not yet dead. When he had gone round the world in the winter of 1892–3, he had examined the political system in Australia and found that the 'Upper Houses of Parliament' seemed strangely alike the world over – 'They all appear to be impressed with the one idea – that they exist solely to maintain the power and influence of property on a basis altogether out of proportion to what property is fairly entitled to.'[50] In his view, there was no need to institutionalize the exclusion of the worst elements of society from government, for he was himself the living proof that the best rose to the top. When he joined the House of Lords, that was merely a just reward: all readers of *Square Deals* would want 'to be especially associated with the congratulations which have been showered on Lord Leverhulme of Bolton-le-Moors'.[51]

Lever admitted no distinction between himself and those who did not match his business achievements – save his choice to apply his will without distraction.[52] It was typical of him that he recorded in his diary in 1895 the strength of character in Rhodes's features: he could admire a man of his own type. Capitalist endeavour benefited everyone: 'You must remember this – that it is high production by means of capital that produces leisure and high intelligence,' he said in an address at Hampstead.[53] The Howe sewing machine was invented by the wife of Elias Howe because 'She was sorry for women who had to sew'; the invention both made a fortune and made life easier for great numbers of people. Even the Standard Oil Company ('I suppose it is more truly called the "slandered" Oil Company today') was a blessing for mankind, despite the fact that in the early days it was not wholly clear what service was being rendered.[54] Lever's life was a life of obsessive method directed towards a goal of self-achievement which, he argued, helped the development of the world; it was an ethic of puritanism and plenty: if there were to be dinners, cigars, wines and exercise in his day-to-day existence they must be recorded with precision, if not penitence, in his diary, 'as a guide for the future'.[55] And if his son was to be given an Eton and Cambridge education – with all the blunting of the business sense that implied – it had to be recognized that the preparation of a man for 'public and social duties'[56] required different vehicles: but the same singlemindedness.

There was no flabby luxury about Lever's Thornton Hall, three miles from Port Sunlight, with his bedroom without adornment or view, open to the night sky which might leave him with a covering of snow on waking in the morning: a suitable prelude to his usual cold bath. Even in his first house, in Park Street, Bolton, he left his mark in the specially designed doors and mantelpieces, and there were perpetual changes and rebuilding to follow in every one of his thirteen houses. He would take what he liked and transform it into his creation: 'I prefer Georgian dining-rooms in which to give large dinners', he wrote. 'For small dining-rooms I prefer Tudor. For drawing-rooms I prefer what is called the Adam style, for entrance halls the Georgian.'[57] His 8,000 Cheshire acres alone made him a large landowner, and he sat on the County Council and the magistrates' bench: but not to follow in the landed tradition, rather to express his own achievement. As he said in New Zealand, when he saw the Maoris benefiting from the new roads and settlements on their land (the land on which they happened to be camping, he called it): the natives had taken to 'the vices of landlordism' – 'that portion of our system of civilisation which enables them to sit in idleness whilst their lands are being developed and made of value without so much as lifting their little finger'.[58]

Lever shared Andrew Carnegie's wish to help the strong to fulfil their potential; he even said that he resented the fact that everyone concerned with 'the human side and human element should be thought a philanthropist'. Philanthropy in business was degradation; good working conditions were merely part of a sound, efficient company.[59] Weakening the strong or impoverishing the wealthy did no one any good; rather, the poor and the weak should be shown how to be wealthy and healthy. The well-to-do should be those who worked, and worked hard. Like Carnegie, Lever carried this view to extremes, but it was one shared by many of his contemporaries; even Thomas Lipton, who was largely responsible for financing the Princess of Wales's scheme to provide 'good, wholesome, well-cooked food at cost price' to the working classes, insisted: 'There is nothing in the form of charity about this, and no person will forfeit the slightest self-respect by taking advantage of it.'[60] If this was a continuation of aristocratic paternalism by other men, it was paternalism with a capitalist face.

The houses built by Lever for his workers at Port Sunlight were models of their kind; Gladstone was so impressed by the new building named after him there that he declared, 'In this hall I have found a living proof that cash payment is not the only nexus between man and man.'[61] The eight-hour day, the Employees' Benefit Fund, the Employees' Holiday Club – all these innovations were in the forefront of progress. The suspicion remains that everything was designed merely to produce the greater efficiency of the business machine; and if you remained poor or destitute with these sort of advantages, it was clearly your own fault.

Lord Riddell compared Lever with George Cadbury – their
model factories serving as an example of what might be done
both in Britain and America.[62] Cadbury, with his brother,
Richard, had inherited a declining business from their father
in 1861 and transformed it by meeting the needs of the same
new markets tapped by Lever. But George's Garden City of
Bournville, built by him a few miles outside Birmingham,
was not merely meant to benefit his own company. The death
rate in Birmingham in 1904 was over nineteen per thousand;
it was less than seven in Bournville.[63] The *British Trade
Journal* doubtless exaggerated in 1880 when it said the
Cadbury partners 'refrain from exercising anything like a
paternal control'; but if everyone had to attend morning
service between 9.15 and 9.30 am, practical considerations
were not neglected. ('We must not omit to add that the all-
important sanitary arrangements of these villas have been
very carefully considered.')[64] Some of the purchasers of
Bournville houses actually resold them at considerable
profit, and when this was prevented by turning the venture
into a charitable trust, considerably less than half of the resi-
dents were Cadbury employees.

The greater part of Cadbury's property was given away
with the creation of the trust – though, as head of a firm
which processed by 1900 a third of all the cocoa that came
into the country, he was not a poor man. He described great
wealth as a curse which his family could well do without; and
there was just one stain on his career: the libel action he
brought against Standard Newspapers for their suggestion
that he had hypocritically condoned the use of what was virtually slave labour in the Portuguese colonies that supplied
cocoa. Even the advocacy of Rufus Isaacs brought him only a
farthing damages. Looked at purely in terms of abstract
morality, it did seem that the firm had taken a long time to
refuse to accept the tainted supplies.

Unlike most businessmen of the period, Cadbury looked to
the press to promote his ideals rather than himself. When he
bought the *Sun* and the *Morning Leader* in 1910, he did so to

prevent papers with a combined circulation of half a million a day from falling into the hands of those who might call for war or oppose social reform. In the Boer War, Lloyd George had approached him to help finance an anti-war paper and, despite some initial doubts, he put up £20,000 to purchase the *Daily News* and a further £20,000 to help it at a later stage. The banning of racing news and advertisements for alcohol did not help the paper's finances, but Cadbury was happy to provide money for such ventures as the *Daily News* exhibition of sweated industries in Queen's Hall in 1906. With Edward Cadbury, he supported the National Old Age Pensions League in 1908: a shilling a day at sixty for every man in the country from the Duke of Westminster downwards – provided the duke was prepared to go to the post office to collect his.

When Gladstone had made a personal appeal to him to stand for Parliament in 1892, he had answered that 'I can be of most service to my fellow men in connexion with religious work, and by taking part in social questions, though I know how dependent we are for progress upon those who take an active part in politics.' If there had to be political life, he later wrote, it should be used as an instrument for lessening suffering, and to help the very old and the very young.

Here was a rich man whose code of conduct was totally opposed to plutocracy, to what he called 'speculators, trust-mongers, and owners of enormous wealth', who are 'the great curse of the world, and the cause of most of the poverty' – a reference, in particular, to those who had profited from specu-lation in South African shares. He declined, respectfully, both membership of the Privy Council and a peerage: for how could these be 'in the interests of the poor suffering people?'[65]

The Cadbury story found all too few echoes elsewhere; but there was at least one of note. Andrew Carnegie had once briefly owned Passmore Edwards's London *Echo*. No paper that the latter controlled was ever used to promote political views with which he disagreed – even if financial considerations suggested that they should. He first tried to enter Parliament at Truro in 1868, where his address – including provisions for an end to the death penalty, the game laws and the army purchase system – 'carried too much reform sail' to captivate a majority of the electorate. When he was at last victorious, at Salisbury in 1880, he received a certain 'stimulation' from the thought that 'the poor Cornish boy, after many buffetings with fortune, should represent a cathedral city in Parliament', but that was tempered by the knowledge that he had been selected in preference to Thomas Hughes, author of *Tom Brown's Schooldays* and champion of the Co-operative movement.

Passmore Edwards rapidly became disillusioned with politics; most MPs seemed to be 'company-promoters on the look-out for opportunities to extend their City connections'; 'scions of the hereditary aristocracy more intent on propping up and perpetuating privilege than benefiting mankind'; or 'members who fought for their seats, to use them as stepping-stones to get into "society", or to secure recognition or titles of one kind or another'. They were all far removed in spirit from a man who sought, in the Commons, to prevent waste and preserve the purity of the air by lowering the gas jet; and it was no surprise that after Edwards's defeat at Rochester in 1885, he settled for the pursuit of his ideal in different spheres, through philanthropy and the press.

Like any successful businessman, he recognized that he lived in a commercial age, in which commerce was the primary source of national prosperity, but he also insisted that the moral strength of the country depended on the morality with which commerce was conducted. He felt that he had accumulated his wealth mainly by the labour of others and that they should therefore benefit; and benefit they did from hospitals at Falmouth and Willesden, Acton and Sutton, convalescent and children's homes, libraries and technical institutes.[66]

Oh, Passmore Edwards, you are beyond contention
Are worthy of *Punch*'s 'Honourable Mention' . . .

There's scarce a project schemed with kindly sense,
But profits by your large benevolence.[67]

For those who felt uneasy at the very idea of newspaper
owners working for the public good, there was much comfort.
Edward Levy, of the *Daily Telegraph*, went through a pleasant
process of change, beginning by adding a hyphenated 'Lawson'
to his name, taking in a knighthood on the way, and finishing,
in 1903, as Baron Burnham, friend of Edward VII. Ernest
Hooley claimed that he offered Alfred Harmsworth £800,000
for the *Daily Mail*; he certainly managed to lose £3,000 a
week for four months when he bought the *Sun* in 1897. And
Harmsworth himself systematically pursued his own ends
through society, politics and the press.

Journalists as such were distrusted in the late nineteenth
century. Long after the invention of daily newspapers, the
men who wrote them remained nonentities.[68] So long as social
exclusivity, and with it social privacy, was a fact, and not
merely an aspiration, communication by the printed word was
an irrelevance. Harmsworth complained in 1903 of 'the
tradition that Grub Street is not a thoroughfare for respectable
wayfarers': an advertisement for a tutor with a good Oxbridge
degree might produce more than a thousand replies for a post
with a salary of £120 per annum; attempts to find a good
sub-editor would have practically no response, despite the
attractions ('I speak of the sub-editors in my own establishment') of £300–£1,000 a year.[69]

The newspaperman who wanted to make a social impact
needed riches and the willingness to adopt the trappings of the
aristocratic life-style. Northcliffe was spending £300 per
annum in subscriptions to West End clubs in the late 1890s;
he took a box at the Royal Opera; and he leased 36 Berkeley
Square – said to be the smallest in the Square, but still next
door to Rosebery. Even so, when Lord Esher called on him in
1908, he recorded in his *Journals*: 'He lives simply, his
house is furnished with taste, without display or ostentation
of his enormous wealth.'[70] Northcliffe was always opposed to

socializing without purpose, bored by gambling, to bed early, up at 5.30, a preoccupied figure asking his wife, but 'what are we dining *about*?'[71]

There were strict calculations of advantage in all his activities. He never enjoyed shooting; he needed to know people who did. In September 1899 he took Thorrington Hall in Suffolk, which answered the need. Sutton Place in Surrey (later the home of Paul Getty), on which he took a lease at £1,750 a year, had 'an ecstasy of oak panellings, quaint furniture, nooks and wonderful stairways, surrounded by park and gardens', one of his young employees found in 1912. After all, as Harmsworth said, 'Little rooms are no good for big ideas.'[72] But in the same year he told Lord Riddell that he could not sleep there; he preferred a bungalow he had built on a hill some miles away.[73]

Harmsworth was not a very good countryman. He built one of the best private golf courses in the world at Sutton Place, but it said much about the man that he once spent an afternoon driving golf ball after golf ball down his own fairway until he collapsed from the effort.[74] He was more at home in pioneering the acceptance of the motor-car – spending, according to *The Tatler*, £500 a year on tyres alone. The paper criticized the volume he edited on *Motors and Motor-driving* for its apparent refusal to register the fact that there were people with less than £10,000 a year.[75] Harmsworth, appropriately given the last word, could at least offer the rejoinder that the car's stable bill was 'of the smallest'.[76]

The attractions of the House of Lords were also connected with self-interest. Harmsworth complained to the Earl of Onslow in October 1897: 'the Party leaders are no doubt quite ignorant of the revolution which the *Daily Mail*, in its infancy at present, is making in London journalism', while 'owners of newspapers of comparatively slight influence are rewarded'.[77] He declined a knighthood, it was publicly noted at the time, on the assumption that he ought to have the higher reward of a baronetcy; and in quick succession he became Sir Alfred Harmsworth in 1905 and Lord Northcliffe the following year.

He decided against the title Lord Elmwood – the name of his house near Broadstairs – on the grounds that 'it's the wood they use for coffins', and settled for the nearby stretch of coastline, North Cliff.[78]

Harmsworth had once said: 'when I want a peerage I will pay for it like an honest man'.[79] Direct evidence for purchase of either baronetcy or barony is lacking, but the *Saturday Review* was blunt enough in its reaction to the news: 'Sir Alfred Harmsworth has a genius for commercial organization, which being translated means the power of getting the most for the least out of one's fellow-creatures. . . . We say advisedly that he has done more than any man of his generation to pervert and enfeeble the mind of the multitude', exploiting 'for his own profit the foibles and the ignorance of the masses'.[80]

It was appropriate that the only biography of Northcliffe published in his lifetime referred to 'that vast development of modern times which controls governments and sways nations – the power of the press'.[81] The great advantage of the newspaper was its sermon-like certainty: judgments received a sanctity in print against which argument was difficult. After declining nomination for Folkestone in 1894, Harmsworth had flirted with Parliament when he stood as a Unionist at Portsmouth the following year. He purchased the Conservative local paper, the *Evening Mail*, for the purpose, and ran in it a sensational serial story, 'The Siege of Portsmouth', painting a frightening picture of a navy unprepared to meet enemy attack. Posters showed the victims of shellings in the Town Hall Square.

He lost the election and it was then that – 'half seriously' – he drew the moral that 'my place is in the House of Lords where they don't fight elections'.[82]

Northcliffe was able to pose as the disinterested newspaperman, free of political corruption. 'Do you think that the bitterness and intrigues of politics have delights for me?' he asked an interviewer from an American paper in 1899.[83] As he told young journalists, 'The newspaper owner should always remember that, while the politicians have nothing to give him, they have much to gain from his newspaper.' The point was that every extension of the franchise made the newspaper more powerful, the politicians less so.[84] And if Northcliffe's aptitude was for making money and organizing, his desire was for power.

He liked money in order to buy the best of everything; he was prepared to use it to win the best journalists. But 'Britain's Man of Power' looked on everything, money and people included, as a means towards the expression of his own will. Everyone who met him saw a Napoleonic figure; he seemed to look like the Emperor: wisp of hair over the forehead, gestures and commands dictatorial, notes sent with the cipher 'N' – Northcliffe or Napoleon?[85] Aggressive and rude, sometimes charming, sometimes witty, inspirational but infuriating, emotional but never intimate: there was no better description than that of his fellow newspaper tycoon, William Randolph Hearst – 'Imagine a face that presents a mixture of Napoleon, Edison and the left-hand cherub leaning over the frame of Raphael's "Sistine Madonna".'[86]

None of this allowed for a consistent political philosophy. Lloyd George compared him to a flea; 'he hopped about and you never knew where to catch him'.[87] Northcliffe himself asserted that if you said a thing often enough it became right or true.[88] His campaigns allowed no variation on a theme of black and white. 'Yes, we detest the Germans cordially,' he said in an interview in 1907. 'They make themselves odious to the whole of Europe. . . . I would not like to print anything which might be agreeable to the Germans.'[89] Capitalism and Empire were at the centre of his creed, but his control over newspapers with large circulations or great influence was what really mattered. Little wonder that he was the object of 'A Study in Malevolence', an open letter from an MP accusing him of being a vain, self-seeking megalomaniac, putting down and setting up governments at his pleasure.[90]

Megalomania was never very far removed from plutocracy. If there was one thing that men as disparate as Northcliffe and Lipton, Lever and Iveagh had in common it was a massive pride in their own achievement. The very depth of this pride made them uncertain about how to persuade the rest of society to register the achievement. Their activities revealed a strange mixture of assurance and the need for reassurance. They sought power – in one sense systematically, but in another with uncertainty – turning from high society to politics and back again as they tried to maximize their control over their surroundings. But whether they succeeded or not, there was no denying that the consequences for English social life and social structure were to be profound.

Chapter 12

The City of Pleasure

The City of Pleasure was built in 1905 south of the River Thames, near Barnes Common and Putney. Josephus Ilam's money purchased 300 acres there, with a marvellous half-mile frontage to the Thames on the east side. It was intended – and soon acknowledged by all the world – to be 'the most gigantic enterprise of amusement that Europe has ever seen'. It became 'the rage, the craze, and the vogue of London'.

The City of Pleasure was the product of Mr Ilam's money and Mr Carpentaria's imagination. 'From every roof floated great crimson flags with the legend in gold: "City of Pleasure. President: Ilam; Director: Carpentaria".' The centrepiece of the firework display was provided by two portraits of these twin Gods of the City, outlined in the powerful, bold lines of living flame.

Visitors came through the gates at the rate of 70,000 an hour, and one shilling a head: one shilling to enter, many more to be spent inside. 80,000 tiny electric lamps were used to light the Central Way alone; 5,000 dinners were served in the restaurants every evening. The City had theatre, music hall, circus, menagerie, concert-hall, Amusement Park, Oriental Gardens. . . .[1]

Arnold Bennett's City was a fiction, but it was not a bad metaphor for London in the era of the plutocrats. As the twentieth century began, London Society took on what one contemporary described as the swagger of a citizen of the world. Here was the sort of fake cosmopolitanism that pronounced 'Dindon' as 'La Turquie'.[2] Yet the reasons for London's designation as the 'metropolis of pleasure' by the disapproving Passmore Edwards were not wholly frivolous.[3] 'We are undoubtedly the greatest nation the world has ever seen,' declared William Lever, and 'We are here in the centre of the greatest city the world has ever seen.'[4] The explosive growth of the Empire and international trade brought wealth from overseas investment, from commerce and from shipping. Much of it gravitated to the City of London and paid for the range of indulgent pleasures that characterized the capital in the early years of the century. Money sustained London Society; and increasingly Society was *London* Society.

No one listened very much when Henry James criticized the 'clumsy conventional expensive materialized vulgarized brutalized life of London'.[5] No one seemed to notice the dust and the smells of summer, the dirty black snow lying in the streets in winter, the grime and the grease which contrived to enter the grandest houses and deposit a layer of filth on furniture and furnishings, the killing, pungent fogs enveloping those who ventured out. Everyone had his heart with Thomas Burke as his train roared along the insipid countryside, furiously intent on taking him to London and a further series of *Nights in Town*.[6] Slowly 'the grey incertitude' began to flower with the lights from thousands of homes, 'each window a little silent prayer'. The suburbs passed quickly, as suburbs should. ('The proper definition of suburbs', said Lord Abbotsworthy in *Mammon & Co*, 'is the place to which one does not go. They are merely a negative geographical expression.')[7] Then, at last, the 'misty sparkle' of Paddington or Euston station, and real excitement in prospect: 'huge black streets rent with loud traffic and ablaze with light from roof to pavement'; 'shop-fronts full of magical things, drowned in . . . lemon light'; and the night itself, for there was no night in all the world so rich in delicate delights as the London night.

The delights of Thomas Burke's London were the delights of the plutocracy. The appearance of 'a kind of high-class public housefeasting, combined with public house morals' – Marie Corelli's definition of a restaurant[8] – gave them ample opportunity for self-publicity. When Baron von Eckhardstein joined the German embassy in London at the end of 1891 he found that the great private houses and historic clubs were the centres of social life; when he came to write his memoirs the public hotels and restaurants had displaced them.[9] Lady Randolph Churchill recalled passing through London in August, when the town houses were usually closed, and facing the prospect of having nowhere to dine; the only 'possible' place was the St James's Hotel, and that provided – in cramped, 'dingy' surroundings – 'an apology for a dinner'.[10] Restaurants implied unconventional behaviour before the late 1890s; but the new century was not very far advanced when *The Tatler* could recommend Pagani's in Great Portland Street as one of a number of restaurants perfectly suitable for women alone in the West End.[11] There may not have been more entertaining in Edwardian times, but it seemed so because the private party became the public occasion. 'Who shall measure the growth of hotels, restaurants, cafés, clubs which has changed the face of London in less than a generation?' asked William Clarke in 1900.[12]

Lieutenant-Colonel Newnham-Davis – the early twentieth-century equivalent of the familiar 'Good Food Guide' man – was commissioned by the *Pall Mall Gazette* to write about the leading hotels and restaurants of London.[13] He was a guest at Woolf Joel's *rouge et noir* dinner at the Savoy, held to celebrate his coup at Monte Carlo – an occasion which was later repeated in white and green in an attempt to 'outdo the luxury' of the original: fruit-trees appeared to grow through the table, and each chair was a little bower of foliage. It was not unusual to encounter at the Savoy a party of South

African stockbrokers, who might not look wealthy but whose combined income surpassed that of half a dozen Balkan principalities. How they enjoyed watching the white-aproned waiters and the *maîtres d'hôtel* and the silver-chained sommeliers all silently moving between the tables: with M. Ritz in firm command of the whole, going from table to table with 'a carefully graduated scale of acknowledgment of the patrons'. M. Ritz gave his name to the famous hotel that was built in 1904 in the style of a French château; his successor at the Savoy was M. Jules, plump, immaculate and autocratic. Little more than a day's notice was necessary for the staging of George A. Kessler's 'Gondola Dinner' there – served on a Venetian gondola and other little boats in several feet of water.[14]

In October 1900 Jack Joel bet £25 that the stockbroker George Howard (189 lbs) could carry the City journalist Douglas MacRae (182 lbs) one hundred yards down Throgmorton Street. The crowd forced him to abandon the wager, but a consolation dinner – costing £10 per person – was held at the Carlton Hotel.[15] The Carlton, in Pall Mall, gained prestige when Edward VII, as Prince of Wales, dined in the public restaurant. Newnham-Davis invited the Boston Princess Lointaine, who had married an Italian aristocrat, to dine with him there. Among the company that evening: a Russian Grand Duke, with three of his fellow countrymen; the prettiest actress of the day *tête-à-tête* with some happy man; a Count from a foreign embassy, talking with a member of the merchant aristocracy; a Duchess as centre of attention at one of the many dinner-parties; the best-known Society painter in London the host at another table; an ambassador, a German prince, a great newspaper proprietor – 'all sumptuous, all luxurious, the mixed cream of all the societies from St James's to the pleasant land of refined Bohemia, in dress-clothes, silk, lace, and diamonds'.

The menu, chosen by M. Echenard himself after the Colonel's request in the morning, included ten courses for a mere £2 19s 6d, including a bottle of Pommery Greno 1889 at £1 1s. 'The suprême de volaille, served on its *socle* of clear ice, was the perfection of a cold entrée; and the ortolans, cooked in an earthenware *cocotte* and served with grapes, the skins and pips of which had been removed, were delicious.' It was as 'a tiny penance for greediness' that they ate only one each. The Colonel was doubtless not the only person who sat after dinner in the palm lounge, listening to the soft music 'in a sort of pleasant dream': seeing himself 'in the Court circle', 'doing the rounds of the studios and hunting with the hounds and going to the most delightful picnics with the most delightful people'.

No wonder that the porter at the Carlton, interviewed in 1912, found quiet only at breakfast time, when 'the Set likes to lie a bed a little . . . to think a bit and plan out the day's wickedness'.*[16]

The theatre atmosphere mirrored that of the restaurant: the thickness of the pile of all those red carpets alone helping to deaden the noisy décor. Social popularity for the theatre developed only in late Victorian times; before, one wit suggested, pleasure-seekers were more likely to make up a party to see a man hanged than to make up a party for the play. 'Good society does not go to the theatres', Taine observed in the 1870s.[17] Black was the only colour ladies were permitted to wear – as Lady Randolph Churchill discovered, when her husband was shocked to discover that she was contemplating anything 'so conspicuous' as pale blue. But by the time London had become 'the pleasure ground of the world' – this said in 1897 – it had also become apparent that the theatre was 'the easiest and the most attractive form of pleasure'.[18] Going to the opera had always been a more acceptable activity; and 'The Opera is, of course, the place of all others to see the glories of evening dress, the cloaks

---

* Cf. the OED's po-faced commentary on the word 'smart': 'The re-appearance of the word in this sense [fashionable] has been the subject of much comment and criticism in newspapers, etc., from about 1885, and the phrases *smart people*, *smart society*, *the smart set*, etc., have been commonly used as a general designation of the extremely fashionable portion of society (sometimes with implication of being a little "fast").'

especially being a constant vision of beauty in themselves.'[19] The performance was scarcely the centre of the activity, '"But then", as Sonia said, "you come to Covent Garden to *see* people."'[20]

Those who did watch Pinero's *Iris* at the Garrick, or Cecil Raleigh's *The Great Millionaire* at Drury Lane in October 1901 found similar subject-matter in the respective performances: 'a Jewish millionaire falling back on the primitive passion for revenge when an aspiration . . . [widely different in the two plays] has refused to be bought with so much gold.'[21] Raleigh's play included Charles Fulton, who entertained duchesses at the rate of £83 6s 8d per five minutes in the Carlton Hotel and who made a corner in wheat involving millions of pounds by making a few shouts down the telephone; and also the spendthrift peer Lord Deerwood, displaced from Deerwood Park by Fulton, and observed ('according to custom') staking his last thousand upon a single card. The fifty-seven London theatres of 1901, soon added to by the Coliseum, the Aldwych, the Scala, the Waldorf, used a simple test of a play's merit – at least through A. M. Thompson's socialist eyes: 'its power to titillate the epicurean sluggishness of Park Lane and Belgravia'.[22]

Balls, too, began to be given in public, in hotels, or to be organized from outside the house. 'Francine' was advised in *The Onlooker* in 1913 'to have a temporary ballroom; but consult the Mayfair Catering Co., who will advise you and who will, moreover, carry out the supper perfectly for you'.[23] The following year, *The Times* carried an angry letter from Baron Michelham (the Jewish banker, Herbert Stern, whose creation less than six months after he had been made a baronet created a storm of protest) complaining of high taxation, 'the means of driving the rich man entirely out of the country' and the cause of the cancellation of 'large bequests to hospitals and other charitable institutions'. Underneath Michelham's letter, in interesting juxtaposition, was a complaint from Sir Philip Burne-Jones that it could not be taken for granted any more that all the guests would know

each other at social gatherings: no longer was there 'a small
and exclusive set of the same people who met each other
night after night'; instead one found 'the rabble of guests
which constitutes a big London ball, say, at the Ritz or
elsewhere, when the majority of men are unknown, even by
sight, to the hostess herself'.

Anonymous correspondents of various kinds responded
next day. 'Tango' thought Sir Philip entirely missed 'the
spirit of the times'; the modern girl would not sit out if she
was unintroduced; she would come to the dance 'armed with
a man, often with more than one man.' 'Three Dances a Week'
was happy to have escaped from 'the gloomy atmosphere of
"correctness" and punctilio', pleased that 'The old social
machinery cannot cope with the "mammoth" gatherings
which fashion now ordains'. The rather less radical 'Student
of Human Nature' agreed the 'whole trouble arises out of the
size of the dances now given'.*[24] Certainly it was news indeed
for a ball to be held without Jews or Americans, tradesmen or
maufacturers. The popularity of the hotel ball, as well as the
garden party, reflected the exodus by the newer members of
Society from the seclusion of the drawing-room.

London men's clubs did not throw open their doors to
anyone passing, least of all the press, but they too underwent
a similar revolution. T. H. S. Escott, in 1897, noted 'the
multiplication of joint stock palaces called clubs, which are
really co-operative homes for poor gentlemen',[25] but it was not
only the impoverished gentry to whom they appealed;
Beatrice Webb's nephew, who became a member of the
Stock Exchange after Oxford, was spending £350 a year on
subscriptions alone immediately before the First World War.[26]
White's, originally a coffee-house, had become a regular club
by about 1730; Boodle's and the Beefsteak were also

---

* This was not the end of the correspondence, but connoisseurs of
The Times will be pleased to note that the last letter of the day was the
comforting report from Whitstone rectory that the nightingale was now
to be found in Exeter, 'a new charm added to the many already possessed
by this part of Devonshire'.

eighteenth-century foundations; but by 1912 there were 108 described as 'Principal Clubs', more than fifty of them with a mainly or exclusively social function.[27] At the City Athenaeum in Angel Court, Barnato and Woolf Joel, Neumann and Whitaker Wright, were found, and financial tips – reliable and unreliable – could be picked up. There was also the City Carlton, St Swithin's Lane, and the City of London, Old Broad Street.[28] But in the main businessmen took good care to look away from the City for their social activities. In time they were to encourage the leather-chair, morning-paper staidness of the Club atmosphere: very different from Trollope's Beargarden, opened with 'the express purpose of combining parsimony with profligacy'.[29]

Away from clubs and restaurants, hotels and the theatre, inside the homes of the plutocracy, the ostentatious grandeur of Society London was carried to its great extremes. The Countess of Warwick may have been right in supposing that the quality of the food deteriorated in proportion to the size of the house and the number of servants.[30] But of the richness of what was served, as of the surroundings, there could be no doubt. Bismarck's physician, the great Dr Schweniging, once dined with Beit, Rhodes, Jameson and their friends in London, and was invited to give his opinion on the suitability of various dishes and drinks – Rhodes, and perhaps Beit, having health worries. Finally, on being confronted with this question and a glass of Napoleon brandy, the doctor walked to the sideboard, mixed small portions of the remaining dishes, and placed the result in front of Beit: 'There, you will now be able to see for yourself,' he said, 'don't you think that this is sufficient answer? Why, it's a chemical impossibility.'[31]

The grand style was essential, if *The Cookery Book of Lady Clark of Tillypronie* (1909) was any guide: 'The turtle', it explained, 'must be put in straw in the cellar and given water every two or three hours. It should be beheaded at night, and left hanging neck downwards.'[32] After that, a bottle of the most popular Society drink of the period – champagne – would be very welcome; but perhaps too an American cocktail, a Manhattan or Brain Duster, indicating that for some at least the 1920s began at the end of the nineteenth century. Curiously, consumption of beer, spirits and wine per head of population declined after 1900,[33] but that had much to do with Lipton's tea and Wills's tobacco: plutocracy intruded at every point. And dinner-table talk? 'Everybody quotes the price of stocks and shares,' Sir Algernon West lamented, 'and I have lived to see the day when a youthful scion of a noble and distinguished house produced from his pocket at dinner a sample bundle of silks to show how cheaply they could be bought at his establishment.' It was an age since – at a house party of Lord Lansdowne's – Macaulay had gone off into the library after breakfast and engaged in flights of the intellect before an admiring audience of fellow guests until dinner.[34]

Staider members of Society had always criticized its wilder elements for their frivolity and lack of intellectual depth; and to some extent they might find they had strange allies in manufacturers and businessmen brought up in a puritan tradition, whether they came from Bolton or Chicago. But money – the pre-eminent prerequisite for all the playthings of modern Society – became associated with the growth of all that was most trivial: of which there was more and more. 'They are frightened of thought', Arthur Ponsonby said of the 'Smart Set', 'because it might plunge them into desperation, they are frightened of knowledge because it might dispel their dearest illusions.'[35]

Even that strange Society group the 'Souls', which flourished in the last decade of the nineteenth century and included Balfour, Curzon, Margot Tennant and Aline, Lady Sassoon, could be accused of doing little more than playing shallow intellectual games which were never removed from the Society drawing-room or dinner-table. Andrew Carnegie was proud of his association with Mark Twain, John Morley and 'My dear friend, Matthew Arnold'; William Waldorf Astor encouraged Wells and Kipling, bought the *Pall Mall Gazette* (and later *The Observer*). According to the editor of *London Opinion*, however, the purchase of the *Gazette* was an obvious first step for a man with his eyes on a seat in the House of Lords;[36] it was, as Astor himself said, to be a paper 'by gentlemen for gentlemen', with one of the 'Souls', Harry Cust, as editor.

It was not only the food and the conversation – punctuated by all too rare intellectual distractions – that gave evidence of money. The clothes of the plutocracy were characterized by ostentation rather than formality as the Edwardian high summer approached. The fate of the unfortunate woman limited to £1,000 a year as a dress allowance was salutary: purchases had to include a velvet gown in November for 50 guineas, six 'sumptuous evening gowns' at £40 each, two 'little frocks as accessories' (£30–£35 each); a tea coat (£25) and a 'larky' billiard coat (£20); three smart summer gowns (£90 in all), plus one in alpaca and one in cotton; serge for Cowes week at 20 guineas; plain serge, bicycle suit, a cheviot (for the moors), golf suit, sporting costume – each with correct headgear – for Scotland; furs and winter gowns, evening coats, lingerie, blouses and petticoats; boots and gloves in due proportion, evening shoes for each evening dress; sunshades and lace collars and umbrellas and belts and sashes . . . and court presentation dress, with train, feathers, veil, bouquet.[37]

Presentation was essential: 'To a young girl', the *Harmsworth Magazine* declared in May 1900, 'it signifies the transition from girlhood to womanhood; from the obscurity of the schoolroom to the brilliancy of society life, in which at-homes, dinners, balls, garden parties, operas and theatres follow each other in a continuous whirl'. What's more: 'Even *trade* is not debarred.'[38] An etiquette book, revised in 1910, confirmed that the list of those received by the King and Queen included 'the wives and daughters of merchants, bankers, and members of the Stock Exchange, and persons engaged in commerce in a large scale'.[39] The attractions were obvious: those who were presented were those who were noticed by Society and Society's lookers-on. 'Another of their Majesties' Courts has come and gone,' sighed *The Tatler*. 'Another set of pretty white-robed *débutantes* have curtseyed themselves into the social vortex.'[40]

This was eighteen months after Edward VII had come to the throne – an event which led to changes in Court life as in everything else. Queen Victoria's drawing-rooms were held, without refreshment, in the early afternoon; Edward replaced them by evening courts. Mary, Lady Monkswell, a Victorian at heart, lamented in her journals that with 'the good old Queen' Court presentation was 'a comparatively simple undertaking'; but 'This new function held at night . . . filled us with a great dread of the unknown – we really did not know *what* might happen to us.' Her husband had been a Lord-in-Waiting to Queen Victoria, but though they had written just after Christmas 1901 to the Lord Chamberlain to say 'we wished to pay our humble duty to their Majesties', some offence followed, since an invitation was not received until the beginning of May the following year. Once there, Lady Monkswell soon pinpointed the key features: supper chairs for 300 people; everybody with diamonds; nobody wearing a gown that cost less than £20. As for the rest . . . it hardly mattered.[41]

The fact was that Society had become organized as a gigantic machine for the furtherance of ostentatious expenditure: at Court, in entertainment – public and private – and lastly in the world of art, a perfect expression and reflection of the quality of life in plutocratic London. One of the chief *Social Transformations of the Victorian Age* was seen in the enormous prices of late-Victorian times, the result not only of an increase in wealth but of the adoption of more lavish standards of expenditure.[42] According to *The Times*, the Jewish financier Lord Swaythling was 'a discriminating collector' – especially of Old English silver – but even his activities 'had somewhat lessened with the extraordinary advance in prices witnessed within the past few years'.[43] Arthur Ponsonby criticized an art world in which prices were unrelated to aesthetic values or even to demand, but to the whim of rich collectors who set the fashion.[44] When Colonel

North, the 'Nitrate King', was asked by Lady Randolph Churchill which painting he had bought for £8,000, he could only remember that it was 12 feet by 8.[45] And even Cecil Rhodes had his portrait painted, though (according to the Society painter P. Tennyson Cole) he put up with artists only because his friends and political supporters thought the painting of his portrait was an essential step in furthering his aims.[46]

The Quaker businessman, George Cadbury – 'Why should I hang fortunes on my walls while there is so much misery in the world' – seemed an oddity indeed.[47]

Joseph Duveen, dealer extraordinary, acted as a key figure in bringing art to the plutocracy.[48] Grandson of a Jewish Dutch blacksmith, he had watched such figures as the Prince of Wales, Sir Edward Guinness and Sir Ernest Cassel patronize his father's Oxford Street shop, which dealt in furniture and décor for the rich. 'It made me sick at my stomach to see people like Lord Iveagh buying mere art objects from us and paintings elsewhere.' He obtained advice from the German museum director (and friend of Alfred Beit), Wilhelm von Bode, who compiled the catalogue of the Hainauer Collection which Duveen purchased in 1906 for $2,500,000; and through his father's banking friend, Horace Farquhar, the firm managed to obtain credit of more than a million pounds early in the century. All the American millionaires – H. E. Huntington, Henry Clay Frick, Andrew Carnegie – proved good customers: it was as well, since his three offices, in London, New York and Paris, cost half a million dollars a year to run. The formula worked to perfection; noted for polishing restored Old Masters until their surface was like a mirror, he explained that the rich wanted only to see reflections of themselves when they looked at works of art.

Art and its social function became inextricably mixed. 'The President of the Royal Academy must ... not only be eminent in art,' it was said. 'He requires other qualities that are rarer among his fraternity' – not least 'social tact'. The consequences were interesting.[49] 'The Royal Academy Exhibition', said *Mayfair* in 1914, 'is no worse this year than usual.'[50] Ever since its foundation by royal charter in 1768 the Academy had been a stronghold of conservatism, with a stranglehold on opinion. It therefore became a natural focus for the plutocracy: in the Boer War, according to one wit, the pick of Englishmen were being shot in South Africa while the pick of the South African millionaires' wives were being hung at the Academy.[51] The May Show at the Academy in 1908 was typical, and *Vanity Fair* complained: 'Painting has become a profession, and the professors to a man are on the strict look out for fine houses and great possessions, and a lordly and dazzling way of life.' The 'anxiety for gold in bulk' had its impact on the paintings – Sargent's *Mr Balfour*, for instance, which presented him as 'being at least twelve feet high, and most gracile'.[52]

John Singer Sargent came on his father's side from an old-established but impoverished New England commercial family. In his early years in England – he was born in Florence – he relied heavily on new-rich patrons, such as the naturalized English banker Carl Meyer. He was the not always willing pioneer of an attitude to art which later found pale expression in the *Mayfair* advertisements that invited readers to have their portraits 'executed by the artists of the Mayfair Salon', thereby joining the Marquess of Crewe, the Duke of Manchester, a good sprinkling of Maharajahs and HIH the Grand Duke Michael Michaelovitch.[53] Tapestries, exotic flowers and fruits, coy Cupids, obtrusive artificial Arcadia, Classical pedestals – all tried to compete with figures that still managed to overpower them.

P. Tennyson Cole, who fought off all rebuffs until he finally obtained commissions to paint Edward VII, observed: 'I have always felt irritated when, just because I am a painter, people expect me to have "a soul above money".' It annoyed him that Lady Wernher (of all people), when agreeing to pay 500 guineas for a portrait of her husband, remarked on the amount of money he must be making.[54] Sargent himself, tall, bearded, firm-faced, looked more like a lawyer or businessman than an artist – described when seen in 1899 in the doorway of 44 Belgrave Square as 'a rather good looking fellow . . . whom at my first sight I took to be a superior mechanic'.[55]

Sargent painted for the plutocracy mirror-images of their wealth. As Sir Osbert Sitwell observed, they loved him not only because he showed them to be rich, but because – by looking at their portraits – they could comprehend just how rich they were.[56] The sheen of the satin and the silk, the richness of the velvet and the brocade, the glinting-gold glittering-diamond dowdiness of it all – 'We must look at these pictures', said Roger Fry looking back from the twenties, 'not as works of art with a value in and for themselves, but as illustrations or reports about other things.'[57] A great contrast with lugubrious Victorian realism, but not an artistic revolution: rather the visible symbol of the transference of power in society. The men might not like it – 'My wife's neck is not green', complained Sir Edgar Speyer – but their wives did.

Sargent expressed it all; but he did not accept it. Edward VII's recommendation in 1907 that he should be knighted was rejected because (Sargent said) he was still an American citizen.[58] The number of his portraits declined from perhaps fifteen in 1906 and again in 1907, to eight in 1908, three in 1909; and finally he abandoned them for landscapes.[59]

'I cannot do a face', he said, 'simply because it happens to belong to somebody who has money to spend.'[60]

Chapter 13

High Times at Home and Abroad

If London – with its grand houses, its Society dinners and art exhibitions and theatre – was the centre of the universe, it was not quite the whole of the plutocrats' universe, especially after the changes wrought by the transport revolution they themselves helped to realize. About one thing the desultory Society magazine *Mayfair* was indisputably correct: 'The horse is best disowned and forsaken even by its best-tried friends. Soon the forlorn animal will betake itself to the Zoological Gardens and beg for the hospitality of a cage.'[1] But that marvellous new invention the car provided a means of escape from a London that could become very wearing. As Lord St Helier observed, it took one from the heart of the metropolis into genuine countryside in a few hours: a case of civilization providing an antidote for its own poison.[2]

The 'poison' was suitably expressed in Consuelo Vanderbilt's 1908 diary:

The London season is at its fag end. Conscience-stricken hostesses with unpaid social debts are sending out belated invitations in a vain effort to fulfil neglected obligations. Every night one is bidden to three or more balls. Today there are six parties, and at one of them a monkey called 'Peter' for whose services in entertaining her guests a hostess paid £150.

The motor-car was used as a speedy – and necessary – method of departure; and Consuelo slept for twenty-four hours solidly at the end of her first Season, after her removal to the seaside 'to recuperate'.[3]

The motor-car was introduced to the English public at a Crystal Palace exhibition in 1896. The 800 cars purchased in 1900 had become 33,800 in the peak pre-war year of 1913. Edward VII was photographed taking his first ride in one in June 1898, and marked the occasion by declaring: 'The motor car will become a necessity for every English gentleman.'[4] His critics appreciated the appeal the new form of transport had for him: novelty, complexity and, above all, costliness – the perfect formula for acceptance at Court.[5] It was, after all, very much a phenomenon of the Edwardian era; the Northcliffe-inspired *Motors and Motor-Driving* traced the motoring movement to Cugnot's steam carriage of 1769 – but recognized that it was only within the last two or three years that concentrated efforts had been made to establish it for both pleasurable and practical purposes.[6]

Wealth and the car went together: Marie Corelli spoke of 'a rapid lady of the new Motor-School of Morals' and of 'the motor-car traffic of plutocrats', with their 'push, effrontery and brazen impudence'.[7] George Bernard Shaw ('this cheery philosopher has more than his fair share of wisdom in motoring matters', it was said) identified the Edwardian phase in the motor-car movement as the 'plundering of plutocrats'.[8] Perhaps that was what was meant by a report in *The Times* that Sir Thomas Lipton had been fined £5 and costs for driving a motor-car at the rate of thirty miles an hour along the Great North Road near Potters Bar.[9] For the moment, however, it was 'The Luxury of the Modern Motor-Car' and not its speed that was remarkable, at least in the eyes of the author of *Motor-Cars and their Story* (1911): the coach-builder, given a free hand, put the latest fashion in drawing-rooms on to wheels.[10] It was no surprise to hear that the stately Sitwells mistook Mr Scrutton for the son of a multi-millionaire when he arrived in 1907 to 'the accompaniment of a great deal of honking of horns and of brass flashing in the sun'. (The youthful plutocrat, it transpired, was only a car salesman in disguise.)[11]

Early motoring was not without its hazards. Lady Gwendolen Cecil's little electric car ran backwards and knocked her down when she was 'dismounted' to open a gate in 1908.[12] But this sort of frivolity could not hide the deep consequences for rural society: here, argued C. F. G. Masterman, was 'an England vulgarized by the clamour and vigour of the newer wealthy, racing each other down from the noise of the town, into the heart of a great silence: the silence that broods over a doomed and passing race'. The 'motoring classes' were the representatives of the arrogance of wealth.[13] If Masterman was not the most objective of observers, it remains clear that the motorists were an important force destroying rural cohesion – directly among the ruling classes, indirectly among those they ruled. The strength of county feeling had always depended on the fact that those who lived on the land had horizons limited by their immobility; now the process which had begun with the development of the railways was completed with the newer form of transport.[14]

The plutocrats' dream! As *Mayfair* said, it had become perfectly possible to go to a ball every night of the week, each in a different county.[15] Lord Montagu of Beaulieu foresaw the car's revolutionary effect on everyday life and its use in every kind of social and sporting activity. No longer would those in search of Scottish salmon have to wait three days to catch up with news brought late to them by *The Times*. Speed ruled; and when in 1902 even Hercules Langrishe, Master of the Kilkenny Fox Hounds, bought a Panhard car to convey him to meets, it could be seen that the wind of social, as well as mechanical change, was blowing like a hurricane.[16]

Rural life and the country house were not the only targets

for the roving motorcrat or his rather more limited kinsman on the railway. Provincial towns with some strong institutional connection – Oxford and Cambridge with their universities, Portsmouth with the navy – had their local seasons. Dublin, under Lord and Lady Dudley, perhaps came nearest to London magnificence, but – as *Society in the New Reign* suggested – London was the magnet for anyone who could afford its pleasures. Bath or Brighton, Buxton or Harrogate displayed 'the veneered vulgarity which is the provincial substitute for smartness'. 'Subscription dances, fancy fairs, theatricals and "at homes" outvie Mayfair in the height of the Season; and toilettes of London-super-mare exaggerate those of London on the Thames.' Invitations to the Mayor's ball were accompanied by more intrigue than royal entertainments at Devonshire House.[17]

New hotels made possible an itinerant society as flashy as the buildings themselves; Harrogate, according to *The Tatler* in 1902, had recently become fashionable, chiefly through the opening of 'a new mammoth hotel which has attracted a number of notable people'.[18] Hotels, seen through the eyes of H. G. Wells, were a practice-ground for the social learner, an aid in the systematic conversion to gentility. Sir Blundell Maple's launching party for the Victoria Station Hotel, Nottingham – erected, fitted and furnished throughout by his firm – was actually described by *Truth* as a 'house-warming'. This building put all its emphasis on the lavishness of its décor: here the 'man of business in his journeys can enjoy a degree of comfort, not to say luxury and splendour, of which his predecessors never dreamed'.[19]

Seaside developments reflected the same forces. The trade unions first passed a resolution in favour of paid annual holidays in 1911, but it was long after that before they became common for working men. In the meantime, comic attempts were made to turn English coastal towns into cosmopolitan equivalents of favoured Biarritz: Eastbourne, for example, sought to emulate the finer social points of French holiday life.[20] Those with sufficient funds, like Lord

Battersea could buy themselves a villa, as he did at Overstrand, near Cromer on the Norfolk coast. Clement Scott, the
author, described it in 1889: 'It is so unpretentious, so tiny,
so completely under the eyes of everybody, that one is
overwhelmed at the idea of a member of the Royal Family
staying there, for Princess Louise actually took her tea on
the wee lawn' while 'the fishermen's wives hung their washing
up in full view . . . and the Royal visitor bought her own
stamps at the shop and strolled unattended on the sands – this
seems incredible.' The Batterseas must have thought so too,
for Lutyens was set to work to evolve from the old cottage a
new home, with its own tennis court and cricket ground.[21]

Also with a home at Overstrand was Sir Edgar Speyer: a
luxurious place which was to be the scene of a strange spying
scandal when life became unpleasant for German-born
financiers on the outbreak of war in 1914. German and
Jewish: Cromer's nickname was 'Jerusalem-on-Sea'.

Of all the activities of the plutocrats outside London, those
of a sporting kind received special attention. Many criticisms
were made of the shooting plutocracy. Their inexperience,
it was said, led them to wound and maim rather than kill the
game. Hypocrisy doubtless went with these judgments –
Andrew Carnegie commented on General Sheridan's 'curious'
ideas of sport, by which he would not shoot animals driven
to him. 'As for hunting down a poor hare – that needs the
deadening influence of custom,' Carnegie sourly concluded.[22]
Certainly there could be no argument about the popularity
of the sport. 'You've no idea how much time and money they
spend on shooting,' the American ambassador wrote in 1913.
'The King has been shooting most of the time for three
months.'[23] It is less likely that those who organized the
co-operative shoots on the edge of towns felt the romance of
it all. More interesting for plutocrats was a typical shooting-
party luncheon: fillets of sole, iced lobster soufflé, fillets of
duckling with goose-liver *farce*, braised stuffed quails, roast
pheasant, Japanese salad and so on.[24] Thus the 1911 study of

John Passmore Edwards
by G. F. Watts

Alfred Harmsworth

George Cadbury in 1890 –
about ten years after the
new factory at Bournville
had been established

Sir Edward Guinness,
later first Earl of Iveagh

King Edward VII as a Sportsman noted that with such technical improvements as the replacement of the breech-loader by the muzzle-loader came 'an increase of luxury in the conditions of shooting':[25] the end of sandwiches in the open and the substitution of lengthy luncheons in tented splendour.

Ironically, it was Andrew Carnegie who pointed out that the prices for deer forest in Scotland were 'absurd': $25–50,000 per annum 'for the right to shoot over a few thousand acres of poorly timbered land, and a force of gamekeepers and other attendants to pay for besides'.[26] His successful contemporaries did not seem to mind. 'Scotland is overrun during the shooting season, not by English squires, for they have not the means, but by wealthy stockbrokers, by the heads of large establishments in London, by the owners of funded property' – the writer was Charles Milnes Gaskell in the *Nineteenth Century* as early as 1882.[27] Cecil Rhodes, over from South Africa in 1901, took the lease of Sir Robert Menzies's Rannoch Lodge: two months for £2,000, with the expectation of shooting 500 brace of grouse and the right to kill 30 deer. Winston Churchill ('a young man who will go far if he doesn't over-balance') stayed, and so did Alfred Beit (but he never shot).[28]

Shooting, like all sport, had provided an important social bond in country life. Galsworthy's description of Mr Pendyce said all that was necessary: 'His wife was a Totteridge, and his coverts admirable.'[29] It was significant, however, that not everything was fair game for the guns. The pseudonymous Baron Hounymhum, a Hungarian nobleman, was said to have been ostracized from Society when he told Sir Harry Tread-win, a sporting baronet, that he had *shot* as many as five or six foxes a day: 'It was nothing that he had been thought guilty of an attempt to assassinate his sovereign, nothing that he was thought to have eloped with a married woman, wrecked her home and shot her husband.' He had shot foxes – and that was 'The Unpardonable Sin'.[30]

In defence against the intrusion of the big-spending *nouveaux riches* the love of sport became associated with a much broader philosophy of life – a 'sporting' code of behaviour. By a grand paradox, the 'sporting' tradition was created at the very time its exponents claimed it was under dissolution; there had not been very much that was 'sporting' about such aristocratic activities as bull-fighting, abolished in the 1830s, in which the bull's horns were sawn, its tail and ears cropped, its nostrils plugged with peppers.[31] The confusion was well expressed in a magazine article of 1896, which remarked with pleasure that Yale was sending a crew to Henley. The Yale men (apparently unlike those from Cornell and other American sportsmen) were 'free from the delusion that the main object of rowing a race is to win the prize'; they would 'come to row rather than to win', and if they lost they would take their defeat 'like sportsmen and gentlemen'. In fact, by the end of the century the Henley Regatta had ceased to be a very exclusive affair; it had long been divorced from the genuine traditions which dated back to the first race between Leander and Oxford in 1829, when the losing Oxford crew had included the wild Marquis of Waterford, later killed hunting.[32] Even *Mayfair* declared, in 1911, that 'Going to Henley is very much like supping at what is known as a cosmopolitan restaurant, because it is frequented by the American million-airage, the stage, and the Stock Exchange.'[33]

Attacks were made on the huntsmen who on weekdays would be found in the City uniform of the Stock Exchange,[34] but the sporting ritual had itself become big business, with £45,000,000 invested in it in 1910, and a further £40,000,000 a year spent on it.[35] The issue became muddled because many of those with the money to devote to sport themselves set out to encourage a sporting ethos. Sir Lewis Michell's 1912 abridged biography of Cecil Rhodes, in which many of the details of the original work were omitted, still gave space to the fact that he won a place in the school first eleven in 1866 at the age of thirteen.[36] In a subtle, but far-reaching way, all these conflicting developments came together in the most important sporting activities: shooting and hunting, card-playing for the less physically active, and, above all, the turf.

'You will never have a revolution in England', Bismarck once told Disraeli, 'as long as you keep up your racing.'[37] Those who witnessed the scenes when Edward VII's Minoru won the Derby would have agreed. Worldly success and horse ownership went together. 'Apart from the Derby having been won by some of the greatest horses in the world', *Bob Sievier's Sporting Annual* declared in 1912, 'it may also be said to have been secured by the greatest of men.'[38] Even Alfred Beit, who was no sportsman, owned horses in Germany, though it is doubtful whether he ever noted when they were racing.[39] Ernest Hooley actually found those who dominated the turf 'a bit too warm for me at that game'. At the height of the Dunlop boom Lord Marcus Beresford, who then trained the Prince of Wales's horses, sold him a thoroughbred yearling foaled at Sandringham for £5,000. 'I gathered that the Derby was the least of the races that it could win,' Hooley recalled.[40] The 'wonder' horse was so useless that he later gave it to a stable lad. Barney Barnato, who was spending at the rate of £10,000 a year on the turf after he came to England in March 1894, also had his horses managed by Lord Marcus Beresford. His nephews, Solly and Jack, both won the Derby; and Jack became involved in a remarkable vendetta with Robert Sievier, a well-known racing personality, which revealed with perfect accuracy the impact of plutocracy on the turf world.

R. S. Sievier, born in 1860, the son of a sculptor, had travelled widely.[41] In Australia, he observed, 'gambling . . . might have been styled the custom of the country – as indeed, it is the custom of any body of free men, especially those who have lost their hymn-books'. Having abandoned a stage career, he seemed to have the perfect background for the race-track: 'if I am not a bold speculator', he said, 'I am nothing.' He married, in 1892, Lady Mabel Brudenell-Bruce, sister of the Marquess of Ailesbury, whose gambling losses played a large part in his downfall. Sievier owned, trained, backed horses; and, at the time of his arrest in the paddock at Sandown Park in 1908 – charged with illegally attempting to obtain £5,000 from Jack Joel – he edited a racing weekly, the *Winning Post*.

The *Winning Post* carried satirical articles on a wide range of personalities, Joel, Cassel and Leopold de Rothschild among them. (Hilaire Belloc's Mr Clutterbuck carried fact into fiction, and was characterized there 'as a sportsman, excused for his personal sobriety, portrayed in a top hat, frock coat, trousers, spats, buttoned boots, and perhaps thirty years less than his actual age'.)[42] Sievier had several grudges against Joel; his trainer, Norton, had been lured away by 'the weight of money'; money too had given Joel a horse that Sievier much wanted. In an open letter in the *Winning Post*, addressed to 'J. B. Joel of Grosvenor Square', he set out to prove that Joel 'was an illicit diamond buyer, a thief's accomplice, and a fugitive from justice, having estreated his bail in one of His Majesty's Colonies for many thousands of pounds'. The core of this was that Sievier had discovered the details of an apparent offence by Joel, who had failed many years before to register a diamond purchase, and had left South Africa before clearing up the matter. The charge was not itself serious – the police had never taken any further action – but Sievier claimed that Joel had employed someone 'to beat and maim' him. Sievier's alleged attempts to obtain money from Joel by extortion eventually led to his trial in July 1908. He was acquitted this time, to the delight of a crowd of five thousand, though he was later discredited in another court case in which he sued, and was sued by, the trainer Richard Wootton.[43]

Sievier was a man with a chip on his shoulder. There had been an upheaval in the 1880s over his presentation at Court, when it was said that he had been 'engaged on the Turf in Australia as a bookmaker' under the name of Sutton. Sir William Grantham later claimed that Queen Victoria would 'sooner have vacated her throne' than that he should have been presented; Sievier shrugged this off – 'I remained a member of Boodle's' – but it was no surprise that he saved his special enmity for plutocrats who succeeded in Society where he failed. The turf, he said had become infested 'with what I can only term an invasion of the scum of the States', placing enormous bets (after all, 'one hundred dollars in America is but £20 in English money'). And worse: 'Twenty years ago there were no Jewburg owners running horses in our English racecourses. Since then dealers in stolen diamonds, fugitives from justice, the scum of swindling speculators who, like leeches, have sucked the life-blood of many a noble family, have taken the place of their victims. . . . With this gang the spirit of the sport doesn't enter into the game; indeed, racing is rather utilized as a key with which to open the door to society.'[44]

The intrusion of large amounts of money into racing certainly encouraged some unpleasant practices. Edward VII's mistress, Lillie Langtry, owned Regal Lodge, just outside Newmarket, where – in the years before the First World War – winners were flashed from the course and bets then telegraphed via the son of a respectable London solicitor to London bookmakers.[45] The Hon. George Lambton encountered doping at Newmarket in October 1896, when Damsel II beat Horace Farquhar's East Sheen in the Trial Selling Stakes; he bought the winning horse for auction at £450, but the same evening found that she 'had been running round her box like a mad thing ever since she came home'.[46] Doping became a menace in the new century, and though it took some time for it to be made a criminal offence, its growth coincided with the great growth in the sport. The number of horses racing in 1878 was 2,097, in 1908 3,706; the number of pre-advertised large meetings was 78 in 1881, 164 in 1909.[47] Racing was expensive and, to that extent, the sporting plutocrat was useful to the turf. On the other hand, unless the sport had given its followers social prestige, the wealthy breeders would not have devoted time and money to it.[48]

It was not all fun. Picture the scene, with *Vanity Fair*, at the Two Thousand Guineas at Newmarket in May 1908. 'The mud was appalling, and those feminine racegoers who had ventured on anything more diaphanous than tailor-made dresses and thick boots had their clothes and footgear pretty well ruined by the rain and the ankle-deep slush.'[49] The King stared fixedly at the race through glasses: if he was disappointed at his horse's performance, he did not show it – besides he would be dining with Cassel in the course of the meet. The weather was usually better for the Derby at Epsom early in the next month; and then, at the apogee of the London Season, came Ascot – attractive enough even for Alfred Beit to take a house at Sunningdale. *The West-End* noted, in 1899, the institution of 'pay parties' there, by which several people would make up a house-party at a cost of £50–£100 per head for the week.[50] Cameras were banned, especially in the royal enclosure[51] – the plutocracy wanted to be seen by the aristocratic social world, not by aspirants from the middle classes.

Goodwood, in August, had been held in the Duke of Richmond's park since 1802. The Duke had the freedom to decide on what terms the public were admitted – it was alleged that the ducal coffers benefited each year to the extent of £5,000. Still, as R. S. Sievier said, what more perfect approach could there be to this 'queen of all meetings': through the lodge-gates, past the mansion, along the tree-lined avenues, up the hill to the famous Birdless Grove for a first sight of the racecourse itself; from the summit countryside stretching as far as the eye could see, perhaps – on a clear day – a glimpse of the blue Solent in the distance.[52] And, just as the private view at the Academy marked the opening of the Season, so did Goodwood give a sign that the mad fashionable months were drawing to a close.[53]

By August, in which the yachting races at Cowes also took place, thoughts were directed to more distant parts. Encouraged by Lipton's success with the King, Ernest Hooley spent £5,000 on the Earl of Lonsdale's *Verena*: 'Most newly made millionaires buy a yacht at some time or another', he said blandly, 'and I was no exception to the general rule.' He tried to buy the royal yacht *Britannia* (incurring Queen

Victoria's displeasure), owned Lillie Langtry's *White Wings* for a few months, gave his partner Martin Rucker Lord Ashburton's *Venetia* – and watched the latter go backwards and forwards between Rucker and Whitaker Wright in exchange for some bogus consols. Wright renamed the yacht, which was later owned by Cornelius Vanderbilt, *Sybarite*, Sybarus being the ancient Greek city in Italy that was famous for luxury – and utterly destroyed in 510 BC.[54] Meanwhile, J. B. Robinson cruised in the Mediterranean and Baltic in *La Belle Sauvage* and had the satisfaction of being shown arm-in-arm with the Prince of Wales in the Johannesburg *Moon*, above the caption, 'A royal Visitor for "La Belle Sauvage" '.[55] Solly Joel, off to the Riviera in *Eileen*, was undismayed by the competition . . . and Lady Pirrie, daughter of an Irish Inspector of Schools, wrote happily in 1912:

Yachting is a delightful way of getting about and a real holiday. . . . We spent quite a delightful week at Kiel. The regatta was on; crowds of people from everywhere; weather is glorious. . . . The Emperor paid us a surprise visit one morning bringing with him some of his Ministers. I had the pleasure of a tête-à-tête visit of nearly half an hour . . . and found him most easy and charming to talk to.[56]

Yachts offered luxury (Arthur Ponsonby described the 'great majority' as 'floating houses of luxury' in 1910)[57] and social prestige. Lady Barnacle, on *Foam Queen* for Cowes week, plotted the marriage of her Algy to Miss Scriven. ('It is essential that you marry money. What with the Licensing Bill and other Socialistic measures, goodness only knows whether this isn't going to be our last year's yachting.') Algy was sensible enough to meet Virginia, the much richer daughter of Jupp, the indigestion pill king from Persepolis, Nebraska, and all was well. Virginia, *inter alia*, noted: 'So that's Erin. Sir Thomas Lipton's, isn't it? He bosses your House of Lords, doesn't he? No? That's a pity.' All the product of R. S. Sievier's imagination – but not too far wide of the mark.[58] Daisy, Princess of Pless, noted in her Cowes diary in August 1908: 'Now I must dress; I hope to get away early to-night after dinner and arrive at Newmarket about midnight with the help of Sir Thomas Lipton's launch and that of his motor which is to meet me on the other side. A dear, nice man,' she added, 'it is most kind of him.'[59]

Yachting, sometimes far afield in the ocean-going variety, was symbolic of a wider process heralded by the age of the pluto-crats. 'What is the life of the rich man of today?' asked Lady Dorothy Nevill in 1906. The answer was 'A sort of firework! Paris, Monte Carlo, big-game shooting in Africa, fishing in Norway, dashes to Egypt, trips to Japan.' When she travelled to Munich as a child, the family party of six had taken two maids, a footman, a French cook, a courier, two *fourgons* to hold the *batterie de cuisine*, six beds (there were no real hotels), the family coach and a barouche, six horses, and two attendant grooms.[60] But by 1914, you could take your car or taxi to Charing Cross, stroll into the Pullman, sit at a chair as comfortable as any at your club, and depart for the Conti-nent 'with a copy of MAYFAIR and the other illustrated weeklies at your elbow'.[61] (Already, as early as 1912, Elaine de Frey – honeymooning in Vienna – discovered that the most ex-pensive hotels in Europe showed 'a depressing international likeness'.)[62]

At the end of the London Season, you would probably need to go to one of the spas – 'Il faut aller aux eaux pour se détruffer' was an accurate, if uninviting expression.[63] Sebas-tian, in *The Edwardians*, reflected that there was very little difference between Marienbad and a Roman *vomitorium*.[64] At Marienbad you would find the American Guggenheim or the South Africans Wernher and Beit; at dinner in the Savoy Hotel, Karlsbad, Jameson spoke with feeling against the use of white labour in the mines: far too expensive, he said, and it would lower them to the level of the natives.[65] At Biarritz, in early 1908, the villa and hotel bookings indicated that 'the same entourage which is generally to be found about King

Edward wherever he goes will once again spend a portion of the season at Biarritz'. Cassel was among those expected. Surprisingly, the casino was 'the dullest and most mousily respectable institution of its kind in the world, not barring the spa at Scarborough or the Winter Garden at Bournemouth'.[66]

The casino at Monte Carlo had been opened in 1871 and until 1914 it used gold plaques worth five pounds at the tables – a reflection not merely of the strength of the English currency, but of the large-scale presence of English gamblers.[67] In 1912 Mr Adolphe Smith published the official lists of the deaths in Monte Carlo from all causes during the year 1911 – his purpose: 'a counter-blast to the many stories of suicides'.[68] According to Frank Harris, Monte Carlo was 'all made up and fictitious, like an over-dressed woman of uncertain virtue, who laid on the powder and the paint, and reddened her lips and darkened her eyelashes, and who, at the end, is not beautiful, but a mere mask'. He advised readers of *Vanity Fair* that if they must go, they should make for the Riviera Palace Hotel 'throned six hundred feet up the mountain side in clear, limpid air, scented with the healthy resin of the stone-pines'.[69] William Lever, who was in Monte Carlo in the winter of 1891–2, eschewed the gambling: 'It appeared such an utterly foolish waste of money and such an absolute certainty that we should lose it'; he found the faces of the players in the casino 'a grand study of human nature'.[70] Ernest Hooley was one of them a few years later; he claimed to have spent £1,000 a week on the Riviera; and at his hotel the *chef d'orchestre* would arrange – for five louis a time – a special musical programme for Madame 'Ooley, wife of the famous millionaire.

In April 1912 an astonishing telegraphed message from Bruce Ismay, Chairman of the White Star shipping line, arrived in New York: 'Deeply regret advise you Titanic sank this morning after collision iceberg, resulting serious loss of life. Full particulars later.'[71] In the decade before a fierce battle

had been fought between rival companies in order to offer the
biggest, grandest, fastest liners to wealthy customers. When
the *Olympic*, sister ship of the *Titanic*, made her maiden
voyage to New York in June 1911, it was entirely in character
that the only problem was due to the beds being too comfortable: their springs, Ismay wrote back to Liverpool,
'accentuated the pulsation in the ship to such an extent as to
seriously interfere with passengers sleeping.'[72] The *Titanic*
itself offered two 'millionaire suites' at a cost of nearly £900
for one crossing of the Atlantic at the height of the season.
Gymnasium and miniature golf course, squash courts and
swimming baths catered for a variety of tastes; special
accommodation was provided for dogs travelling First Class.
'The ship is a monstrous floating Babylon', wrote the journalist
W. T. Stead, who was on board when it departed for New
York for the first and only time; his fellow passengers included John Jacob Astor and Benjamin Guggenheim. As
Filson Young's contemporary account concluded, the ship
in section was like 'a microcosm of civilized society': up above
'the people who rest and enjoy'; down below 'the people who
sweat and suffer'.[73]

The iceberg that sank the *Titanic* was a perfect symbol of
what was to follow. The luxuries of the plutocratic *belle
époque* were to disappear for ever in the wake of the changes
brought about by the First World War. The reign of the
Titanic, like the reign of the plutocrats, had been brief but
brilliant.

England's characteristically quaint originality had lain in
its admission of the plutocracy into Society, while continuing
to subscribe to the values of aristocracy. One of the millionaires – it may have been Wernher – told Beatrice Webb that
he had chosen to settle in England rather than one of the
other European capitals 'because in England there is complete equality'.[74] What he meant was that wealth gave an
equality of opportunity in the battle for a place in a highly
unequal society. In Austria-Hungary, in the early years of the
century, pressure from outside circles had done little to relax

aristocratic control; the Princess of Pless, writing in her diary, confirmed that Vienna Society was 'select and religious'. In Germany considerations of usefulness to the Prussian state helped to break down exclusiveness, except in the army; but Berlin was 'worse than all – bands and beer. . . . The Court is narrow-minded, theatrical and domineering'. Russia, said the Princess, was 'silent, bearded, morose'. The Baroness de Stoeckl, married in 1892 to a Russian diplomat, had to remain in mourning for over a year for her father-in-law, who had died six months before her marriage, and whom she had only seen twice in her life. In France and Italy there were coteries, but no collective body, identified as Society, was known.

But England – in England everything was 'free and easy, sporting, gambling, well-dressed'.[75] Something more than hindsight suggests that it was almost as if Society – launched on a programme of change – was waiting for the decisive upheaval that came with war before openly discarding the standard values and institutions and habits of the landed elite. Unrest and lawlessness in British society as a whole may have reflected the same factors. Industrial civilization had arrived; landed social values survived: the war would pronounce in favour of the former. Suffragettes and syndicalists, strikes and the threat of civil war in Ireland – these were the backcloth against which the rich launched into a last frenzy of conspicuous consumption. For the moment the air was full of a superficially sweet smell of warm earth and lime leaves, giant orchids and malmaisons. But when England declared war on 4 August 1914 those who looked upon it as the chance for a new sort of picnic were to receive the rudest of shocks.

Chapter 14

Casualties of War and Change

War brought change. How could it be otherwise? C. E. Montague, in *Disenchantment*, observed that men who had seen cities turned to rubble and chased emperors from their thrones were hardly likely to share 'the Englishman's old sense of immutable fixity in institutions'.[1] Revolutions removed the rulers of Russia, Germany, Austria and Turkey. Of the kings and royal princes who were at Edward VII's funeral in 1910, one committed suicide, one abdicated, three were deposed, three assassinated, three exiled.[2] Many of them owed their fate to the changes set in motion by the Great, gory War. Casualties of battle resulted in unbelievable statistics: 9,000,000 men mobilized from the British Empire, more than a third of them dead or wounded. The social effects were readily understandable.

C. F. G. Masterman looked back in *England After War* with a sentimentality that might be excused:

In the retreat from Mons and the first battle of Ypres perished the flower of British aristocracy; 'playing the game' to the last, as they had been taught to play it all through their days of boyhood. . . . In the useless slaughter of the Guards on the Somme, or of the Rifle Brigade in Hooge Wood, half the great families of England, heirs of large estates and wealth, perished without a cry.

The landed classes, beaten back to their diminishing estates by triumphant plutocracy, vanished in blood and fire.[3]

For those that remained, more subtle consequences followed from the mixing of social classes. Sir Henry Lucy noted in his diary in 1916 that one of the oldest and best-known clubs, noted for its members' use of the blackball to exclude undesirable aspirants to membership, had decided 'that this is not the time for cultivating exclusiveness'.[4] Conscription of the able-bodied men in the country forced middle- and upper-class women to work and undertake tasks of an entirely new kind to them. Servants too: William Lanceley, who was born in 1854 and ultimately became steward to the Duke of Connaught, explained that 'The war called for hands to help, and many servants responded to the call. The work they were asked to do was a novelty to them, the pay was big and they had short hours, hundreds being spoilt for future service through it. It made those who returned to service unsettled.'[5] Etiquette and the formalities of society tended to dissolve under the pressures of war; eating in restaurants had itself once been frowned upon, but now diners even began to abandon the full rigours of evening wear.[6] The many ingredients in the concoction making up society – of which such trivia were, in aggregate at least, an important part – were all affected in one way or another.

Ostentatious luxury was bound to be less in evidence in the war. Claridge's held austere war concerts; fireworks were abandoned at the fourth of June celebrations at Eton. As the American ambassador observed in the early stages of the war, 'There isn't any formal social life now – no dinners, no parties.' When he stayed the night with the King in 1917, he was offered bread, one egg, and lemonade to drink.[7] The change did not happen all at once; nor was it complete. Armageddon seemed a trifling matter in the drawing-room, where new social games were introduced, based on being in the know: you had to criticize Kitchener, or say something biting about the French, or declare you were sick of the Belgians.[8] Débutantes found time to abandon their canteen war-work for their more serious labours in the ballrooms of society.[9]

Nevertheless, the City Editor of *The Times* had a point when he suggested that the war was at least 'teaching us that the wealth of a nation is not a pile of commodities to be frittered away in vulgar ostentation and stupid self-indulgence'.[10]

He omitted to note that the dominance of the money power might actually be increased once the wild pursuit of consumption was abandoned.

The First World War appeared to result much more from the machinations of aristocratic diplomats than those of international businessmen. But it speedily became clear, as Neville Lytton lamented, that the war was to be conducted by 'engineers, gunners, and businessmen; there was practically no element of sport and practically no hand-to-hand fighting'.[11] Victory would not go to the cavalry, but to those with the best-mechanized transport, telephone communications, artillery and machine guns; and to the nation with the strongest, most efficient and most developed economy, organized to provide supplies of all kinds on a gigantic scale. Weetman Pearson, created Baron Cowdray in 1910 and Viscount in 1917, was a typical success figure of the war – creator of a munitions factory at Gretna Green, builder of a tank-assembly plant at Châteauroux. The motives of men like him were constantly questioned. Lord Henry Bentinck pictured a commercialized and vulgarized society fighting merely to ennoble, decorate, knight and enrich plutocracy:

A force has arisen . . . which has used the war and the passions aroused by it to fortify its position, and now scoffs at all our idealisms. What is the permanent peace of the world to Plutocracy, or Plutocracy to the permanent peace of the world? Its only thought is to turn the British Empire into a bagman's Paradise, and to make the world safe for itself.

While everything generous, self-sacrificing and noble is shedding its blood on the fields of France and Flanders, Plutocracy is on the war-path at home. Its batteries are unmasked and the attack opened.[12]

Lloyd George's ministry of munitions provided enormous profits for the businessmen who ran and supplied it. The plutocracy had always been attacked, but the days when Lipton or Lever could build great fortunes from virtually nothing had their heroic aspect; now, in the midst of the demands of war, there was ample opportunity for profiteering by those without talent or moral sense. The coal profits in 1916, it emerged in a Commons debate of that year, were three times the average of the last five years before the war.[13] The balance of power had shifted decisively from the already ailing squirearchy of Galsworthy's *The Country House* to the hard-faced inheritors of the world of *The Forsyte Saga*.[14]

As the need to make their way in society became less pressing, the plutocrats turned in force to the political scene. In 1910 Lloyd George had played with the idea of a strong government of businessmen under his leadership, and the war gave strong impetus to such notions. 'Put business men over the Departments of State', Lord Charles Beresford wrote in December 1915, 'men who have proved their capability by getting to the top of their profession through long experience of business methods.'[15] When Lloyd George became head of a coalition a year later, it was clear – as Beatrice Webb noted in her diary – that he would represent Mammon ('though Heaven knows that Asquith & Co. do not represent God').[16] Coal (Lord Rhondda), transport (Sir Albert Stanley), shipping (Joseph Maclay), contracting (Lord Cowdray), were among the new Prime Minister's sources of support. Few of these politicians had much political experience, and Maclay would not even sit in Parliament. But Lloyd George himself called all this 'experiment' 'a conspicuous success'.[17] It received additional impetus in the 1918 election, after which the House of Commons contained approximately 260 businessmen – 'hard-faced men who looked as if they had done well out of the war', in Baldwin's famous description.

The aftermath of war also put the seal on the end of landed dominance on all aspects of English life. The value of land, in relation to other commodities, remained very much the same from the first emergence of the English nation until the second half of the nineteenth century; by the time the Second World War began prices still had not recovered to the level of the 1880s.[18] Just before the First World War, the American ambassador was amazed to discover that farming land could be found within thirty miles of London at half the price good corn land would fetch in Iowa. Neville Lytton wrote his book on *The English Country Gentleman* in the 1920s specifically because 'the squire of the old school' and his way of life were quickly becoming forgotten as he was compelled to abandon his ancestral acres.[19]

Well over a million acres found their way on the market in the first two years after the war. When Lord Willoughby de Broke, who had played such a flamboyant role in the Die-Hards' campaign of 1911, sold his family seat of Compton Verney to the soap-boiler Joseph Watson in September 1921, it looked as if the triumph of plutocracy was complete: three months later Watson himself became Lord Manton of Compton Verney.[20] But such evidence is misleading: the rush to sell was not merely the result of high taxation, but connected too with the declining social prestige attached to land. As Masterman pointed out, some of the purchasers were pluto-cratic war-profiteers, but also prominent were tenant farmers and public bodies.[21] England had become a land of cities with a population that retreated into suburban living by night; and its social ideals were at last beginning to reflect that fact.

The great town houses, around which so much of London social life had revolved, almost all passed out of aristocratic hands. The Countess of Warwick noted that the widow of one of the greatest of peers had been forced to live for a while in her former coachman's house; it was even rumoured that a marquis had lived and died in Putney. Few of the beneficiaries were plutocrats, though there were exceptions: Lord Leverhulme's trustees, after he had bought Grosvenor House, put the property up for sale as a 'desirable building site'.[22] But by the beginning of the 1930s only Bridgewater, Londonderry, Holland and Apsely Houses remained in private ownership, aristocratic or plutocratic.[23]

Many aristocrats and landed gentlemen have remained rich to the present day, notwithstanding a plaintive cry made in 1974 by the Duke of Grafton. 'You really can't talk about us as a privileged class any more,' he said. 'Many of us are living in the most dreadful, the most appalling discomfort.'[24] Aristocracy may never have been a question of caste, but its strength had once been based on the realities of social, economic and political power; now, divorced from the centres of power, its story became one without drama. Conspicuous consumption was, in the main, abandoned – not merely to save money, but as a sign that the aristocratic role in modern society was to be a much quieter one, perhaps (as Neville Lytton proposed) as 'a philosophic idea'.[25]

The House of Lords had its numbers increased by 280 through new creations between 1916 and 1945; less than ten of them had inherited status through land or wealth.[26] Lloyd George's coalition had been seen by some as an opportunity to end the sale of honours and a resolution to that effect was adopted by both Houses of Parliament in 1917. In fact more than ninety new Lords owed their titles to him in the next six years, and by no means all of these awards could be traced to the achievements of the war years. If the men concerned were connected with the war, then – in the *Banker*'s judgment – it was because they were profiteers who had been 'shovelled' into the House of Lords in honour of money gained by betraying the nation as it fought for survival. Lloyd George's political fund, containing two million pounds, was largely built up from the sale of honours; and Arthur John Michael Maundy Gregory, with his impressive offices in Parliament Square, provided the perfect intermediary.[27]

A familiar name became involved in a scandal that brought matters to a head. Sir Joseph Robinson, aged eighty-two, had a peerage bestowed on him in June 1922. His baronetcy had been granted by Campbell-Bannerman, on General Botha's recommendation, in 1908. Maundy Gregory, son of a clergyman, schoolteacher come playwright come manager, had helped to launch *Mayfair & Town Topics* in 1910 and Robinson was one of many who paid hundreds of pounds for a laudatory write-up in the 'Men of the Day' feature. He had sold his Park Lane mansion in 1914, but visited England again in 1922 when – according to his trusting biographer – 'he found that he had been offered a peerage' but 'decided not to avail himself of it' after the grant 'aroused opposition in certain quarters'. It was clear that the South African Prime Minister had not suggested the barony, and criticisms centred on the fact that it was impossible to see what he had done to merit recognition. He was described as the chairman of a company which had actually gone into liquidation in 1905; and the information that he had been fined £500,000 by the South African Supreme Court for fraud – a decision upheld on appeal to the Privy Council in November 1921 – was suppressed. When chairman of the Randfontein Estates Company he had bought the freehold of various mining properties and resold it to his own company at great profit to himself. Ironically, it was the purchase of this company by Solly Joel's Barnato Group that brought the whole matter to light.

Robinson, closeted in his suite at the Savoy, at first assumed that the offer of more money would bring an end to the criticism. The facts were nevertheless sufficiently plain to overcome his greed, his deafness and his cantakerous nature: a letter from him to Lloyd George declared that he had not ('as you know') sought the honour. 'I am now an old man to whom honours and dignities are no longer matters of much concern.' This letter, which included the request for permission to decline the barony, was read out in the Lords. George V made his attitude clear when he described the affair as 'little less than an insult to the Crown' in a letter to Lloyd George.

Robinson's biographer could find no one nearer home than the London correspondent of the Milan *Corriere della Sera* to suggest that 'the House of Lords has deprived itself of a good element'.[28] The magnate himself returned to his South African estate and survived, bitter and paranoic, until he was eighty-nine. The *Cape Times* referred to 'the almost incredible malignity of his nature' in its obituary,[29] though he was by no means the only baronet or would-be member of the Lords to be criticized in the British Parliament. Parliamentary debates led to a Royal Commission and eventually to an Act under which Maundy Gregory was to be summoned and given two months' imprisonment in 1933.

The plutocrats had won – and lost. As Neville Lytton observed, it had become accepted that 'the rich capitalists are made barons, viscounts, or earls'.[30] Questions might be raised about the direct sale of honours, but aspirant members of the House of Lords could no longer convince themselves that they were joining an aristocratic elite that dominated the country's social and political life. Once adoption into the aristocracy became (relatively) easy, it became (relatively) pointless. Besides, it was not long before Mr Mitcheson, the Labour MP for Kettering who was full of radical urges to confiscate private capital, became first Sir Gilbert, then Lord Mitcheson:[31] socialism joined plutocracy and aristocracy in a strangely named, new-style House of Lords.

Andrew Carnegie was wandering in the gardens of Skibo one day with Sir Charles Macara when he stopped abruptly. 'Sir Charles', he said, 'the day of the multi-millionaire is over; the people won't have it.'[32] In one sense, the plutocrats had attained their goal. When Hugh Thomas edited a symposium on *The Establishment* in 1959 there was no doubt that the City formed a part of it; by then financial men had developed their own shibboleths and professional traditions, helping to make the City a deeply conservative institution.[33] But the new world was quite different from that of 1914. Such legislation as the Education Act of 1918 and the National Insurance Acts of 1920 and 1921 were symbols of great changes in the state's role in organizing social life. The effective direction of various industries had, at least temporarily, passed into government hands in the First World War.[34] At the same time, the state began to use taxation in a far more active way to force social change. As one economist noted in 1916, 'The war marks, as definitely as the close of the Napoleonic era, the completion of one economic epoch and the beginning of another.'[35] A study of *The National Income, 1924* concluded that when the full effects of taxation were taken into account the real income available to the rich for 'luxurious expenditure' was definitely less than it had been before 1914.[36]

The last budget before the war had raised income tax, super tax and death duties. In 1919 death duties were increased to forty per cent on estates of £2,000,000 or more; income tax at 1s 2d in the pound in 1914 had risen to five shillings by the end of the war. A school textbook on social history, first published in 1903, observed in its third edition of September 1920 that the burden of taxation seemed to fall on the very wealthy and those who had made large fortunes in the war years.[37] The exaggerated complaints of the rich reflected what economists have called 'an unusually big distributive shift' in the years 1913–24, when rents and profits were squeezed and earned income rose significantly as a proportion of home-generated national income.[38]

The Britain of the 1970s retains its rich men, the take-over barons such as Sir Isaac Wolfson, the property magnates such as Harry Hyams. But for fifty years a power neither capitalist nor aristocratic has developed its own position in the social and political structure of the country. Powerful, consolidated trade unions emerged in and after the First World War – the Transport and General Workers in 1921, for example. Election expenditure was severely limited and, within six years of the end of the war, a Labour government came to power: the son of a farm worker took office as Prime Minister. As it happened, this man of the people, Ramsay MacDonald, much enjoyed the company and the customs of aristocracy. But the absence of revolution did not mean that a decisive social change had not taken place.

Organized labour was only one of the centres of power that took away the importance of the individual, aristocrat or plutocrat. The growth in bureaucracy was perfectly symbolized by the introduction of a formal British passport (and by the angry complaint from Bassett Digby, in a letter to *The Times* in 1915, that his own description of his face as 'intelligent' had been altered by some official to 'oval').[39] The business corporation from the 1920s – ICI formed in 1926, Unilever in 1929 – was far removed from the personally run company, however large, of the era of the plutocrats: the scale of long-term investment needed to run modern railways, insurance, banks, energy-supply industries called for a different character of organization; and the salaried managing director was a much paler copy of the aristocratic paternalist than his plutocratic predecessor. Today a mere 150 companies provide half of Britain's industrial output; before 1914 the comparable figure was 2,000. The corporation has taken a stranglehold over the economy which leaves even American big business far behind.[40]

The plutocrats stood at the historical crossroads; in acquiring through their own efforts high status in society they looked forward; in seeking power of a direct and personal kind, they belonged to a tradition now lost to institutions and their captive officials. All historical periods are 'periods of transition', in which the old is mixed with the new, because institutions – and people – are slow or reluctant to accept the realities of political or economic or cultural change. As long as the aims, particularly the social aims, of the plutocrats remained similar to those of the landed classes, they tended to reinforce a system that belonged firmly to the past. But the very fact that the term 'plutocrat' was used as a contrast to 'aristocrat' showed that the old order was breaking up. T. H. S. Escott, surveying the bewildering variety of people and behaviour in the London society of 1904, saw one prominent feature: society's traditional framework had dissolved into a chaos from which the new order had yet to emerge.[41] British social and economic life has been fighting to escape from that confusion ever since.

There were many to argue that the plutocratic preoccupation with luxury and social prestige was an important factor in the economic decline of Britain. Werner Sombart's *The Quintessence of Capitalism* (1915), described by its English translator as 'the Book of the Modern Business Man', asserted forcefully that the Englishman looked for his pleasure to luxury, to an aristocratic way of life and to sport – all of which, as they developed, diverted energies from the business of economic growth. Sombart quoted Schulze-Gaevernitz's devastating analysis of a decadent Britain, where 'the most popular forms of the national sports have a strong plutocratic taint. They presuppose an aristocratic race that lives upon Negro, Chinese, and Hindoo labour, and draws dividends and economic rent from every country under the sun; while the soil of their own land they regard (and value) solely as an article of luxury.'[42] No wonder *The Times* protested (protested too much, perhaps) in 1914 that the supineness and idleness of the English were for ever being compared with the intelligent enterprise and diligence of her industrial rivals.[43]

The transformation of the first and most dynamic of industrial nations into the poor relation of the advanced world within a few decades demands an explanation.[44] The picture was not uniform throughout the country, but in most major industrial activities Britain's growth rate and output looked disconcertingly low compared with that of Germany and America. 'Our ideal prosperity', Bernard Shaw pointed out in 1903, 'is not the prosperity of the industrial north, but the prosperity of the Isle of Wight, of Folkestone and Ramsgate, of Nice and Monte Carlo.' The only workers you saw in the theatre were footmen or parlour-maids, while the heroes and heroines lived off unlimited dividends provided from somewhere off stage.[45] Britain opted for living off the profits of finance and trade, not manufacturing industry, to such an extent that the Marxist picture of a parasitic economy surviving on an exploited Empire and the achievements of the past is in some essentials convincing.[46]

Such capital and labour that was employed in the domestic economy tended to be directed towards distribution and marketing, some light industry, not coal or steel or chemicals. The typical British plutocrat, if not a financier, was William Lever or Thomas Lipton, not Andrew Carnegie, steel manufacturer. Industrial technology and scientific management were unpopular: as early as the 1850s British commissions had praised the mechanization, machines and organization of American industry; as late as 1914 not a tenth of the men who ran Britain's steel industry had experienced a technical training at school or a science education at university.

Many factors determine a country's economic performance; it has been suggested that the attempt by the *nouveau riche* plutocracy to adopt an aristocratic social life was a consequence not a cause of the relative decline of British industry. A number of specific studies certainly indicate that where the choice was between acquiring social status and maximizing economic growth, social status tended to come out on top. The Rathbones of Liverpool and the Marshalls of Leeds provided two examples of families with sufficient wealth not to bother with new methods, and sufficient social or political drive to disregard the interests of business.[47] A preponderance of British steel manufacturers, at any rate after the 1865 generation, married into landed or professional rather than industrial families.[48]

The British educational system reflected to perfection this preference for social rank rather than productivity. The British public schools, especially those – like Marlborough, Haileybury, Wellington, Lancing and Malvern – founded in the middle decades of the century, never closed their doors to wealth. 'Look at the bottle-merchant's son and the Plantagenet being brought up side by side', Matthew Arnold's imaginary Prussian visitor to Eton was told. 'Very likely young Bottles will end up by being a lord himself.'[49] But the public-school children of plutocracy, no less than aristocracy, were brought up to frown on technology and industrial productivity. Richard Rivington, H. G. Wells's scholarship boy at City Merchants school, was provided with an education that would not allow him to consider the profitable production and sale of lavatory basins as a candidate for the highest good.[50] Taine, visiting Eton in the 1860s, was told by a master that sport came before books: three, four or five hours in 'rough and and violent exercises' were the main priority.[51] *Philosophoumen aneu malakis* – 'We are lovers of wisdom without softness': it was fitting that one Etonian should use a Thucydidean tag to describe the 'muscular Christianity' of the public-school system.[52] In 1911 the study of science could only be described as 'pure farce'.[53]

What was learned in these strange institutions? Lord Redesdale recalled in 1916: 'the three R's alone remain to me, and, indeed, of these only two – for owing to my having enjoyed an Eton education in days when arithmetic was deemed to be no part of the intellectual panoply of a gentleman, I can neither add, subtract, nor divide'.[54] But there were compensations, as Shane Leslie pointed out. Three degrees of English gentlemen were recognized unofficially throughout the Empire: sportsmen, sportsmen who had been to Oxford or Cambridge, and Old Etonians. 'To *be* an Etonian', he said, 'seems better than to *become* great or successful.' The school experiences made the man, secure in his sense of superiority: the words of the school song expressed it all –

> . . . nothing in life shall sever
> The bond that is round us now.[55]

No wonder that *Punch* playfully complained that an advertisement in *The Times* for 'a GENTLEMAN *or* Public School man' made an invidious distinction.[56] Or that the American sociologist, Erving Goffman, rather more seriously, described 'the public school system in Britain' as 'a machine for systematically recreating middle-class people in the image of the aristocracy'.[57]

The public schools brought aristocracy and plutocracy together and substituted a peculiar new bond for landed inheritance.[58] The result was to prolong their influence in British society; but it was no longer the influence of those last extraordinary years before the First World War.

Chapter 15

A Resting-place for Memories

In August 1901 the *Westminster Gazette* published a delightful little tale of two old ladies overheard on Basle station. They discussed how much they could afford to tip the waiter, for a franc seemed generous and would mean less for their supper. In Basle they had been put up for the night for one franc fifty centimes and they waited patiently with fourth-class tickets for the slow train to Lucerne. On no account were they going beyond Flüelen because they had not reckoned on that when saving for the journey. But they smiled, and they said: 'If we were millionaires we could not be better off.'[1]

Vanity Fair had its own answer for this sort of sentimentality. 'Millionaires will tell you that money does not make happiness', the magazine declared in 1908. 'This, of course, is the cant of the plutocrat.'[2]

The story of the rise of the plutocrats was in one sense the story of a whole society. Market society and status society came together in superficially unnatural alliance, in the last great age of luxury before the new era of masses and corporative bureaucracy closed in. But it also had its significance in personal terms. 'Setting aside self-indulgence', Arthur Ponsonby commented, 'the chief pleasure of riches is said to be the enjoyment of the power they give.'[3] The centrepiece of the lives of all the plutocrats was the exercise of power: in business, in society, in luxury, in politics; and in the pursuit of happiness. With what success plenty became power, became the satisfaction of a goal achieved, is the most intriguing question of all.

The trouble with conspicuous consumption was that its attractions faded rapidly. Even before the Edwardian period began Consuelo Vanderbilt had discovered how boring it was to walk on an endlessly spread red carpet.[4] Bernard Shaw devoted an article to the plight of the millionaire in the *Contemporary Review* in 1896. The problem was that anyone with a modest £5,000 a year could have the best of everything available; only at his funeral could the millionaire take the opportunity to indulge in a special scale of extravagant pomp. There was no advantage in being able to pay for a peacock's brain sandwich in a society that offered only ham or beef; no one could wear more than one suit at a time, or digest more meals than his butler. The millionaire might seem to have more cares (more money to look after, more begging letters to read), fewer hopes (no dreams of wealth), less sympathy ('The poor alone are pitied') than anyone else.[5]

Those who built great businesses usually had to watch them pass from their control. Sir Thomas Lipton had greeted the First World War in a state of acute depression, for he was involved in 1914 in a scandal over the award of army catering contracts. Heavily criticized both in court and in the House of Lords, especially by Lord Newton, he faced the indignity of having his firm's name struck off the list of War Office contractors – almost the first stain on a career which had brought both success and popularity. After the war, he often looked back to his youth: 'How happy I was then, penniless, and how often I wish that I could once again be called plain Tom Lipton, for riches do not always bring happiness, but very often unhappiness, particularly when one is growing old and feeble and not able to attend to business.' Lipton was ousted as president of his English company in 1928 – for the men who 'grew wealthy under my directorship . . . now when I have grown to be an old man they push me out'.[6]

Profits had dropped bit by bit, and the company's increasing troubles owed much to the problems of reorganization at a time when Lipton was no longer able to cope. Anton Jurgens suggested, in 1926, that without some fast, fundamental improvement Lipton's might not survive at all.[7] There was not much comfort to be had from Sir Thomas's social activities either: the eighty-four volumes of his press cuttings were not even added to after 1926. He was at last admitted to the Royal Yacht Club – gratifying certainly, but wanted thirty years earlier. Beverley Nichols, in the mid-1920s, found a man living on his memories, retelling the same stories, and retelling them again.

Lipton's accurate sense that things were slipping from his grasp was a sad, but relatively mild expression of the continuing desire to be in control. In Northcliffe, the pursuit of power – over his newspapers and over public opinion – gradually dissolved into megalomania. In the First World War, he had adopted the self-appointed role of saviour of the nation, riding on the back of the *Daily Mail* success as 'the paper that foretold the war'; in time he was to be given the task of directing propaganda against the enemy. (One American of German origins, not conscious 'of any particular honour in addressing a Lord – even a new-baked one with a negotiated title', retaliated by suggesting that 'My Lord Poisoner of the Peoples' was the descendant of a family of Frankfurt Jews.)[8] In May 1921, on the twenty-fifth anniversary of the first issue of the *Daily Mail*, Northcliffe spent £7,000 on a single lunch for his employees, and a clergyman was found to describe him 'guiding aright the destinies of this great Empire'.[9] But though that reflected the undisputed success of the mass-circulation newspaper, it was no indication of personal satisfaction, rather the opposite: a wild and desperate bid by Northcliffe to convince himself that the battle for absolute power had been won.

Many of those who were accused of being plutocrats spent

their time proclaiming – in their actions, at least – that there was something better than plutocracy: the pursuit of aristocratic prestige was an admission of the emptiness of the pursuit of money. But the desire for social success often resulted in social unpopularity. William Waldorf Astor was rejected by America after he had rejected it by adopting British citizenship in 1899; Theodore Roosevelt – hardly the most radical of Presidents – would not meet him when he revisited the country. Even the eulogistic journalist who compiled the portraits of those 'In the Public Eye' for *Pearson's Magazine* could find nothing more positive to say of 'The second most wealthy American in the world' than that 'He knows the points of a bulldog, and is popular with those who serve him.'[10] He was made a baron in 1916, a viscount in 1917; but after his admission to the House of Lords he never again attended proceedings. His last home, Western House, Brighton, was – like all the others – surrounded by a tall wall; he dined alone, living off rich and marvellous foods ordered months in advance from his chef. And he died there in 1919, behind the locked doors of his lavatory.[11]

More than twenty years before, Sir Almeric Fitzroy had discovered that Mr Astor's 'burden of £30,000,000 seems to weigh heavily upon him'.[12] His photographs always showed hard, unsmiling features, not tempered at all as he grew older by the development of a puzzled look, as if he was quietly furious that all in life was not clear to him. He craved the attention of Society, but was totally unsuited to it. Without brothers and sisters, privately educated until he went to law school, he did not understand people. Only the thought that scientific progress might help to unravel the secrets of 'the psychic world' was genuinely exciting to him. Astor dealt always in symbols – the symbols of social acceptability, for example – because they were one stage removed from human contact.[13] No one seems to have commented on the significance of the quotation from Walt Whitman he used on the dedication page of his autobiographical writings:

I think I could turn and live with animals;
   they are so placid and self contained;
Not one is dissatisfied – not one is demented with
   the mania of owning things.
Not one kneels to another, nor to his kind that lived
   thousands of years ago.[14]

Only one member of the plutocracy seemed to find the
popularity that evaded Astor: 'He really was a dear man, was
Beit', commented Admiral Lord Fisher.[15] Even Joseph
Robinson – no friend of Beit's – raged at the editor of a
Johannesburg newspaper he owned when an attack on Beit
in *Truth* was reprinted there. Alfred Beit was pleased by his
achievement, but not insufferably so. There is a picture of
him, faintly ridiculous, in the costume of a Stadhouder of
Holland at the Devonshire House Jubilee Ball in 1897; and
another, more revealing, in a family group in the 1890s – next
to his mother, his bearing immensely proud as he sits upright
with his head held high.[16] But his extreme reserve and hatred
of publicity were noted by everyone. There were rumours
about his personal relationships – in 1900 it was said that
he was engaged to Mrs Adolph Ladenburg, whose husband
had been lost overboard between Nassau and New York.[17]
Yet he never married. Instead, he worried, and worried
especially about money. Frank Harris noted the unreal
world in which he was inevitably a prisoner: Beit, with
memories of his poor beginnings, always seemed to over-
estimate the value of small sums of money, but 'the moment
you spoke in thousands, he seemed to treat them as counters.
He would jump from five thousand to fifty thousand as if
there were no intervening figures.'[18]

The result was ill-health – and one recorded impassioned
outburst. In the early 1890s Beit made the long, rough
journey to the group of mud huts that was then Salisbury,
capital of Mashonaland. Round a fire late one night, he
exclaimed: 'what is the use of being a millionaire? Nothing.
. . . A millionaire – suspense, anxiety all day long.'[19] That was

Beit's epitaph. As Wernher had said in the last, unhappy years: 'Poor Beit is better but it does not mean much to me. To me it means dying by inches instead of a sudden end.'[20]

On the other side of the world, some years later, Siegfried Sassoon visited his aunt in Mayfair. Ever since he could remember he had been aware of his rich Sassoon relations. 'I had great-uncles galore, whom I had never met, and they all knew the Prince of Wales, who sometimes stayed with them at Brighton.' His Aunt Rachel lived amid stuffy, unventilated rooms, reached by chilly marble stairs, full of lacquered Oriental furniture and pictures deadened by the weight of the money that had bought them. Her husband's crest was everywhere, even clipped out of the listless-eyed little black poodle, Zulu.[21]

Here too was a world of symbols: the magnificent rings on Rachel's hands a brilliant sign of wealth, the grimy hands beneath them a strange contrast.

Did none of them, then – these giants of successful capitalism – find happiness? When war broke out in 1914, those of German origins were in an especially difficult position. Wernher and Beit were both dead. Wernher's last years had been saddened by the death of his partner – 'To miss dear Beit is another fearful blow,' he had written to Lionel Phillips in August 1906.[22] Even worse, he noticed in his eldest son, Derrick – educated at Eton and Balliol – a lack of desire to work hard, an observation which received unsavoury confirmation in 1910 when he lamented: 'Derrick . . . has fallen in the hands of bookmakers and moneylenders and has been fleeced. . . . I shall never trust him sufficiently to put him in the business and that is final. . . . My wife and self are both heart-broken.' Wernher himself died two years later: Derrick emigrated to America.[23]

Wernher, Beit & Co. passed into the control of the Central Mining & Investment Corporation, which contained on its board a number of naturalized British citizens of German origin. Liquidation was at least a possibility once Britain and Germany were at war.[24] In theory international bankers had everything to lose from a world-wide conflict, but they provided a convenient scapegoat. *Punch*, on 19 August, was delighted to announce that the thousand fresh herrings a certain cosmopolitan millionaire had purchased at the beginning of the war had all gone bad; and *Mayfair*, the following month, warned of 'The German Peril in England' – the peril from naturalized Englishmen whose signature on a scrap of paper was not going to make them forsake their fatherland.

According to Saemy Japhet, Cassel had not believed that war would come, though – once it did – he was prepared to discuss his firm's financial affairs as if he had nothing else in the world to care about. Early in July 1914 Cassel had determined on a visit to his Swiss villa, high up in the mountains. On the evening of the 24th – the day after the Austrian ultimatum to Serbia – he played bridge at Brook House late into the evening with Winston Churchill, Sir Felix Semon and his niece, Mrs Jenkins. He was in the closest contact with the financial community throughout Europe and America, but stuck to his plans for departure to the Continent the following day. Stranded there as war began, he found that all his millions could not buy him a seat on the twenty-hour journey from the French frontier to Paris, and during the further seventeen hours from Paris to Folkestone.

Margot Asquith suggested that in spite of all his subsequent suffering at the hands of 'our contemptible spy-hunters', 'no one was ever more loyal or generous to the country of his adoption'.[25] He certainly made some of the biggest subscriptions to the war loans, and in September 1915 went to New York to use his influence to raise an Anglo-French loan in America. But a few months later an action was brought against both Cassel and Sir Edgar Speyer, in an attempt to remove them from the Privy Council.

Lady Augusta Fane had been staying at Overstrand, near Cromer, when war was declared. The Speyers' house on the cliffs could be seen for miles out to sea, and its lights continued to shine each night into the early hours. Local gossip con-

Reuben Sassoon;
from *Vanity Fair*,
20 September 1890

Sir Albert Sassoon;
from the *Illustrated London
News*, 1 June 1872

Andrew Carnegie

William Waldorf Astor

nected the Speyers with a wireless receiver found behind a winnowing machine in a barn, and there was a general feeling of relief when they left for London in November, with their German governesses and chauffeur; they had never before spent such a lengthy period at Overstrand.[26] Sir Edgar abandoned his connections with the Frankfurt and pro-German New York houses of his firm. *The Times* reported his severance from New York by noting his prominence in financial circles in England; he had become a public figure through his role in financing the London transport system.[27] But Lord Reading (the ennobled Rufus Isaacs) and Sir Almeric Fitzroy discussed the Privy Council case in December 1915, and gloomily noted that the New York Speyer branch had been employed as a depository for German funds intended to pay for supplies which were then used by vessels engaged in the destruction of British commerce.[28]

A long press campaign had been conducted against Speyer. The *Morning Post* (on 27 May) was typical:

The New York House is managed by Sir Edgar Speyer's brother, who is openly helping in the German campaign against England in America. . . . He is the friend of Herr Dernburg, the Black Hand Diplomatist, who arranged the matter of the 'Lusitania'. . . . His kith and kin are fighting us either personally or financially.

The *Bulletin* in Sydney, Australia, was more directly personal: 'He married Fraulein von Stosch, so he can't even talk about his dear English wife and children.' And the *Financial Mail* was full of articles suggesting that anyone having anything to do with Speyer flotations was foolish, disloyal, or both: 'Another Speyer fiasco'; 'the Brazil Railway Scandal' – 'The Worst Default of Modern Times'; 'Speyer & Co. and Missouri-Pacific. Candid Comments on Another Big Scandal'.[29]

Cassel and Speyer reacted very differently to the attempt to remove them from the Privy Council. The former submitted an affidavit earnestly protesting his loyalty to king and country; the latter, though formally represented, was plainly impolite. Lord Reading contrasted the two attitudes, describing the one as 'utmost correctness', the other as 'studiously disrespectful'. Both men remained members of the Council, but in December 1921 the naturalization of Speyer and his family was revoked and he was struck off the list of Privy Councillors. According to Fitzroy, the order expunging his name 'was hailed with satisfaction by everyone present', but by this time an embittered Speyer had abandoned England for America. Fitzroy claimed that the Prime Minister in 1915, Asquith, should have realized that the accusations against Speyer had some foundation, though it appears to have been the King who was especially reluctant to allow the financier to renounce his baronetcy.[30] Other charges of helping Germany during the war were included in a White Paper in January 1922, Speyer dismissing them as 'trivial beyond words'.[31]

Cassel, too, faced continuing criticism, and in 1916 Lord Alfred Douglas's *Plain English* accused him of conspiring with Winston Churchill to mislead the public about the consequences of the Battle of Jutland in order to take advantage of the drop in the stock market in the resulting panic. The Attorney-General advised that it would be a mistake to give an 'obscure' and 'contemptible' paper publicity by bringing a prosecution. Nevertheless, the story was repeated several times and Douglas was eventually sent to jail for criminal libel.[32] Cassel was left deeply embittered by this and his other wartime experiences, for public disapproval came to him after a lifetime of sadness in his private affairs.

His wife Annette, to whom he appears to have been devoted, died three years after their marriage. They had a daughter – Maud – who married Wilfred Ashley in the month that Queen Victoria died. This was a moment of happiness – the Prince of Wales, who wrote to Cassel just before Christmas to ask if the time of the wedding could be postponed so that he could attend, was the star guest;[33] and Major Ashley, ex-Boer War battalion commander, educated at Harrow,

Cambridge and Sandhurst, and grandson of the Earl of Shaftesbury, seemed a suitable husband. He was not rich, but he had inherited a splendid estate in Hampshire – and Cassel was hardly in difficulties about providing financial support. (Clement Attlee later described Ashley, who became Lord Mount Temple, as 'a nice old Tory, not very bright, but one of the nice old boys':[34] not an inaccurate judgment.) But later that year, at the end of November, Cassel received another letter from Edward VII. 'I am indeed distressed to hear . . . that you are in anxiety about your daughter's health since her confinement. I sincerely hope . . . that you will soon be quite happy about her. The Baby', he added, 'is I trust strong and well.'[35]

The baby was Edwina, who narrowly escaped being christened Edwardina in tribute to the King, and she soon became the especial focus of Cassel's attention. Her delicate mother enjoyed Society life, if not the deadening traditions of Wilfred Ashley's family and estate; she played bridge, and poker too, for high stakes. According to the Duchess of Sermonetta, she had an intellect as fine as her complexion and much-noted hazel eyes, but she grew quickly tired as she succumbed to the consumption that was to kill her in 1911 when only thirty. The Duchess described the last years. Cassel tried everything to prolong them, and after the death of Edward VII retreated from Society to concentrate his energies on improving her health. In Egypt he booked three entire floors of the Assouan Hotel to give her peace, then paid for a special ship to carry her back to London. In the remaining months, which she spent in a bungalow in the gardens of her husband's estate, he gave her all the presents that money could buy. She was too weak to respond.

Her death, said the Duchess of Sermonetta, broke his heart.[36]

To some extent he continued his former life. We find the new King, George V, writing him a polite note in June 1913 accepting an invitation to dine at Moulton Paddocks.[37] Earlier that month, however, Sir Almeric Fitzroy had seen him with Speyer at dinner at the Schroeders'. 'Cassel is a dejected and pathetic figure – a sermon, if you like, on the vanity of great wealth; nothing seems to raise his interest except a reference to his grandchildren.' In his attitude to those grandchildren, Fitzroy confided to his diary, it was interesting to see 'the softer side of this man outside the thrall of material ambitions'.[38] Maud had given birth to a second daughter in 1904, but Cassel must have found it difficult to express his true feelings to either of his grandchildren. Sonia Keppel remembered him appearing in the nursery at Biarritz, silently puffing at his cigar while Edwina, Mary and (his great-niece) Marjorie Jenkins sprang to their feet at the sight of him. Sonia was soon able to distinguish the King from Cassel, Tweedledee from Tweedledum – Tweedledee laughed more easily and was always willing to join in nursery games.[39]

From his sister, who had brought up Maud, he inspired complete devotion, though the Duchess of Sermonetta may have been correct in supposing that she was rather afraid of him. She had the job of organizing constant entertainment for guests – kings or financiers – and rushed round with nervous cheerfulness inviting everyone in her strong German accent to 'come to their hair and tidy their rooms'.[40] Later, Edwina took on the role of hostess, but Cassel's grimness was enhanced by the problems of the war years. He would have been gratified to know that the attendance at his funeral indicated the importance of his achievement – perhaps something more: 'So large and varied a congregation', Fitzroy noted, 'was testimony enough to the esteem in which the dead man had come to be held, in spite of all the prejudices to the contrary.'[41]

This was 1921. He was found dead at his writing-desk in Brook House. For many years past the house had seemed like a gigantic, gaudy mausoleum – perfect resting-place for the memories of an astonishing era in history, and one of its most astonishing figures.

Reference Notes

Titles and authors are given in full at first reference only

Preface
1 R. D. Blumenfeld, *RDB's Diary 1887–1914*, London 1930, p. 87 (12 October 1900)
2 Ellis T. Powell, *The Evolution of the Money Market*, London 1915, p. vii
3 Sir Frederick Ponsonby, *Recollections of Three Reigns*, London n.d., p. 36

1 The Land and the People: England Before the Plutocrats
1 Andrew Carnegie, *Our Coaching Trip: Brighton to Inverness*, New York 1882, p. 75
2 Cf. Harold Nicolson, *Good Behaviour*, London 1955, p. 188
3 R. W. Emerson, *Essays and English Traits*, New York 1909, p. 418
4 *Truth*, 14 November 1901
5 F. M. L. Thompson, *English Landed Society in the Nineteenth Century*, London 1963, pp. 77–8
6 Ralph Nevill (ed.), *The Reminiscences of Lady Dorothy Nevill*, London 1906, p. 84
7 Lady Frances Balfour, *Ne Obliviscaris*, Vol. 1, London 1930, p. 32
8 Thomas Carlyle, *Past and Present*, collected edition of *Sartor*

294

Resartus, Heroes and Hero-Worship, Past and Present, London n.d., p. 121

9 Richard Greville Verney, *The Passing Years*, London 1924, p. 56

10 *Some Memories*, London 1958. David Spring, 'Some Reflections on Social History in the Nineteenth Century', *Victorian Studies*, Vol. 4, No. 1, September 1960

11 John Langton Sanford and Meredith Townsend, *The Great Governing Families of England*, Vol. 1, London 1885, p. 18

12 W. Bence Jones, 'Landowning as a business', *Nineteenth Century*, March 1882

13 Ramsay Muir, *Peers and Bureaucrats: Two Problems of English Government*, London 1910, p. 7

14 Sanford, Vol. 1, p. 15

15 Harold Perkin, *The Origins of Modern English Society 1780–1880*, London 1969, p. 39

16 Walter Bagehot, *The English Constitution*, London 1867, reprinted (introduction R. H. S. Crossman) 1963, pp. 173–4

17 Price Collier, *England and the English: From an American Point of View*, London 1911, p. 48. See also Gerald Macmillan, *Honours for Sale: The Strange Story of Maundy Gregory*, London 1954, pp. 222–3

18 James McMillan, *The Honours Game*, London 1969, p. 43

19 S. Baring-Gould, *Old Country Life*, London 1889, reprinted 1913, pp. 140–2

20 Sanford, Vol. 1, p. 8

21 Emile Boutmy, *The English People: A Study of their Political Psychology*, transl. E. English, London 1904, p. 233

22 G. S. Street, *People & Questions*, London 1910, pp. 186–7

23 Consuelo Vanderbilt Churchill, *The Glitter and the Gold*, London 1952, p. 40

24 Bagehot, pp. 121, 123

25 An argument used by W. E. H. Lecky in *The Rise and Influence of Rationalism*. See Arthur Ponsonby, *The Decline of Aristocracy*, London 1910, pp. 14–15

26 Sir Bernard Burke, *Vicissitudes of Families*, London 1883, Vol. 1, p. 25, Vol. 2, p. 54

27 George W. Smalley, *Anglo-American Memories*, First Series, London 1911, p. 327

28 See the discussion in Peter Laslett, *The World we have lost*, 2nd ed., London 1972, pp. 23, 27

29 G. D. H. Cole, *Studies in Class Structure*, London 1955, reprinted 1968, p. 1

30 See, for example, Perkin, p. 26

31 John Burnett, *A History of the Cost of Living*, Harmondsworth 1969, p. 171

32 Cole, p. 84

33 For the development of local government, see Sir Robert Ensor, *England 1870–1914*, Oxford 1936, reprinted 1966; Edward Jenks, *An Outline of English Local Government*, 2nd ed., London 1901; J. M. Lee, *Social Leaders and Public Persons: A Study of County Government in Cheshire since 1888*, London 1963; K. B. Smellie, *A History of Local Government*, 4th ed., London 1968; W. Thornhill (ed.), *The Growth and Reform of English Local Government*, London 1971; J. P. D. Dunbabin, 'Expectations of the new County Councils, and their realization', *Historical Journal*, Vol. 8, No. 3, 1965

34 Smellie, p. 17

35 David Spring, 'The English Landed Estate in the Age of Coal and Iron: 1830–1880', *Journal of Economic History*, Vol. 11, No. 1, 1951

36 T. H. S. Escott, *Social Transformations of the Victorian Age*, London 1897, p. 265

37 *Ibid.*, p. 13

38 R. E. Pumphrey, 'The Introduction of Industrialists into the British Peerage: A Study in Adaptation of a Social Institution', *American Historical Review*, Vol. 65, No. 1, October 1959

39 B. van Oven, *Ought Baron de Rothschild to Sit in Parliament?*, 2nd ed., London 1848, p. 5

40 E. J. Hobsbawm, *Industry and Empire: An Economic History of Britain since 1870*, London 1968, reprinted 1969, p. 65

41 Bagehot, p. 141

42 Cf. Douglas Sutherland, *The Landowners*, London 1968, p. 32

43 Perkin, p. 431

44 Nevill, p. 127

45 Bagehot, p. 122

2 Rural Dearth and Business Plenty: The Economic Revolution After 1870

1 John Galsworthy, *The Country House*, London 1907, reprinted 1919, pp. 9, 128, 134, 172

2 Oscar Wilde, *The Importance of Being Earnest*, first performed 1895, London 1951, p. 176

3 Bence Jones, *Nineteenth Century*, March 1882

4 Helen Bosanquet, *The Standard of Life and Other Reprinted Essays*, 2nd ed., New York 1906, p. 158

5 Charles Milnes Gaskell, 'The Country Gentleman', *Nineteenth Century*, September 1882

6 For the depression in agriculture, see S. B. Saul, *The Myth of the Great Depression 1873–1896*, London 1969, reprinted 1972; T. W. Fletcher, 'The Great Depression of English Agriculture, 1873–1896', *Economic History Review*, 2nd Series, Vol. 13, No. 3, April 1961; Ensor; Hobsbawm

7 O. F. Christie, *The Transition to Democracy 1867–1914*, London 1934, p. 163

8 The Marchioness of Londonderry, *Henry Chaplin: A Memoir*, London 1926, p. 229

9 Saul, p. 36

10 Burnett, p. 228

11 Thompson, p. 309

12 W. L. Guttsman (ed.), *The English Ruling Class*, London 1969, p. 108

13 George Cadbury Jnr and Tom Bryan, *The Land and the Landless*, 1909, p. 19

14 James Howard, *Nineteenth Century*, April 1882

15 David Spring, *The English Landed Estate in the Nineteenth Century: Its Administration*, Baltimore 1963, *passim*

16 *Ibid.*, p. 127

17 George Bourne (pseudonym for George Sturt), *Change in the Village*, London 1912, reprinted 1955, p. 77

18 A. H. H. Matthews, *Fifty Years of Agricultural Politics: Being the History of the Central Chamber of Agriculture 1865–1915*, London 1915, pp. 2, 147, 214

19 Cf. Milnes Gaskell, *Nineteenth Century*, September 1882

20 Guttsman, p. 6

21 Thompson, p. 321

22 Milnes Gaskell, *Nineteenth Century*, September 1882

23 Sutherland, p. 53

24 C. F. G. Masterman, *The Condition of England*, London 1909, reprinted 1960, J. T. Boulton (ed.), p. 77

25 C. H. Feinstein, 'Income and Investment in the United Kingdom, 1856–1914', *Economic Journal*, Vol. 71, 1961

26 R. C. K. Ensor, 'The English Countryside', in Lucian Oldershaw (ed.), *England: A Nation. Being the Papers of the Patriots' Club*, London 1904, p. 106

27 John Roberts, *Europe 1880–1945*, London 1967, pp. 37–8

28 See the discussion in Charles Wilson, 'Economy and Society in Late Victorian Britain', *Ec.H.R.*, 2nd Series, Vol. 18, No. 1, August 1965

29 See Geoffrey Barraclough, *An Introduction to Contemporary History*, London 1964, reprinted Harmondsworth 1967, *passim*

30 S. G. Checkland, *The Rise of Industrial Society in England 1815–1885*, London 1964, p. 421

31 Andrew Carnegie, *The Gospel of Wealth and Other Timely Essays*, Edward G. Kirkland (ed.), Cambridge, Mass., 1962, p. 82

32 W. E. H. Lecky, *The Map of Life: Conduct and Character*, London 1899, reprinted 1901, p. 294

33 See the pioneering work of W. D. Rubinstein, 'British Millionaires, 1809–1949', *Bulletin of the Institute of Historical Research*, Vol. 47, No. 116, November 1974; and the same author's 'Wealth, Elites and the Class Structure of Modern Britain', *Past and Present*, No. 76, August 1977

34 Boulton, pp. 57, 72

35 Arthur Ponsonby, *Decline of Aristocracy*, pp. 148–9

36 See Lady Bell, *At the Works: A Study of a Manufacturing Town*, London 1907; also Boulton, pp. 77, 85, 122

3 Towards One World: South Africa and its Wonders

1 *Millionaires and How They Became So. Showing How Twenty-Seven of the Wealthiest Men in the World Made Their Money*, London 1884, pp. 1, 101. Of 700 millionaires in the world, 200 were said to be British, 100 American

2 *Pearson's Magazine*, January 1896.

3 W. Ashworth, 'The Late Victorian Economy', *Economica*, New Series, Vol. 33, No. 129, February 1966

4 Paul H. Emden, *Money Powers of Europe in the Nineteenth and Twentieth Centuries*, London 1937, p. 322

5 Baron von Eckhardstein, *Ten Years at the Court of St. James' 1895–1905*, transl. and ed. George Young, London 1921, p. 53

6 S. Japhet, *Recollections from my business life*, printed for private circulation only, London 1931, p. 154

7 John Buchan, *Prester John*, London 1910, reprinted 1950, pp. 20, 219–20

8 J. B. Robinson, 'The South African Settlement', *Nineteenth Century*, September 1882

9 J. B. Robinson, 'South Africa As It Is', *Nineteenth Century*, June 1887

10 H. W. Struben, *Recollections of Adventures: Pioneering and Development in South Africa 1850–1911*, Cape Town 1920, p. 180

11 For the story of the gold and diamond discoveries, see especially Paul H. Emden, *Randlords*, London 1935

12 Osbert Sitwell, *Left Hand Right Hand! An Autobiography*, London 1945, p. 242

13 Louis Cohen, *Reminiscences of Kimberley*, London 1911, p. 68
14 J. B. Taylor, *A Pioneer Looks Back*, London 1939
15 *D.N.B.*
16 Struben, p. 131
17 Stanley Jackson, *The Great Barnato*, London 1970, p. 136
18 Phyllis Lewsen (ed.), *Selections from the Correspondence of J. X. Merriman*, Vol. 1, Cape Town 1961, p. 203
19 Emden, *Randlords*, pp. 47, 257
20 C. Seymour Fort, *Alfred Beit*, London 1932, p. 58
21 Sir Alfred Beit and J. G. Lockhart, *The Will and the Way, being an account of Alfred Beit and the Trust which he founded*, London 1957, p. 5
22 Emden, *Randlords*, p. 153
23 *D.N.B.*
24 In his appendix to 'Imperialist' (J. R. Maguire), *Cecil Rhodes A Biography and Appreciation*, London 1897, p. 393
25 *Richard Burton Haldane: An Autobiography*, London 1929, p. 144
26 Jackson, *The Great Barnato*, p. 40
27 Ian D. Colvin, *Cecil John Rhodes 1853–1902*, London 1913, p. 33
28 'Vindex', *Cecil Rhodes: His Political Life and Speeches 1881–1900*, London 1900, p. 779
29 *Ibid.*, p. 5
30 *John Bull*, 28 July 1906
31 J. G. Lockhart and Hon. C. M. Woodhouse, *Rhodes*, London 1963, p. 108
32 *John Bull*, 28 July 1906
33 Jackson, *The Great Barnato*, p. 57
34 Richard Lewinsohn, *Barney Barnato*, London 1937, p. 22
35 'Imperialist', p. 283
36 Beit and Lockhart, p. 19
37 *John Bull*, 4 August 1906
38 Lady Sarah Wilson, *South African Memories: Social, Warlike & Sporting*, London 1909, pp. 29–30
39 Lockhart and Woodhouse, p. 386
40 Lionel Phillips, *Some Reminiscences*, London 1924, p. 88
41 Louis Cohen, *Reminiscences of Kimberley*, p. 110
42 *D.N.B.*
43 *Vanity Fair*, 15 January 1908
44 Emden, *Randlords*, p. 173
45 Seymour Fort, p. 92
46 William P. Taylor, *African Treasures: Sixty Years Among Diamonds and Gold*, London 1932, p. 213

47 Baron Ferdinand Rothschild, *Three Weeks in South Africa: A Diary*, printed for private circulation only, London 1895, p. 94

48 Taylor, *Pioneer Looks Back*, p. 109; Emden, *Randlords*, p. 161

49 *John Bull*, 4 August 1906

50 Leo Weinthal, *Memories, Mines and Millions: Being the Life of Sir Joseph B. Robinson, Bart.*, London 1929, p. 227

51 Louis Cohen, *Reminiscences of Kimberley*, p. 92

52 Marie Corelli, *Free Opinions*, London 1905, p. 106

53 Lewsen, Vol. 1, p. 277

4 The Financiers: New-style

1 For this and the quotations that follow, see Japhet, pp. 23, 40, 58

2 Checkland, *Rise of Industrial Society*, p. 204

3 Joseph Sykes, *The Amalgamation Movement in British Banking, 1825–1924*, London 1926, p. 95n

4 *Alfred Spalding Harvey 1840–1905*, printed for private circulation only, London 1907, p. 458

5 Hartley Withers, *The Meaning of Money*, 2nd ed., London 1909, p. 91

6 *Ibid.*, p. 98

7 S. G. Checkland, 'The Mind of the City, 1870–1914', *Oxford Economic Papers*, Vol. 9, No. 3, October 1957

8 Ignatius Balla, *The Romance of the Rothschilds*, London 1913, pp. 7, 34

9 T. H. S. Escott, *Society in the New Reign*, London 1904, p. 69

10 *Men and Manners*, 23 August 1893

11 Virginia Cowles, *The Rothschilds: A Family of Fortune*, London 1973, p. 168

12 For this and the quotations that follow, see Japhet, pp. 104–5, 110

13 W. S. Adams, *Edwardian Portraits*, London 1957, p. 55

14 Japhet, p. 126

15 *Daily Telegraph*, 24 December 1910

16 Emden, *Money Powers*, p. 331

17 Cyrus Adler (ed.), *Jacob H. Schiff: His Life and Letters*, Vol. 2, London 1929, p. 329 (April 1894)

18 Afaf Lutfi al-Sayyid, *Egypt and Cromer: A Study in Anglo-Egyptian Relations*, London 1968, p. xi

19 Japhet, p. 128

20 Robert Keith Middlemas, *The Master Builders*, London 1963, p. 144; see also pp. 141–53 *passim*

21 Sidney Low, *Egypt in Transition*, London 1914, p. 132

22 Sigmund Münz, *King Edward VII at Marienbad*, London 1934, p. 247

23 *Pearson's Magazine*, February 1896

24 George W. Edwards, *The Evolution of Finance Capitalism*, London 1938, p. 10

25 *Ibid.*, p. 21

26 Escott, *Society in the New Reign*, p. 203

27 Alan Jenkins, *The Stock Exchange Story*, London 1973, p. 91

28 *The Times*, 13 January 1911

29 Hartley Withers, *Stocks and Shares*, London 1910, pp. 354–5

30 *Financial Times*, 28 February 1898. For comments on the Hooley affair, see *The Hooley Book*, London 1904, especially pp. 24, 34, 36, 52, 54, 102, 112; and for Hooley's own comments, Ernest Terah Hooley, *Hooley's Confessions*, London 1924, pp. 9, 13, 48, 149

5 The Discovery of the Consumer: Plutocracy at Home

1 For general background on Lever, see Charles Wilson, *The History of Unilever*, 2 vols, London 1954; Nigel Nicolson, *Lord of the Isles: Lord Lever in the Hebrides*, London 1960; William Hulme Lever, *Viscount Leverhulme*, London 1927; W. P. Jolly, *Lord Leverhulme*, London 1976

2 Adams, p. 147

3 *Town Topics*, 16 November 1912

4 Sir William Lever, Bart., *Day by Day – That's All* ... (Address in Wigan, 1 December 1915), Port Sunlight n.d.

5 Wilson, *History of Unilever*, Vol. 1, p. 8

6 *Square Deals*, January 1909

7 Nigel Nicolson, *Lord of the Isles*, p. 5

8 Lever, *Day by Day*, Address in Wigan

9 *Square Deals*, January, October 1909

10 Lever, *Day by Day*, New Year Address at Gladstone Hall, Port Sunlight, 2 January 1916

11 Wilson, *History of Unilever*, Vol. 1, p. 43

12 *Ibid.*, p. 40

13 Lever, *Day by Day*, Address in Wigan

14 W. H. Lever, *Following the Flag: Jottings of a Jaunt Round the World*, London 1893, p. 7

15 *Town Topics*, 16 November 1912

16 *Square Deals*, January 1909

17 Lever, *Viscount Leverhulme*, p. 5

18 Withers, *Stocks*, p. 29

19 *Nineteenth Century*, March 1891. Kirkland, pp. 74–5

20 Wilson, *History of Unilever*, Vol. 1, p. 187

21 *Ibid.*, p. 115
22 *Daily Mirror*, 22 October 1906. Reproduced in Jolly, facing p. 120
23 For general background on Lipton, see Alec Waugh, *The Lipton Story: A Centennial Biography*, London 1951; Sir Thomas J. Lipton, Bt., *Leaves from the Lipton Logs*, London 1931; Captain John J. Hickey, *The Life and Times of the Late Sir Thomas J. Lipton: From the Cradle to the Grave*, New York 1932; Charles T. Bateman, *Sir Thomas Lipton and the America Cup*, Edinburgh and London 1901
24 Bateman, p. 15
25 Hamilton Fyfe, *Northcliffe: An Intimate Biography*, London 1930, p. 82
26 Lipton, pp. 50–1
27 Bateman, p. 11
28 *Ibid.*, p. 12
29 Lipton, pp. 67, 80
30 *Ibid.*, p. 163
31 *Pearson's Magazine*, January 1896
32 Bateman, p. 21
33 Hickey, p. 23
34 Lipton, p. 95
35 Waugh, p. 47
36 Bateman, p. 23
37 *Ibid.*, p. 20
38 *Ibid.*, p. 15
39 Peter Mathias, *Retailing Revolution*, London 1967, p. 98; see also pp. 41, 97–114 *passim*
40 Lipton, p. 196
41 Mathias, pp. 112–13
42 Discussed in 1913. *Ibid.*, p. 114
43 Hickey, p. 26
44 John Galsworthy, *The Island Pharisees*, London 1904, reprinted 1970, p. 173
45 Alison Adburgham, *Shops and Shopping 1800–1914*, London 1964, p. 142
46 James B. Jefferys, *Retail Trading in Britain 1850–1950*, Cambridge 1954, pp. 21–5
47 Dorothy Davis, *A History of Shopping*, London 1966, p. 266
48 Jefferys, p. 37. Philp's book was published in 1866
49 Barraclough, p. 49
50 The First Viscount Devonport, *The Travelled Road: Some Memories of a Busy Life*, printed for private circulation only, Rochester, Kent, 1946, p. 24

51 For the department store and those that developed it, see John William Ferry, *A History of the Department Store*, New York 1960; H. Pasdermadjian, *The Department Store: Its Origins, Evolution and Economics*, London 1954; Adburgham; Davis; Jefferys

52 *Punch*, 7 December 1911

53 There is a copy in the British Library. Pages unnumbered

54 Pasdermadjian, p. 125

55 Jefferys, p. 281

56 Arthur Lawrence (ed.), *Journalism as a Profession*, London 1903, p. 171

57 Janet Roebuck, *The Making of Modern English Society*, London 1973, p. 42

58 Quentin Crewe, *The Frontiers of Privilege: A century of social conflict as reflected in the Queen*, London, 1961, p. 89

59 H. G. Wells, *The New Machiavelli*, London 1911, reprinted Harmondsworth 1946, pp. 268–9

60 Stephen McKenna, *Sonia: Between Two Worlds*, London 1917, reprinted Harmondsworth 1949, p. 231

61 Marie Corelli, *Temporal Power: A Study in Supremacy*, London 1902, *passim*

62 J. Passmore Edwards, *A Few Footprints*, London 1906, p. 29

63 For general background on Northcliffe, see Reginald Pound and Geoffrey Harmsworth, *Northcliffe*, London 1959; Paul Ferris, *The House of Northcliffe: The Harmsworths of Fleet Street*, London 1971; A. P. Ryan, *Lord Northcliffe*, London 1953; Harry J. Greenwall, *Northcliffe: Napoleon of Fleet Street*, London 1957; Andrée Viollis, *Lord Northcliffe*, Paris 1919; Tom Clarke, *My Lord Northcliffe Diary*, London 1931; William E. Carson, *Northcliffe: Britain's Man of Power*, London 1918; *D.N.B.*; Fyfe

64 Viollis, title-page

65 Pound, p. 28

66 Viollis, p. 9

67 Carson, p. 67

68 Lawrence, p. 188

69 Interview in *Illustrated Magazine*, 1896. Pound, p. 73

70 *Answers*, 25 May 1895. *Ibid.*, p. 178

71 Ferris, p. 82

72 Escott, *Social Transformations*, p. 386

73 *Daily Mail*, 1 August 1914

74 Lawrence, p. 188

75 Maurice V. Brett (ed.), *Journals and Letters of Reginald*

Viscount Esher, Vol. 2, London 1934, p. 256 (16 November 1907)
76 *The Times*, 17 March 1908. Pound, p. 321

6 In at Last: The Social Revolution
1 G. S. Street, *On Money and Other Essays*, London 1914, pp. 1–2
2 Burton J. Hendrick, *The Life and Letters of Walter H. Page*, London 1924, p. 140
3 Phillips, p. 280
4 Thorstein Veblen, *The Theory of the Leisure Class: An Economic Study of Institutions*, New York 1899, reprinted (introduction C. Wright Mills) London 1970, pp. 37, 42, 54
5 *The Times*, 6 May 1914, 13 May 1914
6 Wilton J. Oldham, *The Ismay Line: The White Star Line, and the Ismay Family Story*, Liverpool 1961, p. 69
7 C. F. M. Cornwallis-West, *Edwardian Hey-Days or A Little About a Lot of Things*, London and New York 1930, pp. 132, 149
8 *Contemporary Review*, December 1900
9 Collier, p. 81
10 Boulton, pp. 20, 35
11 Lady Colin Campbell (ed.), *Etiquette of Good Society*, London 1911, p. 106
12 Arthur L. Bowley, *The Change in the Distribution of the National Income 1880–1913* Oxford 1920, pp. 20–1
13 Corelli, *Free Opinions*, p. 111
14 Simon Nowell-Smith (ed.), *Edwardian England 1901–1914*, London 1966, p. 238
15 *Pearson's Magazine*, April 1896
16 *The Times*, 4 January 1912
17 Charles F. G. Masterman, *England After War*, London 1922, p. 32
18 T. H. S. Escott, *Society in the Country House*, London 1907, p. 484
19 Bernard Shaw, *Man and Superman: A Comedy and Philosophy*, New York 1903, reprinted Harmondsworth 1946, p. 196
20 Kenneth Rose, *Superior Person: A Portrait of Curzon and his Circle in late Victorian England*, London 1969, p. 7
21 Oldershaw, dedicatory preface
22 R. D. Mackerness (ed.), *The Journals of George Sturt*, Vol. 1: 1890–1904, Cambridge 1967, pp. 302–3
23 Described for rather different reasons in William Makepeace Thackeray, *The Book of Snobs* (introduction G. K. Chesterton), London 1911, p. 133

24 H. G. Wells, *Tono-Bungay*, London 1909, reprinted London 1964, p. 57

25 Churchill, p. 59

26 Henry Pelling, *The Social Geography of British Elections 1885–1910*, London 1967, p. 83

27 Wells, *Tono-Bungay*, p. 8

28 Thompson, p. 298

29 Rose, p. 287

30 *Punch*, 11 January 1914

31 Boulton, p. 158

32 *The Tatler*, 20 August 1902

33 Hon. E. C. F. Collier (ed.), *A Victorian Diarist. Extracts from the Journals of Mary, Lady Monkswell*, Vol. 1, 1873–95, London 1944, pp. 43–4, 110, 116–17

34 Pamela Hinkson (ed.), *Seventy Years Young. Memories of Elizabeth, Countess of Fingall*, London 1937, pp. 113, 116

35 Hendrick, *Walter H. Page*, p. 158 (22 December 1913)

36 Adburgham, p. 169

37 Phillips, pp. 182–3

38 Sir Henry Lucy, *The Diary of a Journalist*, Vol. 1, London 1920, p. 71 (13 May 1896)

39 *Society Pictures Drawn by George du Maurier Selected from 'Punch'*, Vol. 2, London 1891, p. 168

40 H. Belloc, *Mr Clutterbuck's Election*, London 1910, p. 58

41 Christopher Hussey, *The Life of Sir Edwin Lutyens*, London 1950, pp. 156, 203, 217–19, 222, 225. See also A. S. G. Butler, 'Country-Houses', *The Architecture of Sir Edwin Lutyens*, Vol. 1, London 1950. Drogo became the first house designed by Lutyens to pass into the possession of the National Trust in 1975

42 Lever, *Day by Day*, New Year Address, 1916

43 *Truth*, 5 September 1901

44 Street, *On Money*, p. 4

45 David Owen, *English Philanthropy 1660–1960*, London 1965, p. 475

46 Carnegie, p. 137

47 Lucy Cohen, *Lady de Rothschild and her daughters 1821–1931*, London 1935, p. 203

48 *Truth*, 5 December 1901

49 Frank D. Long, *King Edward's Hospital Fund for London: The Story of its Foundation and Achievements 1897–1942*, London 1933, pp. 24–5

50 *The Times*, 4 January 1912

51 *The Times*, 1 May 1914

52 Shaw, p. xxvii
53 Corelli, *Free Opinions*, p. 106
54 Veblen, p. 226
55 Owen, p. 490
56 Hickey, p. 5
57 Escott, *Society in the New Reign*, p. 118
58 Sir Lionel Cust, *King Edward VII and his Court*, London 1930, pp. 79–80, 198
59 Sir George Arthur, *Not Worth Reading*, London 1938, p. 156
60 Ralph G. Martin, *Lady Randolph Churchill*, Vol. 1, London 1969, reprinted 1974, pp. 107–8
61 Clare Sheridan, *Nuda Veritas*, London 1927, p. 19
62 Ethel Smyth, *What Happened Next*, London 1940, p. 140
63 Arthur, p. 56
64 Bagehot, p. 95
65 Lucy, Vol. 2, 1922, p. 323 (10 September 1910)
66 Philip Magnus, *King Edward VII*, London 1964, reprinted Harmondsworth 1975, p. 303
67 *Ibid.*, p. 305
68 William Scovell Adams, *Edwardian Heritage: A Study in British History 1901–1906*, London 1949, p. 15
69 Horace G. Hutchinson (ed.), *Warriors and Statesmen. From the 'Gleanings' of the Late Earl Brassey*, London 1918, p. 26
70 Sir Charles W. Macara, Bart., *Recollections*, London 1921, p. 62
71 Edward Legge, *King Edward in His True Colours*, London 1912, p. 118
72 *The Tatler*, 3 July 1901
73 *Truth*, 19 September 1901
74 Cust, p. 14
75 Frances, Countess of Warwick, *Afterthoughts*, London 1931, p. 15
76 Lucy Cohen, *Lady de Rothschild*, p. 277
77 *Truth*, 17 October 1901
78 *Ibid.*, 21 November 1901, 28 November 1901
79 *Ibid.*, 19 September 1901
80 *The Tatler*, 25 June 1902
81 *Ibid.*, 20 August 1902
82 Corelli, *Free Opinions*, p. 132
83 E. T. Raymond, *Portraits of the New Century: The First Ten Years*, London 1928, pp. 24–5
84 Escott, *Society in the New Reign*, pp. 27, 211
85 Harold Nicolson, *Small Talk*, London 1937, pp. 78–9
86 Escott, *Society in the New Reign*, p. 28

87 Alfred E. T. Watson, *King Edward VII as a Sportsman*, London 1911, p. 119
88 T. H. S. Escott, *Society in London*, 9th ed., London 1886, p. 22
89 Frederick Ponsonby, *Recollections*, pp. 59–60
90 Watson, p. 329
91 Collier, *England and the English*, p. 340
92 Daisy, Princess of Pless, *From My Private Diary*, Major Desmond Chapman-Huston (ed.), London 1931, p. 172 (1 November 1905)
93 John Boon, *Victorians, Edwardians, and Georgians*, Vol. 1, London 1928, p. 243
94 Magnus, p. 477 (3 February 1907)
95 *Mayfair*, 15 December 1910
96 Escott, *Society in the New Reign*, pp. 11, 207
97 *A King's Story: The Memoirs of H.R.H. the Duke of Windsor K.G.*, London 1951, p. 48
98 *The Times*, 20 January 1912

7 In at Last: Public Life Succumbs

1 Guttsman, p. 181
2 Christie, p. 168
3 Dunbabin
4 *The Times*, 23 October 1888. Thornhill, pp. 60–1
5 Dunbabin
6 Lee
7 Thompson, p. 325
8 Boutmy, p. 240
9 Muir, p. 108
10 Letter to Lady Dorothy Nevill, 17 September 1876, in Nevill, p. 139
11 John Buchan, *Comments and Characters*, W. Forbes Gray (ed.), London 1940, p. 41 (10 December 1908)
12 L. G. Chiozza Money, *Riches and Poverty*, London 1905, revised ed. 1910, reprinted 1913, p. 247
13 Elie Halévy, *The Rule of Democracy 1905–1914*, transl. E. I. Watkin, London 1934, reprinted 1961, p. 271
14 Christie, pp. 171, 178
15 George W. Smalley, *Anglo-American Memories*, Second Series, London 1912, p. 62
16 Howard Evans, *Our Old Nobility*, 5th ed., London 1907, p. 12
17 Verney, pp. 246–7
18 Forbes Gray, p. 31 (22 October 1907)
19 Barbara Drake and Margaret I. Cole (eds), *Our Partnership by Beatrice Webb*, New York 1948, p. 433

20 Mrs Humphry Ward, *The Coming Election: Letters to My Neighbours*, in *The Lords' Debate on Lord Rosebery's Resolution*, reprinted from *The Times* of March 15, 16, 17, 18, 22 and 23, 1910, p. 3

21 *The Standard*, 22 November 1909

22 *Lords' Debate*, 16 March 1910

23 Wilfrid Scawen Blunt, *My Diaries: Being a personal narrative of events, 1888–1914*, Vol. 2, London 1920, p. 377 (22 August 1911)

24 Lord Newton, *Lord Lansdowne*, London 1929, illustration facing p. 386

25 *Parl. Debates*, 3rd series, CCCXXIII (1888), pp. 763, 782, 795

26 Muir, p. 107

27 Evans, p. 2

28 Roy Jenkins, *Mr Balfour's Poodle*, London 1954, reprinted 1968, p. 125

29 Brian Guinness (ed.), *The Guinness Family*, privately printed, 2nd ed. 1969

30 Escott, *Society in the New Reign*, p. 154

31 Lady Colin Campbell, p. 24

32 H. J. Hanham, 'The Sale of Honours in Late Victorian England', *Victorian Studies*, Vol. 3, No. 3, March 1960

33 *Punch*, 1 July 1914

34 Sir Almeric Fitzroy, *Memoirs*, Vol. 1, London 1925, p. 387 (22 November 1909)

35 Hanham

36 *Hooley Book*, pp. 72–4

37 Hooley, pp. 20–1

38 Lord Riddell, *More Pages from my Diary 1908–1914*, London 1934, p. 67 (1 June 1912)

39 Thompson, p. 60

40 Sutherland, p. 38

41 Pumphrey

42 Arthur Ponsonby, *Decline of Aristocracy*, p. 97

43 Collier, *England and the English*, p. 49

44 Sutherland, p. 38

45 *The Times*, 5 April 1917

46 *Ibid.*, 31 January 1925

47 Collier, *England and the English*, p. 467

48 Halévy, p. 310n

49 *Candid Quarterly Review of Public Affairs*, February 1914

50 Evans, p. 7

51 Speech in Commons, late 1880s. Algar Labouchere Thorold, *The Life of Henry Labouchere*, London 1913, p. 218

52 Evans, p. 8
53 Roy Jenkins, *Mr Balfour's Poodle*, p. 26
54 A. Lawrence Lowell, *The Government of England*, Vol. 1, New York 1908, new ed. 1920, p. 406
55 Hanham
56 *Saturday Review*, 16 December 1905
57 Hanham
58 Macmillan, p. 241
59 *Candid Quarterly Review of Public Affairs*, May 1914
60 *The Tatler*, 14 May 1902
61 *Autobiography of Andrew Carnegie*, London 1920, p. 301
62 Burton J. Hendrick, *The Life of Andrew Carnegie*, London 1933, pp. 311, 516
63 Lowell, Vol. 1, pp. 412–13; Vol. 2, p. 508
64 *Truth*, 12 September 1901
65 Bagehot, p. 279
66 Kirkland, p. 167
67 Sanford, Vol. 1, pp. 6–7
68 *Manchester Guardian*, 27 January 1910. Paul Thompson, *The Edwardians: The Remaking of British Society*, London 1975, p. 243
69 Lee, p. 32
70 Christie, p. 76. See also W. L. Guttsman, 'The Changing Structure of the British Political Elite 1886–1935', *Brit. Journ. of Sociology*, Vol. 11, No. 2, June 1951
71 Donald Read, *Edwardian England 1901–15: Society and Politics*, London 1972, p. 113
72 Robert Blake, *The Conservative Party from Peel to Churchill*, London 1970, reprinted 1972, p. 194
73 A. J. P. Taylor, *Beaverbrook*, London 1972, p. 45
74 Riddell, p. 122 (2 September 1913)
75 *Review of Reviews*, March 1912
76 Emerson, p. 419
77 Nevill, p. 147
78 Neal Blewett, 'The Franchise in the United Kingdom 1885–1918', *Past & Present*, No. 32, December 1965
79 T. H. S. Escott, *Gentlemen of the House of Commons*, Vol. 2, London 1902, p. 328
80 *The Times*, 13 January 1912
81 Chiozza Money, p. 339
82 'F.O.L.', *Men About Town*, London 1912, preface
83 Lowell, Vol. 2, p. 511
84 Pelling, p. 119
85 *Ibid.*, p. 111

86 McKenna, p. 138
87 Belloc, pp. 87, 147, 214, 274
88 Lucy, Vol. 2, p. 288 (23 September 1909)
89 McMillan, p. 117
90 *Fortnightly Review*, February 1884. Thorold, p. 210
91 W. E. Adams, *Memoirs of a Social Atom*, Vol. 1, London 1903, reprinted New York 1967, p. 260
92 Lincoln Springfield, *Some Piquant People*, London 1924, p. 131
93 *Candid Quarterly Review of Public Affairs*, February 1914
94 F. Schnadhorst, 'The Caucus and Its Critics', *Nineteenth Century*, July 1882
95 Escott, *Society in the New Reign*, p. 270
96 *Candid Quarterly Review of Public Affairs*, May 1914
97 Viscount Grey of Falloden, *Twenty-Five Years 1892–1916*, Vol. 1, London 1925, reprinted 1935, p. 68
98 Brett, Vol. 2, p. 321 (6 June 1908)
99 13 December 1964. *Sunday Times*, 2 February 1975
100 Lowell, Vol. 2, p. 511
101 *The West-End*, 17 May 1899
102 Corelli, *Free Opinions*, p. 267
103 Frank Hardie, *The Political Influence of the British Monarchy 1862–1952*, London 1970, p. 3
104 Peter Rowland, *The Last Liberal Governments: The Promised Land 1905–1910*, London 1968, p. 21
105 Devonport, p. 49
106 B. W. E. Alford, *W. D. & H. O. Wills and the Development of the U.K. Tobacco Industry 1785–1965*, London 1973, pp. 238, 279–80
107 Colin Cross, *The Liberals in Power, 1905–1914*, London 1963, p. 26
108 Grey, Vol. 1, p. 117
109 Edwin R. A. Seligman (ed.), *Encyclopaedia of the Social Sciences*, Vol. 12, New York 1934, p. 177
110 Alan Jenkins, *Stock Exchange Story*, pp. 129–30
111 Frances Donaldson, *The Marconi Scandal*, London 1962, pp. 166–7
112 Oldershaw, p. 37
113 *Candid Quarterly Review of Public Affairs*, February 1914
114 Riddell, p. 161 (14 June 1913)
115 Rowland, p. 228
116 C. J. C. Street, *Lord Reading*, London 1928, p. 131
117 *The Autobiography of Margot Asquith*, Vol. 1, London 1920, reprinted 1936, p. 17

118 Escott, *Society in London*, p. 110
119 Blake, p. 157
120 W. Macqueen-Pope, *Twenty Shillings in the Pound*, London 1948, p. 334
121 Taylor, *Beaverbrook*, p. 74
122 Hartley Withers, *International Finance*, London 1916, pp. 90–1
123 Thorold, p. 392

8 Through Contemporary Eyes: the Plutocrat in Fact and Fiction
1 Sitwell, p. 241
2 Corelli, *Temporal Power*, dedication
3 Riddell, p. 16
4 Corelli, *Free Opinions*, p. 99
5 John Fore, *Edwardian Scrapbook*, London 1951, p. 98
6 *Hooley Book*, p. 26
7 See the discussion in Montagu Frank Modder, *The Jew in the Literature of England*, New York and Philadelphia 1960, pp. 276–7, 378
8 Escott, *Society in London*, p. 144
9 Collections of Du Maurier cartoons, including those quoted, were published in *English Society Sketched by George du Maurier*, London 1897, and *Society Pictures*
10 Blake, p. 18
11 E. F. Benson, *Mammon & Co.*, London 1899, pp. 8–9, 13, 24, 317
12 *Hooley Book*, p. 26
13 Mrs H. de Vere Stacpole, *London 1913*, London 1914, p. 89
14 McKenna, pp. 140, 221, 253, 278–9
15 Collier, *England and the English*, p. 135
16 By Peter Laslett. Nowell-Smith, p. 142
17 Roebuck, p. 72
18 Chiozza Money, pp. 47–9
19 Jackson, *The Great Barnato*, p. 3; Smalley, Second Series, p. 243
20 Arthur Ponsonby, *The Camel and the Needle's Eye*, London 1910, pp. 28, 30
21 Boulton, pp. 19, 25 51
22 Boris Ford (ed.), *The Modern Age*, Vol. 7 of 'The Pelican Guide to English Literature', 3rd ed., Harmondsworth 1973, p. 29
23 Corelli, *Free Opinions*, p. 109
24 See Amy Cruise, *After the Victorians*, London 1938, p. 209

25 T. W. H. Crosland, *The Wicked Life*, London 1905, pp. 10, 13, 28, 30–2, 36
26 *Nineteenth Century*, January 1887
27 Lecky, *Map of Life*, pp. 53–4, 62–3, 85
28 Werner Sombart, *The Quintessence of Capitalism*, transl. M. Epstein, London 1915, p. 176
29 *Novels of George du Maurier*, London 1947, introduction by Daphne du Maurier, pp. xiii–iv
30 George du Maurier, *Social Pictorial Satire*, London 1898, pp. 74–6
31 Thackeray, pp. iv–v, 137–9, 142, 165, 255, 257
32 H. Taine, *Notes on England*, London 1872, p. 242
33 Brett, Vol. 1, p. 383 (2 March 1903)
34 Patrick Balfour (Lord Kinross), *Society Racket: A Critical Survey of Modern Social Life*, London 1933, p. 33
35 Laslett, p. 230
36 N. Mitford (ed.), *Noblesse Oblige*, London 1956, p. 73
37 Taine, pp. 172–3
38 Sonia Keppel, *Edwardian Daughter*, London 1958, p. 201
39 Guttsman, *English Ruling Class*, pp. 61–2
40 Cf. Harold Nicolson, *Good Behaviour*, p. 225
41 Louis Cohen, *Reminiscences of Kimberley*, p. 56
42 Boutmy, p. 310
43 Andrew Sinclair, *The Last of the Best: The Aristocracy of Europe in the Twentieth Century*, London 1969, p. 3
44 E. F. Benson, *As We Were: A Victorian Peep-Show*, London 1930, reprinted Harmondsworth 1938, p. 294
45 Louis Cohen, *The Memoirs of Priscilla Countess Whopper*, London 1932, pp. 7, 171
46 Escott, *Society in the New Reign*, p. 93
47 Fitzroy, Vol. 2, p. 499
48 Shane Leslie, *The End of a Chapter*, revised ed., London 1917, p. 165
49 John Foster Fraser, *The Conquering Jew*, London 1915, pp. 115–16
50 'Saki' (H. H. Munro), *The Unbearable Bassington*, London 1912, reprinted Harmondsworth 1947, p. 51
51 Escott, *Society in the New Reign*, pp. 192, 198
52 See especially, Charles Merrill Mount, *John Singer Sargent*, London 1957, p. 217
53 Paul H. Emden, *Jews of Britain*, London 1944, p. 427
54 Macara, p. 1
55 Anonymous article on 'Money and Investments', *Contemporary Review*, July 1896

56 Herbert H. Bassett (ed.), *Men of Note in Finance and Commerce: A Biographical Business Directory*, London 1900–1, p. 5
57 Escott, *Social Transformations*, p. 155

9 The World Comes to Mayfair
1 Jackson, *The Great Barnato*, pp. 188–9
2 *D.N.B.*
3 H. O'Kelly Webber, *The Grip of Gold*, London 1936, p. 96
4 Altiora and Oscar Bailey, in Wells, *New Machiavelli*, pp. 150, 218
5 Drake and Cole, p. 346
6 *Ibid.*, p. 268
7 Haldane, p. 144
8 Drake and Cole, p. 301
9 *Ibid.*, p. 311
10 G. S. Street, *The Ghosts of Piccadilly*, London 1907, reprinted 1914, p. 82
11 The party is described in Drake and Cole, pp. 346–7
12 *Ibid.*, p. 413
13 For the estate and its development, see E. I. Musgrave, *Luton Hoo: The Wernher Collection*, Derby 1951
14 G. W. Stamper, *What I Know*, London 1913, p. 105
15 Drake and Cole, pp. 412–13
16 *Ibid.*, p. 412
17 Seymour Fort, p. 155
18 *John Bull*, 28 July 1906
19 Oldershaw, p. 16
20 Prince von Bülow, *Memoirs*, Vol. 2 1903–9, London and New York, 1931, pp. 183–7
21 Wilson, *South African Memories*, pp. 4–5
22 Seymour Fort, p. 176
23 Weinthal, p. 226
24 *Mayfair*, 8 December 1910
25 Weinthal, p. 115
26 P. Tennyson Cole, *Vanity Varnished*, London 1931, p. 185
27 Weinthal, p. 231
28 Sir Lewis Michell, *The Life and Times of the Right Honourable Cecil John Rhodes 1853–1902*, London 1912, p. 264
29 Diana Cooper, *The Rainbow Comes and Goes*, London 1958, p. 24
30 Michell, p. 161
31 *Ibid.*, p. 355
32 Philip Jourdan, *Cecil Rhodes: His Private Life*, London 1911, p. 197

33 *Truth*, 17 October 1901
34 Hutchinson, p. 325
35 Jackson, *The Great Barnato*, p. 185
36 Springfield, p. 150
37 Emden, *Randlords*, p. 134
38 Harry Raymond, *B. I. Barnato: A Memoir*, London 1897, p. 174
39 Jackson, *The Great Barnato*, p. 228
40 For the Sassoons, see Cecil Roth, *The Sassoon Dynasty*, London 1941; Stanley Jackson, *The Sassoons*, London 1968
41 Fitzroy, Vol. 1, p. 193 (15 March 1904)
42 Ernest Dudley, *The Gilded Lily*, London 1958, p. 46
43 Duke of Manchester, *My Candid Recollections*, London 1932, p. 60
44 Jackson, *Sassoons*, p. 87
45 Mount, p. 225
46 Duke of Portland, *Men, Women and Things*, London 1937, p. 51
47 Jackson, *Sassoons*, p. 54
48 Sir Seymour Fortescue, *Looking Back*, London 1920, pp. 178–9
49 Jackson, *Sassoons*, p. 71
50 *Ibid.*, p. 72
51 *Vanity Fair*, 19 February 1908
52 Mrs Hwfa Williams, *It Was Such Fun*, London 1935, p. 95
53 Frederick Ponsonby, *Recollections*, p. 207
54 Fortescue, pp. 259–60
55 Watson, pp. 327–8
56 Emerson, p. 407
57 Richard Hofstadter, *The American Political Tradition*, London 1967, p. 164
58 Anon., *Our Best Society*, New York and London 1905, pp. 34, 165
59 Elizabeth Drexel Lehr, *King Lehr and the Gilded Age*, London, 1935, p. 55
60 Boulton, pp. 28–30
61 J. O. Field, *Uncensored Recollections*, London 1924, p. 320
62 James Bryce, *The American Commonwealth*, Vol. 2, New York 1910, p. 815. S. N. Lipset, *Political Man*, London 1963, p. 400
63 Carnegie, pp. 94–5
64 *The Onlooker*, 22 March 1913
65 Corelli, *Free Opinions*, p. 135
66 Lehr, p. 171
67 Lucy Kavaler, *The Astors: A Family Chronicle*, London 1966, p. 177

68 *Autobiography of Margot Asquith*, Vol. 2, London 1922, reprinted 1936, p. 76
69 Wells, *Tono-Bungay*, p. 80
70 Smalley, Second Series, p. 263
71 Warwick, p. 112
72 Smalley, Second Series, p. 265
73 Harvey O'Connor, *The Astors*, New York 1941, pp. 371–2
74 Warwick, p. 112
75 William Waldorf Astor, *Silhouettes 1855–1885*, London 1917, p. 21
76 Kavaler, p. 194
77 Smalley, Second Series, pp. 266–8
78 Martin, Vol. 2, London 1972, reprinted 1974, p. 85
79 Joseph Frazier Wall, *Andrew Carnegie*, New York 1970, p. 437 The best modern life of Carnegie
80 Cf. Kirkland, pp. 18, 62–3
81 Carnegie, p. 255
82 *Review of Reviews*, January 1912, March 1912
83 Macara, p. 256
84 Smalley, Second Series, pp. 256, 259
85 Fitzroy, Vol. 2, p. 463 (11 October 1911)
86 Harley Williams, *Men of Stress*, London 1948, p. 240
87 Wall, pp. 942, 944
88 Smalley, Second Series, p. 256
89 Kirkland, p. vii
90 Hendrick, *Life of Carnegie*, pp. 31, 280
91 Carnegie, p. 160
92 Wall, p. 847
93 *Ibid.*, pp. 806, 1042
94 T. H. S. Escott, 'Andrew Carnegie', *Contemporary Review*, September 1919
95 Kirkland, p. 31; Wall, p. 808
96 *Town Topics*, 7 December 1912

10 Finance to the Helm
1 Edward Legge, *More About King Edward*, London 1913, p. 265
2 Hooley, pp. 24, 105, facing p. 276
3 *Hooley Book*, pp. 92–3
4 Hooley, pp. 55, 61, 63, 145
5 *Hooley Book*, p. 141
6 For the Rothschilds, see Cowles; Balla; Frederic Morton, *The Rothschilds: A Family Portrait*, London 1962, reprinted Harmondsworth 1964
7 Escott, *Society in London*, p. 44

8 Magnus, p. 141
9 Escott, *Social Transformations,* p. 65
10 Escott, *Society in the New Reign,* pp. 193–4
11 From J. Wade, *The Black Book of Corruption Unmasked!!!,* London 1820 and many later eds. Sutherland, p. 3
12 Morton, p. 150
13 Hanham
14 Escott, *Society in the New Reign,* p. 66
15 Lucy Cohen, *Lady de Rothschild,* p. 207
16 Constance Battersea, *Reminiscences,* London 1932, p. 324
17 Horace G. Hutchinson (ed.), *Private Diaries of the Rt. Hon. Sir Algernon West, G.C.B.,* London 1922, p. 46 (8 August 1892)
18 Cowles, pp. 191–2
19 Fitzroy, Vol. 1, p. 89 (6 December 1902)
20 Cowles, p. 170
21 Hon. George Lambton, *Men and Horses I Have Known,* London 1924, reprinted 1963, pp. 225, 230
22 Cowles, p. 170
23 Escott, *Society in London,* p. 45
24 Cowles, p. 171, 190
25 Escott, *Society in London,* p. 46
26 Magnus, pp. 213–4
27 Stamper, p. 64
28 Frances Balfour, *Ne Obliviscaris,* Vol. 1, p. 221
29 Hutchinson, *Diaries of Sir Algernon West,* p. 314
30 Battersea, p. 38
31 Vittoria Colonna, Duchess of Sermonetta, *Things Past,* London 1929, pp. 73–4
32 Manchester, p. 61
33 Escott, *Society in the New Reign,* p. 68
34 Legge, *More About King Edward,* p. 232
35 *Pearson's Magazine,* February 1896
36 Mrs George Cornwallis-West, *The Reminiscences of Lady Randolph Churchill,* London 1908, p. 218
37 Watson, p. 338
38 Magnus, p. 273
39 Lady Augusta Fane, *Chit-Chat,* London 1926, p. 282
40 Eckhardstein, p. 54
41 *Autobiography of Margot Asquith,* Vol. 1, p. 86
42 Adler, Vol. 2, pp. 83 (4 December 1888), 84 (3 May 1889)
43 Broadlands Archive
44 Keppel, p. 22
45 Münz, p. 246

46 Henry C. Semon and Thomas A. McIntyre (eds), *The Auto-biography of Sir Felix Semon*, London 1926, p. 181

47 Madeleine Masson, *Edwina: The Biography of The Countess Mountbatten of Burma*, London 1958, p. 26

48 Colonna, p. 137

49 Keppel, p. 23–4

50 Masson, p. 16

51 Adler, Vol. 2, p. 332

52 Fitzroy, Vol. 1, pp. 97 (8 September 1902), 102 (11 September 1902)

53 Blunt, Vol. 2, p. 316 (related to Blunt, 7 May 1910)

54 Hinkson, pp. 187–8

55 Lady Angela St Clair Erskine, *Fore and Aft*, London 1932, p. 23

56 Escott, *Society in the New Reign*, p. 249

57 Warwick, pp. 90–2

58 Fitzroy, Vol. 2, p. 516 (8 July 1913)

59 Masson, p. 26

60 Cornwallis-West, *Edwardian Hey-Days*, p. 150

61 *Town Topics*, 14 September 1912

62 Blunt, Vol. 2, p. 276 (19 August 1909)

63 *The Tatler*, 21 May 1902

64 Keppel, pp. 44–5

65 Rowland, p. 96

66 Münz, p. 244

67 Emden, *Money Powers*, p. 339

68 Blunt, Vol. 2, p. 8 (21 April 1901)

69 Gordon Brook-Shepherd, *Uncle of Europe: The Social and Diplomatic Life of Edward VII*, London 1975, p. 132

70 Masson, p. 17

71 Warwick, p. 90

72 *The Tatler*, 2 July 1902

73 Haldane, p. 297

74 Edward VII to Sir Ernest Cassel, 10 December 1909. Broad-lands Archive

75 Semon and McIntyre, p. 181

76 Brook-Shepherd, p. 387

77 See especially the account in W. H. Edwards, *The Tragedy of Edward VII: A Psychological Study*, London 1928, pp. 328, 330, 332–3, 335–7, 339

78 Brook-Shepherd, p. 347

79 Haldane, p. 239

80 Emden, *Money Powers*, p. 340

81 Halévy, pp. 568n, 569n

82 *Daisy, Princess of Pless by Herself*, London 1928, pp. 238, 252
83 Brett, Vol. 2, pp. 266 (3 December 1907), 295 (14 March 1908)
84 Von Bülow, Vol. 2, p. 309
85 Blunt, Vol. 2, p. 63 (27 June 1903)
86 Cassel recorded the meeting in a letter to Maud. Masson, p. 51
87 *Autobiography of Margot Asquith*, Vol. 2, p. 103
88 Adler, Vol. 2, p. 329 (31 May 1910)
89 V. Sackville-West, *The Edwardians*, London 1930, reprinted 1935, p. 225
90 Münz, pp. 243, 247, 249

11 Home-grown Plutocracy

1 Waugh, p. 84
2 Beverley Nichols, *Twenty-five*, London 1926, reprinted 1935, p. 195
3 Hickey, p. 23
4 Keppel, p. 24
5 Waugh, p. 139
6 Lucy, Vol. 2, p. 282 (2 September 1909)
7 Waugh, p. 163
8 *Truth*, 10 October 1901
9 Bateman, p. 55
10 Blumenfeld, p. 105 (21 October 1900)
11 Bateman, pp. 63–4
12 *Ibid.*, pp. 71, 74
13 Fitzroy, Vol. 1, p. 51 (24 May 1900)
14 Sir Sidney Lee, *King Edward VII*, Vol. 2, London 1927, p. 73 (26 May 1901)
15 T. C. Bridges, H. Hessell Tiltman, *Kings of Commerce*, London 1928, pp. 160–1
16 *The Tatler*, 2 October 1901
17 Lipton, p. 114
18 Waugh, p. 73
19 Escott, *Society in the New Reign*, p. 63
20 Lipton, pp. 28, 224
21 Nichols, p. 195
22 See the Earl of Cardigan, *The Wardens of Savernake Forest* London 1949, for a sensitive account of what follows
23 Rose, p. 75
24 Blumenfeld, p. 55 (9 April 1892)
25 George Martelli, *The Elvedon Enterprise*, London 1953, p. 43
26 *Mayfair*, 1 December 1910, 8 December 1910
27 *Vanity Fair*, 20 May 1908
28 Gore, p. 34

29 *Mayfair*, 6 July 1911
30 Hinkson, p. 287
31 Stamper, p. 161 (2 January 1908)
32 *Vanity Fair*, 1 January 1908, 8 January 1908
33 Martelli, p. 50
34 *Mayfair*, 8 December 1910
35 *Ibid.*, 1 December 1910
36 Martelli, pp. 53–5
37 *Evening Standard*, 4 September 1975
38 *The Tatler*, 25 June 1902
39 *The West-End*, 17 May 1899
40 *Town Topics*, 16 November 1912
41 Lever, *Day by Day*
42 *Ibid.*
43 Augustus John, *Chiaroscuro*, London 1952, pp. 150–1. The painting was restored long after Lever's death; see the account in Jolly, pp. 190–6
44 Riddell, p. 114 (4 January 1913)
45 *Town Topics*, 16 November 1912
46 Carnegie, p. 18
47 *The Tatler*, 3 July 1901
48 *The Times*, 29 March 1913
49 Lever, *Viscount Leverhulme*, p. 11
50 Lever, *Following the Flag*, p. 117
51 *Square Deals*, August 1917
52 Harley Williams, *Men of Stress*, p. 339
53 Lord Leverhulme, *Capital and Capitalism*, Port Sunlight n.d. (Address at Lyndhurst Road Congregational Church Hampstead, 7 March 1920)
54 Lever, *Day by Day* (New Year Address, Gladstone Hall, Port Sunlight, 2 January 1916)
55 Lever, *Viscount Leverhulme*, p. 102 (14 September 1891)
56 *Ibid.*, p. 245
57 Nigel Nicolson, *Lord of the Isles*, p. 10
58 Lever, *Following the Flag*, p. 72
59 Leverhulme, *Capital and Capitalism*
60 Bateman, p. 38
61 Wilson, *History of Unilever*, Vol. 1, p. 46
62 Riddell, p. 114 (4 January 1913)
63 Chiozza Money, p. 227
64 *Bournville: A Descriptive Account of the Growth of Cocoa and of its manufacture by Cadbury Brothers*, reprinted from the *British Trade Journal*, 1 November 1880, Bournville 1880, pp. 11, 22

65 A. G. Gardiner, *The Life of George Cadbury*, London 1928, pp. 75, 79, 81, 86
66 Edwards, *Footprints*, pp. 32–3, 40–3, 45, 68
67 Owen, p. 433
68 Escott, *Society in London*, p. 139
69 Lawrence, p. 167
70 Brett, Vol. 2, p. 327 (11 July 1908)
71 Pound, p. 222
72 Clarke, pp. 45, 49 (1 January 1912)
73 Riddell, p. 68 (8 and 10 June 1912)
74 Pound, p. 401
75 *The Tatler*, 21 May 1902
76 Lord Northcliffe (ed.), *Motors and Motor-Driving*, 4th ed., London 1906, p. 41
77 Pound, p. 234
78 Ferris, p. 125
79 Pound, p. 295
80 *Saturday Review*, 16 December 1905
81 Carson, p. 11
82 Pound, p. 186
83 Ferris, p. 74
84 Lawrence, pp. 172, 186
85 Cf. Ralph D. Blumenfeld, *RDB's Procession*, London 1935, p. 205
86 Pound, p. 268
87 Ryan, p. 10
88 Clarke, p. 18
89 J. A. Farrer, *England under Edward VII*, London 1922, p. 143
90 *A Study in Malevolence: An Open Letter to Lord Northcliffe from a Member of Parliament*, London 1920, unnumbered pages

12 The City of Pleasure

1 Arnold Bennett, *The City of Pleasure*, London 1914, pp. 9–10, 12, 30, 85, 93
2 Escott, *Society in the New Reign*, pp. 4, 7
3 Edwards, *Footprints*, p. 66
4 Sir William H. Lever, Bart., *Art and Beauty and the City*, Port Sunlight, n.d., p. 14
5 Ford, p. 29
6 The quotations that follow are from Thomas Burke, *Nights in Town*, London 1915, reprinted 1925, pp. 15, 20–1
7 Benson, *Mammon*, p. 113
8 Corelli, *Free Opinions*, p. 226
9 Eckhardstein, pp. 42–3

10 Cornwallis-West, *Lady Randolph Churchill*, p. 52
11 *The Tatler*, 10 July 1901
12 *Contemporary Review*, December 1900
13 For Newnham-Davis's experiences, see his *Dinners and Diners: Where and how to dine in London*, London 1899, revised ed. 1901, pp. 4, 7–10, 25, 30, 36
14 James Laver, *Edwardian Promenade*, London 1958, p. 41
15 Blumenfeld, *Diary*, p. 112 (26 October 1900)
16 'F.O.L.', p. 105
17 Taine, p. 266
18 Escott, *Social Transformations*, p. 211
19 *The Tatler*, 3 July 1901
20 McKenna, p. 162
21 *The Tatler*, 2 October 1901; see also *Truth*, 26 September 1901
22 A. E. Wilson, *Edwardian Theatre*, London 1951, pp. 166–7
23 *The Onlooker*, 4 January 1913
24 *The Times*, 19 May 1914, 20 May 1914; see also 'Cynicus' on 20 May
25 Escott, *Social Transformations*, p. 410
26 Col. the Hon. F. H. Cripps, *Life's a Gamble*, London 1957, p. 197
27 Arthur Ponsonby, *Decline*, p. 72
28 W. Pett Ridge, *I Like to Remember*, London 1925, p. 287
29 Anthony Trollope, *The Way We Live Now*, Vol. 1, London 1875, reprinted 1941, p. 24
30 Warwick, p. 257
31 Taylor, *Pioneer Looks Back*, pp. 201–2
32 Robert Cecil, *Life in Edwardian England*, London 1969, p. 104
33 A. R. Prest, assisted by A. A. Adams, *Consumer's Expenditure in the United Kingdom 1900–1919*, Cambridge 1954, p. 8
34 Sir Algernon West, *One City and Many Men*, London 1908, pp. 7, 22–3
35 Arthur Ponsonby, *Camel and Needle's Eye*, p. 96
36 Springfield, p. 69
37 *Truth*, 17 October 1901
38 John Montgomery, *1900: The End of an Era*, London 1968, pp. 94–5
39 *Manners and Rules of Good Society or Solecisms to be Avoided: by a member of the Aristocracy*, 31st ed., London 1910, p. 74
40 *The Tatler*, 7 May 1902
41 Collier, *Victorian Diarist*, Vol. 2, 1895–1909, London 1946, pp. 90–1 (13 June 1902), 132 (13 May 1904)
42 Escott, *Social Transformations*, pp. 50, 52
43 *The Times*, 17 January 1911
44 Arthur Ponsonby, *Camel and Needle's Eye*, p. 107

45 Martin, Vol. 1, p. 251
46 Cole, *Vanity Varnished*, p. 166
47 Gardiner, p. 117
48 For Duveen, see S. N. Behrman, *Duveen*, London 1952; Edward Fowles, *Memories of Duveen Brothers*, London 1976
49 *Pearson's Magazine*, January 1896
50 *Mayfair*, 16 May 1914
51 Arthur, p. 141
52 *Vanity Fair*, 13 May 1908
53 *Mayfair*, 3 January 1914
54 Cole, *Vanity Varnished*, p. 218
55 Mount, p. 190
56 Sitwell, pp. 207, 226
57 Roger Fry, *Transformations*, London 1926, p. 128. Richard Ormond, *John Singer Sargent*, London 1970, p. 45
58 Mount, pp. 218, 238
59 Ormond, p. 66
60 Warwick, p. 175

13 High Times at Home and Abroad

1 *Mayfair*, 17 November 1910
2 Northcliffe, p. 315
3 Churchill, pp. 85, 154
4 Ethel Raglan, *Memories of Three Reigns*, London 1928, p. 230
5 Escott, *Society in the New Reign*, p. 113
6 Northcliffe, p. viii
7 Corelli, *Free Opinions*, pp. 100, 219
8 *The Bystander*, 23 December 1903
9 *The Times*, 16 November 1911
10 Frederick A. Talbot, *Motor-Cars and their Story*, London 1912, pp. 124, 133
11 Osbert Sitwell, *The Scarlet Tree*, London 1946, p. 286
12 *Vanity Fair*, 1 January 1908
13 Boulton, pp. 54, 156
14 Cf. T. H. White, *Farewell Victoria*, London 1933, reprinted Harmondsworth 1943, pp. 61–2
15 *Mayfair*, 24 January 1914
16 Northcliffe, pp. 25, 30–1, 349
17 Escott, *Society in the New Reign*, pp. 220–1, 230
18 *The Tatler*, 20 August 1902
19 *Truth*, 28 November 1901
20 Escott, *Social Transformations*, p. 207
21 Battersea, pp. 378–9; see also Lucy Cohen, *Lady de Rothschild*, p. 221

22 Carnegie, p. 247
23 Hendrick, *Walter H. Page*, p. 157 (22 December 1913)
24 John Burnett, *Plenty and Want: A social history of diet in England from 1815 to the present day*, London 1966, p. 176
25 Watson, pp. 49–50
26 Carnegie, p. 247
27 *Nineteenth Century*, September 1882
28 Jourdan, p. 247
29 Galsworthy, *Country House*, p. 6
30 Baring-Gould, pp. 205–6
31 Leslie, p. 152
32 *Pearson's Magazine*, May 1896
33 *Mayfair*, 6 July 1911
34 Cf. Leslie, p. 152; Escott, *Social Transformations of the Victorian Age*, p. 413
35 Arthur Ponsonby, *Camel and Needle's Eye*, p. 64
36 Michell, p. 9
37 Lambton, p. 226
38 Robert S. Sievier (ed.), *Bob Sievier's Sporting Annual 1912–13*, London 1912, p. 1
39 Seymour Fort, p. 52
40 Hooley, pp. 98–9
41 For Sievier's early life, see his own account, *The Autobiography of Robert Standish Sievier*, London 1906, pp. 37, 53, 77, 107, 144
42 Belloc, p. 145
43 The Joel–Sievier conflict is discussed in Sievier, *Autobiography* pp. 214, 348; Stanley Jackson, *Rufus Isaacs*, London 1936, pp. 120–9; Gerald R. Isaacs, *Rufus Isaacs: First Marquess of Reading*, New York 1940, pp. 198–201
44 Sievier, *Autobiography*, pp. 163–4, 194–5
45 Dudley, p. 154
46 Lambton, p. 253
47 Arthur Ponsonby, *Camel and Needle's Eye*, pp. 65–6
48 Escott, *Social Transformations*, p. 413
49 *Vanity Fair*, 13 May 1908
50 *The West-End*, 17 May 1899
51 *The Tatler*, 18 June 1902
52 Sievier, *Autobiography*, p. 143
53 *The Tatler*, 31 July 1901
54 Hooley, pp. 85, 107, 238
55 Weinthal, p. 165
56 Herbert Jefferson, *Viscount Pirrie of Belfast*, London 1948, p. 89 (4 July 1912)
57 Arthur Ponsonby, *Camel and Needle's Eye*, p. 68

58 *Sievier's Monthly*, February 1909
59 Chapman-Huston, p. 249 (8 August 1909)
60 Nevill, pp. 35, 124
61 *Mayfair*, 28 February 1914
62 'Saki', p. 131
63 Arthur, p. 53
64 Sackville-West, p. 35
65 Münz, pp. 105, 110
66 *Vanity Fair*, 8 January 1908, 11 March 1908
67 Sinclair, p. 29
68 *Town Topics*, 2 November 1912
69 *Vanity Fair*, 17 June 1908
70 Lever, *Viscount Leverhulme*, p. 58
71 Geoffrey Marcus, *The Maiden Voyage*, London 1969, p. 196
72 Oldham, p. 173
73 Marcus, pp. 28–9, 55, 94, 206. Filson Young, *The Titanic*, was published in 1913. See also Oldham
74 Beatrice Webb, *My Apprenticeship*, London 1926, reprinted 1950, p. 44
75 Princess of Pless, p. 114 (17 May 1906); George D. Kinnand (ed.), Baroness de Stoeckl, *My Dear Marquis*, London 1952, p. 48; Escott, *Society in the New Reign*, p. 129

14 Casualties of War and Change
1 C. E. Montague, *Disenchantment*, London 1922, reprinted 1968, p. 70
2 Noted by Sir Lionel Cust. Christie, p. 6
3 Masterman, pp. 31–3
4 Lucy, Vol. 3, 1923, pp. 269–70 (22 July 1916)
5 *Hall-Boy to House-Steward*, London 1925. John Burnett (ed.), *Useful Toil: Autobiographies of Working People from the 1820s to the 1920s*, London 1974, p. 193
6 Crewe, p. 119
7 Hendrick, *Walter II. Page*, p. 336
8 Colonna, p. 239
9 Cf. Thompson, p. 328
10 Hartley Withers, *International Finance*, London 1916, p. 159
11 Neville Lytton, *The English Country Gentleman*, London 1925, p. 183
12 Lord Henry Bentinck, *Tory Democracy*, London 1918, p. 1
13 Arthur Marwick, *The Deluge: British Society and the First World War*, London 1965, p. 123
14 Gerhard Masur, *Prophets of Yesterday: Studies in European Culture*, London 1963, p. 245

15 Blumenfeld, *Procession*, p. 67
16 Margaret I. Cole (ed.), *Beatrice Webb's Diaries 1912–1924*, London 1952, pp. 71–2 (7 December 1916)
17 *War Memoirs of David Lloyd George*, Vol. 1, London n.d., p. 641
18 Anthony Sampson, *The New Anatomy of Britain*, London 1971, p. 558
19 Lytton, pp. 19–20
20 Thompson, p. 333
21 Masterman, pp. 40, 44
22 Michael Harrison, *Lord of London: a biography of the 2nd Duke of Westminster*, London 1966, p. 207
23 Sutherland, p. 49
24 *The Observer*, 6 June 1974
25 Lytton, p. 167
26 Sinclair, p. 105
27 For Maundy Gregory and the debates on the sale of honours, see Macmillan; McMillan and the more recent study by Tom Cullen, *Maundy Gregory: Purveyor of Honours*, London 1974
28 Robinson's side of the story is given in Weinthal, pp. 191–3
29 Lockhart, Woodhouse, p. 113
30 Lytton, p. 45
31 McMillan, p. 134
32 Macara, p. 262
33 Hugh Thomas (ed.), *The Establishment*, London 1959, reprinted 1962, pp. 15–16
34 For these developments, see Marwick, *passim*
35 J. C. Stamp, *British Incomes and Property*, London 1916, preface
36 Albert L. Bowley and Sir Josiah Stamp, *The National Income, 1924*, Oxford 1927, p. 59
37 John Finnemore, *Social Life in England*, 3rd ed., London 1920, p. 240
38 E. H. Phelps Brown and B. Weber, 'Accumulation, Productivity and Distribution in the British Economy, 1870–1938', *Economic Journal*, Vol. 63, 1953
39 *The Times*, 15 February 1915. See Kenneth Gregory's article in the same paper, 15 February 1975
40 S. J. Prais, *The Evolution of Giant Firms in Britain*, Cambridge 1977, *passim*
41 Escott, *Society in the New Reign*, p. 267
42 Sombart, pp. 150–1
43 *The Times*, 1 January 1914. Read, p. 12
44 Cf. Hobsbawm, p. 149
45 Shaw, p. xxvii

46 See especially Hobsbawm, p. 155
47 S. Marriner, *Rathbones of Liverpool, 1845–73*, Liverpool 1961; W. G. Rimmer, *Marshalls of Leeds. Flax-Spinners, 1788–1886*, Cambridge 1960; D. H. Aldcroft, 'The Entrepreneur and the British Economy, 1870–1914', *Ec.H.R.*, 2nd series, Vol. 17, No. 1, August 1964
48 Charlotte Erickson, *British Industrialists: Steel and Hosiery, 1850–1950*, Cambridge 1959, p. 45
49 *Friendship's Garland*, 1871. Checkland, *Rise of Industrial Society*, p. 292
50 Wells, *New Machiavelli*, p. 126
51 Taine, p. 128
52 Leslie, p. 36
53 Edmond Holmes, *What Is and What Might Be*, London 1911, reprinted 1917, p. 260
54 Lord Redesdale, *Further Memories*, London 1917, p. xx
55 Leslie, pp. 33, 42–3
56 *Punch*, 5 August 1914
57 Robert Miller, *The New Classes*, London 1966, p. 109
58 Cole, *Class Structure*, p. 64

15 A Resting-place for Memories

1 *Westminster Gazette*, 7 August 1901. *Two Millionairesses: An Incident at Basle Station*, London 1901
2 *Vanity Fair*, 15 April 1908
3 Arthur Ponsonby, *Camel and Needle's Eye*, p. 110
4 Churchill, p. 119
5 'Socialism for Millionaires', *Contemporary Review*, February 1896
6 Hickey, pp. 5, 125
7 Wilson, *History of Unilever*, Vol. 2, p. 260
8 Ferdinand Hansen ('the "Unrepentant Hun"'), *The Unrepentant Northcliffe: A Reply to the London 'Times' of October 19, 1920*, Hamburg 1921, pp. 7, 18
9 *D.N.B.*
10 *Pearson's Magazine*, January 1896
11 Michael Astor, *Tribal Feeling*, London 1963, p. 21
12 Fitzroy, Vol. 1, p. 6 (4 December 1898)
13 O'Connor, p. 373
14 Astor, *Silhouettes*, dedication page
15 Emden, *Jews*, p. 414
16 Reproduced in Beit and Lockhart, facing p. 12
17 Blumenfeld, *Diary*, p. 135 (9 November 1900)
18 *John Bull*, 4 August 1906

326

19 Seymour Fort, p. 116
20 A. P. Cartwright, *The Corner House: The Early History of Johannesburg*, London 1965, p. 256
21 Siegfried Sassoon, *The Old Century and seven more years*, London 1938, reprinted 1968, pp. 92–3, 97, 100
22 Cartwright, p. 262
23 A. P. Cartwright, *Corner House: The story of the industrialization of South Africa*, Cape Town 1968, pp. 19–21
24 Emden, *Randlords*, p. 203
25 *Autobiography of Margot Asquith*, Vol. 2, p. 188
26 Fane, pp. 247–9
27 *The Times*, 7 October 1914
28 Fitzroy, Vol. 2, pp. 613–14 (19 December 1915)
29 A. Moreton Mandeville, *The House of Speyer: A Candid Criticism of Speyer Flotations*, London 1915, pp. 25, 29, 36, 50
30 Fitzroy, Vol. 2, pp. 613–14 (19 December 1915), 770 (13 December 1921); Emden, *Jews*, p. 345
31 *D.N.B.*
32 *Sunday Times*, 18 April 1976
33 Prince of Wales to Ernest Cassel from Marlborough House, 22 December 1900. Broadlands Archive
34 Alden Hatch, *The Mountbattens*, London 1966, p. 188
35 Edward VII to Ernest Cassel from Sandringham, 29 November 1901. Broadlands Archive
36 Sermonetta, pp. 136, 141
37 George V to Sir Ernest Cassel from Buckingham Palace, 24 June 1913. Broadlands Archive
38 Fitzroy, Vol. 2, pp. 512 (5 June 1913), 516 (8 July 1913)
39 Keppel, p. 44
46 Sermonetta, p. 140
41 Fitzroy, Vol. 2, p. 762 (26 September 1921)

Index